Selling
Yellowstone

DEVELOPMENT OF WESTERN RESOURCES

The Development of Western Resources is an interdisciplinary series

focusing on the use and misuse of resources in the American West.

Written for a broad readership of humanists, social scientists, and

resource specialists, the books in this series emphasize both historical and

contemporary perspectives as they explore the interplay between resource

exploitation and economic, social, and political experiences.

John G. Clark, University of Kansas, Founding Editor

Hal K. Rothman, University of Nevada, Las Vegas, Series Editor

Selling
Yellowstone

CAPITALISM AND

THE CONSTRUCTION

OF NATURE

Mark Daniel Barringer

 University Press of Kansas

Published by the University Press of Kansas (Lawrence, Kansas 66049), which was
organized by the Kansas Board of Regents and is operated and funded by Emporia State
University, Fort Hays State University, Kansas State University, Pittsburg State University,
the University of Kansas, and Wichita State University

Library of Congress Cataloging-in-Publication Data

Barringer, Mark Daniel, 1962–
    Selling Yellowstone : capitalism and the construction of nature / Mark Daniel Barringer.
        p. cm — (Development of western resources.)
    Includes bibliographical references and index.
    ISBN 0-7006-1167-3 (cloth : alk. paper)
        1. Yellowstone National Park — History.   2. Yellowstone National Park —
Economic conditions.   3. Yellowstone National Park — Environmental conditions.
4. Concessions (Amusements, etc.) — Yellowstone National Park — History.   5. Resort
development — Yellowstone National Park — History.   6. Land use —Yellowstone
National Park — History.   7. Capitalism — Social aspects — Yellowstone National Park —
History.   8. Capitalism — Environmental aspects — Yellowstone National Park —
History.   9. Nature — Effect of human beings on — Yellowstone National
Park — History.   I. Title.   II. Series.
    F722 .B27 2002
    978.7'52— dc21   2001006732

British Library Cataloguing in Publication Data is available.

Printed in the United States of America

10 9 8 7 6 5 4 3 2 1

The paper used in this publication meets the minimum requirements of the American
National Standard for Permanence of Paper for Printed Library Materials Z39.48-1984.

CONTENTS

Few places are as familiar to tourists as the national parks of the United States. Yellowstone, Yosemite, the Grand Canyon — all remain among the most popular vacation destinations in the country and host an impressive number of visitors each year. Recent events have created an even greater amount of interest in Yellowstone. The great fires of 1988 focused world attention on this, the first and most well-known national park. More recently, the controversial decisions to reintroduce wolves and reduce bison numbers, as well as to ban snowmobiles from the park, have generated an immense amount of publicity and numerous debates over federal management policies. And through all the controversy, tourists come to the park in greater numbers every year. Yellowstone remains, more than 125 years after its founding, a cherished national possession.

The park also serves as a vast outdoor laboratory. Many scientists converge on Yellowstone to conduct research on plant and animal life, while others explore its unique geology. Economists scrutinize the impact of tourism on surrounding areas, the potential wealth contained in the park's geothermal resources, or the biomedical benefits of algae growing in hot springs. Policy analysts investigate the effects of political decisions such as the snowmobile ban, endangered species rules, or other contemporary issues. Historians have also devoted a significant amount of attention to the park, as more frequently visitors have expressed interest in the cultural past of Yellowstone as well as its natural attractions. Two in particular have provided interested individuals with a wealth of information and inspiration for further study. In 1977 Aubrey L. Haines, longtime Yellowstone historian, published his exhaustive two-volume *The Yellowstone Story*, a comprehensive chronicle of human experience in the park. Richard A. Bartlett has also written two books on the subject, *Nature's Yellowstone* (1974) and *Yellowstone: A Wilderness Besieged* (1985), which are more interpretive and place the history in a broader regional and national context. Literally hundreds of other books and articles analyze portions of the story. Until now, however, the impact of concessioners on tourism, the environment, and popular perceptions of the park has remained largely unexamined.

This study grew out of a personal desire to spend more time in Yellow-

[viii] SELLING YELLOWSTONE

stone. Moving from Montana to Texas for graduate school, I desperately needed a reason to return north in the summertime. In 1994 I began searching through the park archives at Mammoth Hot Springs for a suitable dissertation topic. Thanks largely to Lee Whittlesey, I discovered that the archives contained hundreds of boxes of Yellowstone Park Company records, as yet unindexed and virtually unexplored. The documents became my excuse to travel northward, as well as the basis for this book.

As noted, Lee Whittlesey was instrumental in launching this project and is deserving of many thanks. At the risk of inadvertently omitting some persons or organizations that helped make this book possible, I also gratefully acknowledge debts of gratitude to Ben Procter and William Beezley at Texas Christian University, who provided wise direction, insightful criticism, and invaluable friendship while overseeing the dissertation from which this book was drawn. Also at TCU, Donald E. Worcester and Ken Stevens helped clarify ideas and suggest avenues of inquiry, as did Nancy Scott Jackson at the University Press of Kansas. Spencer Tucker and Paul F. Boller Jr. provided departmental financial assistance at TCU for the research. At Yellowstone, Barbara Zafft, Vanessa Christopher, Elsa Kortge, Susan Kraft, John Dalheim, and the rest of the staff at the research library and curator's office helped during the months spent there and later helped track town photos. Dan Sholly, Yellowstone's chief ranger during my summers in the archives, kindly waived the fourteen-day camping restriction and allowed me to remain close to my sources for months on end. Rick Ewig and the staff at the American Heritage Center in Laramie, Wyoming, also provided research assistance. Those who read parts of the manuscript and offered constructive criticism, direction, or inspiration include Lee Whittlesey, Tamsen E. Hert, Elinor Melville, Robert T. Smith, Mark Beasley, Page Foshee, Barry MacIntosh, Edison McIntyre, Daniel Newcomer, Matthew Esposito, Wendy Waters, Robert Righter, and Richard West Sellars. Colleagues who were kind enough to discuss some of these issues and help me formulate ideas include James Pritchard, Gene Gressley, William Hunt, Mark Harvey, John Clark, Brad Raley, Donald Jackson, Scott L. Bills, Bobby Johnson, Archie P. McDonald, Sylvia McGrath, and Roger Tuller. Texas Christian University, the National Society of The Colonial Dames of America in the State of Texas, the Sagamore Hill Library Foundation, and the American Heritage Center all provided financial support.

Finally, this book is dedicated to Sheila, Patrick, and Emma.

There is a story with which Americans have long lived, the one about the Old West, the frontier. For much of the twentieth century it remained among the most familiar of American myths, one that told people who they were and from where they had come. Historian William Cronon endowed it with "the ability to turn ordinary people into heroes and to present a conflict-ridden invasion as an epic march toward enlightened democratic nationhood." Still a powerful tale today, the frontier mythology has shaped Americans' perception of the world, defined individual and collective identities, and brought citizens together as a nation. Such stories, according to noted author William Kittredge, "are valuable precisely to the degree that they are for the moment useful in our ongoing task of finding coherency in the world." They bring order, structure, understanding. And for a very long time, indeed for much of the past hundred years, the story of the Old West proved itself useful in shaping popular ideas about what an American, as well as America as a nation, was.[1]

The story itself is familiar, the once upon a time not so long ago. Usually the tale begins with Lewis and Clark, who in 1805 embarked from the Mandan villages in North Dakota on a trek across the unexplored, virgin wilderness of the West in a valiant attempt to expand the boundaries of America, a country newly independent and eager to explore new lands and new possibilities. Their success opened the trans-Mississippi West to waves of settlement, to civilization. Then came the fur trappers, the mountain men, brave enough to face the wilderness and the Indians — who, in this story, were little more than geographic features to be overcome — to capture the elusive beaver. The trappers, men like William Henry Ashley, Jedediah Smith, Jim Bridger, and Thomas Fitzpatrick, mapped and charted the West, making the wilderness understandable. Ashley invented the rendezvous, a celebration of the wealth and opportunity that the region and its resources promised. Later, these same men made the West accessible to others, acting as guides for wagon trains along the western trails. The mountain men began the stories, too, those that would shape popular opinions about the West and what it was.

The next chapter opened with those wagon trains pulled by teams of oxen slowly plodding along the trails to Oregon and California, led by long-in-the-tooth mountain men toward the valleys of the Willamette or the American River. The men, women, and children who occupied these prairie schooners were, in the stories, hardy pioneers brave enough to seek new lives in lands far away. They were also avowed nationalists, helping extend American hegemony to areas contested by the English, Mexicans, or Indians, in search of opportunity, the chance at the American Dream. Then came prospectors, striking gold in California, Colorado, Idaho, and elsewhere, and the rush to the West took on new stridency. Soon boom towns sprang up — San Francisco, Denver, and hundreds of others — and with them new opportunities. Boosters advertised land, wealth, adventure, even health in the dry western air. They said that it was God's will, our "manifest destiny," to occupy the continent from sea to shining sea. They sold the West with promises of paradise, stories about free land, abundant water, gold and silver, and above all, opportunity. Perhaps most famously, New York newspaper editor Horace Greeley exhorted Americans to migrate: "Go West, young man, and seek your fortune." Many did, lured by the stories of paradise.[2]

The story continues. By the 1860s, railroads arrived and created new opportunities in the West. Hunters reduced the buffalo herds nearly to extinction, while the cavalry battled and conquered the Indians, forcing them to accept the changes wrought by civilization and pushing them onto reservations and out of the story. A cattle kingdom, originating in Texas, spread across the Great Plains, turning this previously worthless, arid land into a valuable resource. And now a seminal figure appeared in the story: the cowboy. Cowboys epitomized the Old West, living romantic lives on horseback, singing songs around nightly campfires, and roaming the landscape beholden to no one. They drove vast herds of cows to railroad towns like Dodge City and Abilene, drew their pay and celebrated their good fortune, then rode back to the campfires.

In the final chapter of the story, homesteaders arrived in the Old West. Armed with plows, reapers, and barbed wire, they marked the beginning of the end. Lured westward by government land giveaways, they turned the soil, built houses of sod, and, family by family, civilized and tamed the land, turned it into something productive. Market towns appeared alongside the railroad tracks, bringing schools and churches and city life to the West. Then the railroads penetrated into the deeper recesses of the region, making long cattle drives unnecessary and ending the era of the open range. The gold played out, and boom towns were abandoned. Silver strikes in Nevada, Idaho, Montana, and Colorado required heavy equipment, capital, and labor and gave birth to larger, more urban settlements. Sawmills in Idaho, Washington, California, and elsewhere employed hundreds of workers, and timber companies transformed forests into lumber to build cities and towns. By the 1890s, farms dotted the landscape of plains and river valleys, cattle had been fenced on corporate ranches, industrial mines occupied mountainsides, and cities had appeared that were much like those elsewhere, populated by ethnically diverse immigrant groups and suffering from all the maladies that plagued such urban places.

The Old West, the frontier, was gone.

And this was good, for a time, because its passing created a useful place, a civilized landscape. The stories that had drawn people west with promises of wealth and opportunity — promises of paradise — required also that they claim possession of the land and transform it into something of worth. The Old West may have been paradise, but it needed some alteration to fulfill the promise of the American Dream. The grasslands had to be grazed or turned and planted with cash crops, the minerals extracted and turned into money, the trees sawn and utilized in the building of great cities. This was development, the extraction of wealth from the bountiful natural resources of the region, a step in the right direction along some linear progression toward the ultimate society, the quintessential Good Place. Those who were brave enough, who believed in themselves enough to risk everything for a shot at paradise, now owned the West and its wealth.[3]

Soon, however, nostalgia crept in. By 1893, when Frederick Jackson Turner articulated what many were already feeling, that the frontier, with its opportunities for wealth and adventure, representing something unique in America, was in fact gone, many wanted it back. Fortunately, there existed another chapter in the story of the Old West, a kind of epilogue tagged on to the end for those who tarried or arrived too late to assist in remaking paradise, as well as for those now lamenting the transformation that had taken place. And it said that there were places still out there, unclaimed, where the Old West lived on. These places were different. They were desert canyons or mountain valleys ringed by waterfalls, or majestic mountains that inspired awe and wonder. They were places harboring natural curiosities, geysers and hot springs, that almost defied description. In the story, they held some kind of spiritual value above and beyond that which could be extracted from their natural resources. They were untouched, untrodden wilderness lands that became symbols of America itself; according to Kittredge, remnants of "the vast continent we found, natural and almost magically alive, capable of inspiring us to awe and reverence." And according to the story, altruism and a sense of national responsibility required that these places be protected from development, that the commercial forces transforming the rest of the West into farms, mines, and cities be held at bay.[4]

Anything valuable enough to escape the general frenzy of western development, the story went, had to be special indeed. So these places were designated national parks, symbols of our identity, and beginning with the establishment of Yellowstone in 1872, visitors flocked to the West to see these repositories of our national mythology, these reminders of our past. After Yellowstone came Yosemite in 1890, Mount Rainier in 1899, Glacier in 1910, Rocky Mountain National Park in 1915, and Grand Canyon in 1919; later, Zion, Bryce Canyon, and Grand Teton National Parks joined the list, along with many others. And for decades, upon arrival in any of these places, tourists found exactly what they had come looking for, those things lost to progress elsewhere but preserved in the parks: nature, wildlife, the frontier, or just a simpler past, all of those things that the stories told them they would find. They saw mountains, waterfalls, canyons, glaciers, and geysers. They watched herds of bison and elk grazing in meadows, and bears alongside wagon roads. They traveled by railroad and stagecoach, stayed overnight in hotels hewn from immense logs or in tent camps, and sang cowboy songs around campfires. Upon leaving they told their own stories, and before long national parks had become even more popular as places not only of nature and history but also of recreation and leisure. For most of the twentieth century, the parks lived up to expectations, and people assumed that these places had always been this way and would remain so forever.[5]

They assumed it in part because the government promised to protect the national parks and preserve them as symbols of America's heritage. In the 1872 act establishing Yellowstone, Congress charged the secretary of the interior with maintaining the park in its natural condition. In 1916, following a controversial decision to allow the construction of a dam and reservoir in Yosemite's Hetch Hetchy Valley, the National Park Service (NPS) was founded and assumed custodial responsibility for all national parks. The law specifically stated that the NPS was both to promote the parks and leave them "unimpaired for the enjoyment of future generations." For the next fifty years, as more and more travelers descended upon Yellowstone and the others, it seemed that the agency was doing just that, and the national parks continued to provide visitors with the scenery, wildlife, natural wonders, and sense of history that they expected.[6]

Recently other stories have challenged the premise that the Old West was a place worthy of veneration, insisting instead that the frontier mythology so many sought in visiting national parks masked a reality of conquest and destruction. Critics charged that the old story demonized Native Americans, ignored precontact Indian cultures, and marginalized ethnic minorities, women, and the environment itself. They constructed new narratives in which Euro-American expansion deprived native people of their lands and wreaked havoc on a fragile landscape. Others even objected to the idea that national parks were altruistic creations of forward-thinking individuals, insisting instead that these places held no value, that they were allowed to escape the transformative, exploitative processes of development only because they "encompassed only those features considered valueless for lumbering, mining, grazing, or agriculture," were "worthless" in the traditional sense.[7]

Many of these critics and revisionists were correct, of course, but the very nature of mythology requires simplification and necessitates the exclusion of complicating factors. The Old West was without question a more complex place than the popular stories suggested. There were people other than ranchers, prospectors, homesteaders, and cowboys, other ethnic groups and even women who populated the region and shaped its reality. But none of this really mattered for a long time, because the old myth of the frontier stood unchallenged. In the American imagination the Old West was a place of mountain men and cowboys, and national parks were special places, preserved and protected from the forces that had transformed the region into something less interesting, created for all to enjoy. The story said so, and most people believed it.

Those who questioned the mythological origins of the parks were right as well, for regardless of how much we wish it were otherwise, altruism had little to do with the establishment of many, or even most, of these places. But assertions that the parks were worthless lands, like the myth that claims them as symbols of national sacrifice and goodwill, are mistaken. In reality, commercial development did not bypass national parks, as both the traditional interpretation and newer theories claim, but rather assumed a different form. Even before parks like Yellowstone, Yosemite, Mount Rainier, and the others were established, promoters staked claims near natural features such as hot springs, geysers, waterfalls, and canyons. After Congress created Yellowstone in 1872, the Department of the Interior leased parcels of land in national parks to entrepreneurs who agreed to provide visitor services. Some of these businesses, called *concessions,* were more successful than others — mainly due to the financial backing from railroads. But by 1916, when the NPS took over management of national parks, concessioners had already entrenched themselves in Yellowstone, Yosemite, Glacier, Grand Canyon, and Mount Rainier National Parks and partnered with government administrators in shaping the parks to fit visitor expectations. Together, the NPS and concessioners designed the national parks to fit popular beliefs about what they should be.

As the years went on, these custodians of what were more and more being referred to as "national treasures" built elaborate hotels so visitors could appreciate the sublime mountains, canyons, and waterfalls. They cleared roads so tourists could marvel at the wonders of nature like geysers, hot springs, and petrified trees. They eliminated predators and banned hunting to bolster herds of deer and elk, and in Yellowstone they bred bison to fill the valleys. Later, they offered tent camps, lodges, and cabins as tourism was democratized and national parks became available for all Americans to appreciate. They provided recreational opportunities such as dance halls, swimming pools, and bear-feeding shows to reflect the belief that nature's bounty had created the most affluent society on earth, able to afford such whimsical pursuits. And tourists came to expect all of these things, for the national parks had for so long been everything they wanted them to be.

Although some scholars contend that "our wild parks are sacred earth which cannot be bought and sold," that is not entirely true. Sacred ground, as noted by others, is "inevitably contested space, a site of negotiated contests over the legitimate ownership." So while it is true that places like Yellowstone could not be purchased, the myths that made them valuable could be appropriated and used to generate wealth, to turn them into "neatly packaged cultural experiences of environment on which substantial profits are recorded each year." Ownership of the land was not necessary—simply the ability to use it to sell an idea, a symbol to market a story. National parks, rather than escaping commercial development because they were "worthless," or because they were too valuable as public treasures, actually became the most commodified pieces of real estate in the country. True, park development took on a different character. Instead of the environmental industrialization affected by mining, farming, and lumbering, national parks were designed to fit specific commercial needs in a more subtle, less obviously transformative fashion. In fact, as this story will demonstrate, parks like Yellowstone were the sites of some of the most intensive commercial activity in the American West.[8]

This, then, is the tale of those who owned Yellowstone, of the public administrators and especially the private entrepreneurs who shared stewardship of the park from its creation. This is not a morality play meant to assign blame for making the park less than some believe it should be. Rather, it is an account intended to illuminate how together the NPS and concessioners falsely raised expectations, how they designed and marketed Yellowstone as a museum of mythology, a landscape created to look like what Americans wanted to believe the Old West once was. It is about the people who constructed Yellowstone's many identities and shaped popular perceptions of the park over the years, and their reasons for doing so. It is about how they altered the physical landscape to fit these constructed images, and how eventually imagination outstripped their ability to transform the land itself. It is essentially a story about how Yellowstone was invented in the American imagination, altered again and again to fit the desired image, then creatively advertised as being all things to all groups of people. It is also a tale about what happens when reality no longer lives up to expectations.

Beginnings

1

Isolation characterized many of the early images of Yellowstone. For a place later deemed the repository of so much national heritage, Yellowstone National Park has a history that spans a relatively brief period, in both geologic and human terms. Approximately six hundred thousand years ago — long after most of the North American continent had assumed its present shape — a volcanic eruption formed an immense caldera (a crater or basin), fashioning what is now Yellowstone Lake and the immediate vicinity. Later, the resultant lava flows created a level plain high in the mountains of the northern Rockies; unstable and thin-crusted, the plateau, averaging seventy-five hundred feet above sea level, remained an active geothermal basin strewn with geysers, hot springs, and boiling mud pots. Surrounded by some of the most rugged peaks on the continent, isolated from American westward expansion for much of the nineteenth century by the brutal landscape and harsh climate, the region that would become the world's first national park remained almost unexplored by European-Americans until after the Civil War.[1]

The mountains around this plateau defined the physical boundaries of the latter-day park. To the northeast lay the Beartooth range, almost impenetrable; not until well into the twentieth century would regular entry to the reservation be viable from that direction. Southward, running along the eastern border of the park, the Absaroka Mountains stretched from the Montana border far into central Wyoming. The Tetons, the Wind River range, and the high plateaus of the Continental Divide thwarted encroachment from the south. Westward, the jagged peaks of the Gallatin range guarded Yellowstone.[2]

Most local Indians used the region as a passageway to summer hunting grounds, following rivers and streams through the mountains and across the plateau. Crows, Bannocks, Blackfeet, Shoshones, and Nez Perces, among others, all of whose tribal lands bordered the high country, utilized the region during certain seasons. Some, like the Crows, camped along the Yellowstone River north of the present-day park boundary in the winter months to hunt the herds of elk migrating from the mountains onto the lower riverside plains. The Bannocks and Shoshones crossed the Yellowstone plateau from their homes in Idaho and Utah to reach the buffalo plains to the east, as did the Nez Perces who regularly traversed the park. One such travel route, known as the Great Bannock Trail, led from Henry's Lake through the Targhee Pass to the Duck Creek drainage, then northeast along Cougar Creek to the Gardner River valley near Obsidian Cliff, an important quarry for tools and weapons. The trail then headed north to the future settlement of Mammoth Hot Springs and east along Lava Creek, over the Blacktail Deer Plateau, and eventually reached the Yellowstone River just above Tower Falls. It then passed into the Lamar Valley in the northeast corner of the park and branched, one section following the Lamar River southeast toward the Stinkingwater River (later renamed the Shoshone) and the other up Soda Butte Creek and across the Absarokas to the Clark's Fork drainage. Yet another fork left the main trail at the Yellowstone crossing and led southward to the lake and beyond. Obsidian Cliff attracted other tribes from vast distances, and artifacts from faraway regions have suggested that the glasslike black stone found there provided trade goods throughout the Northwest.[3]

Native people first shaped the physical characteristics of the landscape. The well-worn trails demonstrated that this area, despite its geographic isolation from mainstream patterns of both native and Euro-American settlement, was no more pristine, untouched, or untrodden than any other part of the North American continent. Native hunting pressures in the areas around the plateau had doubtless contributed to concentrating game animals in the future park. Likewise, native methods of hunting and gathering — especially the use of fire to clear forests and brush for campsites, to herd game animals, and to maintain areas for the harvest of tubers — shaped a landscape of open meadows interspersed within the lodgepole forests that future Euro-American explorers instinctively, if mistakenly, recognized as "natural." In this respect, the Indian peoples of the Yellowstone region were the first to design a landscape — in this case, completely inadvertently — that appealed to those who came later.

Despite the heavy seasonal native use by many different groups, the harsh climate of the Yellowstone plateau discouraged most Indians from remaining year-round. By the 1870s, however, when Yellowstone was designated a national park, American mythology had already transformed nature from threatening hostile "wilderness" into a place of spiritual renewal. Likewise, denizens of the forests and mountains had evolved in our imaginations from savages to noble savages. Nature, to be natural, needed such inhabitants, and despite the fact that native populations were transient on the plateau, stories about native occupation appeared. Most of these tales focused on a small band of Shoshones, called "Sheepeaters," who according to legend inhabited the mountain forests of Yellowstone. These people lived in woven huts and hunted the acrobatic bighorn sheep that shared the mountainous terrain. They were timid souls, adept at subsisting on available resources despite the heavy snows, frigid temperatures, and short summers. Shoshone mythology provided a model, the supernatural "Little People," who were said to inhabit the mountains. The Sheepeaters, most likely a fictive device borrowed from Shoshone stories, provided a necessary element to Euro-American stories about nature, and hence became useful in constructing images of Yellowstone during the latter years of the nineteenth century. The sense of isolation, of naturalness, to which this Sheepeater myth contributed eventually consituted one of the most attractive tourist draws.[4]

The maps and journals of explorers and trappers who invaded the northern Rockies between 1790 and 1840 increased public awareness of this immense and foreboding landscape. The geographically isolated Yellowstone country, however, received only cursory attention. British adventurer David Thompson, wintering at the Mandan villages in 1797 and 1798, learned about a great tributary to the Missouri and adopted the French name "Roche Jaune," which was translated as "Yellow Stone" on his maps. In 1806, returning from his epic journey to the Pacific, Captain William Clark of the U.S. Army crossed Bozeman Pass and reached the Yellowstone River at the site of present-day Livingston, Montana, about fifty-five miles north of the park. But neither of these men ever entered the future reservation because it was simply out of their way. One of Clark's men, John Colter, left the main party and likely crossed the Yellowstone plateau and descended the Stinkingwater, or Shoshone, River while returning east in 1807. Many believe Colter to be the first Euro-American to venture into the future Yellowstone National Park. His accounts led Captain Clark to include on maps an area known for the next several decades as "Colter's Hell."[5]

Other trappers passed through the park occasionally over the next thirty years, and stories about "Colter's Hell" added color to the already legendary mountain man mythology. In 1826 a party of trappers that included David Jackson, William Sublette, and Daniel Potts followed the Snake River north from Jackson Hole, across an intimidating mountain plateau, and into a fanciful land of geysers, hot springs, and mud volcanoes. While Colter's visit to the latter-day park remains in dispute (many believe that he was describing thermal features farther east, near present-day Cody, Wyoming), this group most certainly explored parts of Yellowstone. A letter Potts wrote described "a number of boiling springs . . . of most beautiful fine clay . . . the clay is white and of a pink and water appears fathomless as it appears to be entirely hollow under neith." Potts also described "Sublette Lake," later to be renamed Yellowstone Lake, in terms tinged with awe. But the wonders of the region had their most powerful impact on a twenty-two-year-old trapper who accompanied old hands Jackson and Sublette on this journey. His name was Jim Bridger, and more than any others, his tales would become the ones that invented the Yellowstone region in the popular imagination.[6]

Bridger's stories evoked a mysterious place full of wondrous natural phenomena. He told of a meadow high in the Rockies where a single stream divided, one rivulet running westward toward the Pacific and the other turning east to the Atlantic. A trout, he insisted, could cross the Continental Divide all by itself. Another story recounted Bridger's amazement at discovering "peetrified" trees full of "peetrified" birds singing "peetrified" songs. Yet another tale described how Bridger and his horse once rode right across a yawning chasm between two mountains — right on the very air! Bridger explained, of course, that this was possible only because "gravitation" was "peetrified" as well in this strange country of the Yellowstone. Hot springs and geysers became passages to hell itself in these stories, which garnered much interest across the land and were published in numerous outlets over the years. Thus, throughout this era of haphazard exploration, Yellowstone and its mythological wonders became shrouded in legend; such a place could not possibly exist in reality, most thought, for Bridger and his ilk were known to be accomplished embellishers of fact.[7]

The trappers' tales of the place "where Hell bubbled up" circulated widely. As the fur trade died, mining camps appeared in Montana and Idaho; settlements began springing up near the high-country plateau; and the resident population stimulated renewed interest in the upper Yellowstone. Bridger guided a government expedition under Captain William F. Raynolds that attempted to reach Yellowstone Lake from the south in 1859, but heavy snow prevented the party from gaining its objective. Bridger, Raynolds, and their men detoured west in frustration after coming close enough to see Two Ocean Plateau, that place where the waters did indeed divide, but "official" discovery of the wonders of the plateau was stymied by the weather. The outbreak of the Civil War ended any further bid. Soon, however, more miners flooded into Montana. Gold strikes at Alder Gulch (Virginia City) in 1863 and Last Chance Gulch (Helena) in 1864 began the rush; later, gold was discovered at Bear Gulch (Jardine) and Crevice Gulch in the Yellowstone Valley north of the park, and in 1868 at the Clark's Fork district (Cooke City) to the northeast. Farmers and ranchers followed the miners, laying claim to the fertile lands of the river valleys, and the military moved in to protect the new settlers from hostile Indians — Blackfoot lands had long been dangerous for whites. The U.S. Army built Fort Ellis, just east of Bozeman, in 1867, and soon prospectors penetrated the mountain barriers and panned the streams throughout the region. Their tales of natural phenomena, like those of the trappers before them, led only to disbelief. Who would believe that there existed a lake where a man could catch a fish and, moving a few paces, cook it in a hot spring without ever taking it off the hook?[8]

In 1869 a small party of Montana citizens, excited by the miners' accounts and familiar with the stories of Bridger and other trappers that had by now become legendary, set out to find the wonders and lend some much-needed credibility to the mountain man stories. These men were the first Yellowstone tourists. Leaving Diamond City, on the Missouri River southeast of Helena, they traveled south to the Yellowstone River at its junction with the East Fork (now the Lamar River), well within the boundaries of the future park. From there they trailed along the east side of the Yellowstone to the canyon, the falls, and Yellowstone Lake, then west into the Lower Geyser Basin, where the Great Fountain Geyser erupted in greeting. Following the

Firehole River downstream to the Madison, the men returned home, having spent over a month on their trip. Their report reverberated throughout Montana. They had beheld yellow-walled canyons too deep to descend, waterfalls to rival Niagara. They had discovered geysers erupting hundreds of feet into the air, boiling springs of crystal water, meadows where the ground rang hollow and thin-crusted, the men a single false step away from disaster. For the first time, respected citizens verified the old trappers' tales, and by the following summer everyone in Montana was eager to see the natural wonders. The explorers were certain that these same natural features would appeal to all Americans as symbols of national pride.[9]

Thus the stage was set for quite possibly the most famous creation story in the American West. This tale has become a staple of Yellowstone mythology, perhaps the most important factor in shaping the image of the park in America's collective consciousness. The story goes as follows.

In 1870 a group of fifteen prominent Montanans set out to investigate the reports coming out of the Yellowstone plateau area. These men, noble, public-spirited citizens all, initiated a series of events that culminated in Yellowstone being declared a national park. Accompanied by a military escort from Fort Ellis, this well-provisioned party established the truth behind the tall tales of Bridger and the rest. In August it followed the Yellowstone River south and confirmed the wonders of this isolated corner of the West. On September 19, 1870, after an extensive tour of the area, the men camped in a lush, well-watered meadow. Then, around the nightly campfire, one of the men, Cornelius Hedges, proposed a novel idea. He suggested that the area's uniqueness deserved protection from private ownership and exploitation so that others could experience it. The group supported his idea and promised to work toward making it a reality. This conversation occurred in what would later be known as National Park Meadows, at the junction of the Gibbon and Firehole Rivers, in the future Yellowstone National Park.[10]

This story, long recounted as the genesis of the national park idea, is almost certainly apocryphal. The party did camp in those meadows that final evening, but diaries kept by its members include no accounts of such a conversation. Only later, after the public reservation had become immensely popular and the idea spread to other locales, did the story emerge. The members of this group probably did discuss their intentions for the future of the area. Quite possibly the idea of a national reserve, consisting of lands protected from private claims under existing land disposal laws, arose, as the artist George Catlin had proposed such a plan for a large portion of the Rocky Mountain West decades before. In addition, Yosemite's creation as a state preserve in 1864 had established a precedent for such actions. Whatever happened around the campfire that night, the group returned to Fort Ellis with a plan to convince government officials to treat this land differently than most of the rest of the West. But its motives for seeking federal protection for the area were much more complex, and less altruistic, than the romantic, nationalistic account told and retold around countless Yellowstone campsites over the past decades suggests.[11]

Nevertheless, the members of the group possessed both the will and the resources to garner support for their vision of a federally protected reserve. General Henry D. Washburn was the surveyor-general of Montana, with government connections in Washington; Nathaniel P. Langford, destined to become the first superintendent of Yellowstone, was closely allied with the Northern Pacific Railroad, whose executives were even then planning future resorts along its yet-to-be-completed transcontinental line north of the park. Cornelius Hedges was a popular political figure in Montana, later a U.S. attorney, state senator, and judge. Samuel T. Hauser was president of the First National Bank of Helena, soon to be appointed territorial governor. All produced accounts for regional newspapers and excited interest in the idea of a national park. Langford, the most persistent of the group, lectured in Helena, Minneapolis, New York, and Washington, describing what he had seen and spearheading a publicity campaign orchestrated and financed by Jay Cooke of the Northern Pacific. Among those who heard Langford's presentation was Dr. Ferdinand V. Hayden of the U.S. Geological Survey, who immediately began lobbying Congress for funds to inspect the area officially.[12]

The Hayden Survey of 1871 represented the most ambitious and thorough study of the region yet undertaken, as well as the most important in forging a national identity for Yellowstone. On July 15, accompanied by twenty men of the "scientific party" and fifteen laborers, cooks, and hunters, Hayden embarked from Fort Ellis on the first government-financed tour of the Yellowstone plateau. As part of his scientific team Hayden had included photographer William Henry Jackson and landscape painter Thomas Moran. Like the previous explorers, he and his party headed south along the Yellowstone, three days later reaching the mouth of the Gardner River. The adventurers then diverged from usual practice, electing to follow the smaller stream, and thus became the first of the three major exploring parties to see Mammoth Hot Springs. Heading east, they advanced to Tower Falls and then to the Grand Canyon of the Yellowstone, mapping the territory to the lake. Using a twelve-foot boat brought for the purpose, two of the party sailed the shoreline and charted the bays, islands, and tributaries. Next the men established camp on the west bay and explored the three main geyser basins, crossing and recrossing the wandering Continental Divide. Moving around the south shore of the lake, they circled back to the outlet and downstream to the newly completed Baronett's Bridge, crossed the Yellowstone, and proceeded along that river toward Fort Ellis and home.[13]

Upon returning to Washington, Hayden joined the members of the Washburn party in lobbying for congressional action to protect the Yellowstone region from private control, to preserve the natural curiosities for future visitors to appreciate. Within a few months, by means of a sophisticated public relations campaign, the work produced results. The government expedition had returned with geologic, zoological, and botanical specimens, as well as photographs and sketches documenting the wonders of the plateau. Most famous was a painting by Moran of the Lower Falls of the Yellowstone, which he sold to Congress in 1871. On December 18, 1871, bills to withdraw Yellowstone from public entry were introduced into both houses of Congress. Hayden prepared and displayed his souvenirs in the Capitol rotunda, and supporters of the legislation distributed copies of *Scribner's Monthly* from May and June 1871, containing Langford's memoir of the Yellowstone, to every lawmaker's desk. In addition, the members of the Montana exploration party lobbied heavily for the park, as did Northern Pacific president Cooke, who envisioned the profits that would accrue to his enterprise as the line nearest this proposed reservation that would contain powerful symbols of the growing American belief in natural wonders as icons of a civil nature religion. The alliance of enthusiastic park supporters and powerful railroad interests had the desired effect. Both bills passed swiftly, and on March 1, 1872, President Ulysses S. Grant signed the legislation into law.[14]

The act created the world's first national park, although the language referred only to the reservation as being a "public park or pleasuring ground." Beyond that, little evidence suggests any coherent administrative plan for the reserve. Models existed, in California's Yosemite preserve and other attractions, such as Niagara Falls, designed to utilize nature as symbols of nationalism. But Yosemite belonged to the state, and although it was already a popular excursion destination for residents of San Francisco and other nearby cities, Yellowstone was much more remote. And Niagara had by this time become not only a symbol of nature but also a symbol of how such attractions could fall prey to commercial exploitation. Some were concerned that Yellowstone might suffer the same fate; when Hayden discovered the Mammoth Hot Springs in the northern part of the park, he also found several small-time entrepreneurs busily constructing ramshackle lodgings and promoting the "healing qualities" of the waters. But Congress demonstrated little inclination to spend much time or money on a place so remote, both physically and psychologically, from mainstream America. Thus administration and funding for the new reservation were provided in an indirect fashion. The secretary of the interior, to whom Congress assigned control over the park, was responsible "for the preservation, from injury or spoilation, of all timber, mineral deposits, natural curiosities, or wonders within said park, and their retention in their natural condition." To carry out this charge, Secretary of the Interior Columbus Delano appointed Nathaniel P. "National Park" Langford, Jay Cooke's public relations star, as superintendent of Yellowstone, without salary, since no appropriations accompanied the act. To provide operating funds, the secretary could, at his discretion, "grant leases for building purposes for terms not exceeding ten years, of small parcels of ground, at such places in said park as shall require the erection of buildings for the accommodation of visitors." All necessary moneys to operate the park would accrue from this leasing scheme.[15]

As Hayden had already discovered, frontier capitalists had earlier begun positioning themselves to take advantage of the increased public interest in the region among both miners and tourists. Perceived as entrepreneurs by some and as opportunistic squatters by others, they began a long tradition of private enterprise in the park. Early in 1871 one resourceful businessman, Collins J. "Yellowstone Jack" Baronett, had constructed a toll bridge over the Yellowstone near the mouth of the Lamar River to collect revenue from prospectors traveling to the Clark's Fork district. He was the first to recognize the opportunities presented by the region, but he was not alone for long. In June 1871, just before Hayden's arrival, James C. McCartney, commonly referred to as Yellowstone's "pioneer proprietor," erected a flimsy hotel and several small bathhouses at Mammoth Hot Springs to accommodate potential tourists attracted by the so-called healing waters. Hayden, who discovered upwards of fifty people shuttling in and out of the small curative shanties, described the lodgings as "very primitive," but he noted that "there is no reason why this locality should not at some future period become a noted place of resort for invalids." Members of the government survey also encountered Henry Horr, described by a contemporary as "a drunken worthless sort of man," who was busily constructing a bathhouse and tarpaper hotel near the springs adjacent to McCartney's claim. Another of these visionaries, Matthew McGuirk, arrived a year later only to find the supposed healthful waters of the hot springs already appropriated. He moved two miles northeast to Boiling River, the point where runoff from the Mammoth Hot Springs entered the Gardner River, and built a hostelry that catered to the infirm. While many accounts of the Mammoth settlement were derogatory, others described these enterprises in different tones. To some witnesses, McCartney and Horr were simply "two young gentlemen from Bozeman," and the tourists camped thereabouts "rather a motley, though quite a lively, group."[16]

The establishment of Yellowstone offered Americans a new symbol in which to invest national meaning. This was nature religion on a new scale. Those who had lobbied for the creation of the park claimed proudly that Yellowstone represented a new era, the first time any people in the history of the world had thought enough of nature to preserve it altruistically from rapacious exploiters. Such claims, combined with the accounts of early explorers, ignited a decade of surveys and tourism. In the summer of 1872 Hayden returned to expand upon his earlier work, while another government survey party also explored the park. Such official inspections occurred annually for the remainder of the decade. At the same time, parties of tourists, mostly from Montana, discovered attractions that previous pathfinders had bypassed, such as the Norris Geyser Basin. No roads existed; only McCartney, Horr, and McGuirk provided accommodations of any kind. Yet the sightseers flocked in, camping in shaded groves near the geysers or the canyon, taking day trips to other curiosities, exploring the still-mysterious corners of the vast "national pleasuring ground."

Despite popular belief that commercialization was precluded, private enterprise also flourished in the park. Harry Norton of Virginia City compiled the first guidebook, *Wonder-Land Illustrated,* in September of that first year. By 1874 regular passenger service between Bozeman and Mammoth Hot Springs commenced; "Zack Root's express" departed every Monday with freight and passengers bound for McCartney's hotel. One early traveler, the earl of Dunraven, referred to the inn in glowing terms: "The last outpost of civilization — that is, the last place where whiskey is sold." Indeed, intoxicating liquors were the most attractive features of the rudimentary accommodations. But Dunraven found much more to appreciate once separated from "civilization." His description of the spiritual qualities available in the park, published in 1876, remains a prime example of why nature — not just curiosities but the more mundane forests, meadows, and such — was itself an increasingly powerful draw. Dunraven wrote that Yellowstone was a place where one could become "saturated with the glories of Nature," where one could experience "pride that he too forms part of the same scheme, is a higher manifestation of the same power, a more perfect combination of the same material." He concluded that he "feels at one with Nature; the birds that fly, the beasts that roam the forests, the very trees and leaves and flowers are his brethren." About the same time, Secretary of War W. W. Belknap, accompanied by several high-ranking military officers, toured the park but declined to lodge with McCartney or Horr. Belknap's extremely well-provisioned party camped in luxury and, like Dunraven and so many others who have traveled to Yellowstone over the years, published an account of the trip, further spreading the fame of the region.[17]

Yellowstone epitomized the transition from wilderness as a threat to nature as an attraction. Much in the same way that the rest of the West was being tamed by agriculture, mining, ranching, and lumbering, Yellowstone was being transformed into something understandable, something orderly. The landscape had not yet changed, but the stories told about it were undergoing dramatic revision. Wilderness, in the old stories, was a place inherently frightening, lacking order and beyond control or understanding. In newer versions nature was a pleasant landscape able to provide spiritual sustenance. And Yellowstone National Park was rapidly becoming, in popular constructs, nature rather than wilderness. Occasionally, however, reality intruded upon the tranquillity of the natural scene. Such was the case during the summer of 1877, when Chief Joseph and his Nez Perce followers abandoned their reservation in Idaho and bolted for Canada. Their route took them through the park and into conflict with vacationers; thus, the mythic Old West, already an important part of the American metanarrative, collided with the still-under-construction stories of the New West as a place where nature could be appreciated in tranquillity. When the Nez Perces entered the park via the Madison River, several parties of campers were in their path. They encountered one group headquartered in the Lower Geyser Basin, became entangled with the tourists, and inflicted casualties as a result. Another party from Helena participated in the fighting, and one man was killed by Nez Perce warriors as he stood in the doorway of McCartney's Mammoth hotel. For two weeks the Indians, who had chosen this route across the plateau to avoid white settlements to the north, struggled to exit the park to the east but continued surprising tourists. Eventually they made their way to Clark's Fork and north into Montana, only to suffer defeat less than fifty miles short of the Canadian border in the Bearpaw Mountains.[18]

Two years later, park superintendent Philetus W. Norris officially removed all Indians from Yellowstone. By so doing, he was helping construct an image of the park that fit popular constructs about what nature should be. In 1876 Dunraven had referred to Yellowstone as a place where one could "comprehend in the smallest degree the greatness and grandeur of the Creator's works." Nature was available for such spiritual revitalization only if those seeking it believed that the natural world remained untouched, as designed by "the Creator." Reality — the fact that the park had long been utilized by Native Americans, that it had been cleared with fires and inhabited by humankind for centuries — infringed upon the usefulness of the mythology. So Norris expelled the Indians, assuring that reality would not intrude on the imagined, natural park. At the same time he promulgated the Sheepeater myth, a story about nonthreatening, nonlandscape-altering Indians who had retreated to the plateau to escape the changing world — again, a useful image to promote Yellowstone to those seeking their own escapes. Similar actions later took place in Glacier National Park, where Blackfeet were excluded to construct a more perfect image of "nature" for visitors. In Yosemite, native people continued to reside in the valley well after its designation as a national park. There, possibly because perceived threats from Indians had faded more into memory, they became attractions that added a historic, cultural element to the wonders of nature — another thread in the story.[19]

Indian removal was important in assuring Yellowstone visitors their expected experiences. It was also, not unimportantly, good for business, and by the early 1880s Yellowstone businesses had undergone considerable alteration and had begun the long process of shaping the park to fit popular images. Early entrepreneurs Horr and McGuirk had departed the park, pressured by new superintendent Philetus Norris into surrendering their squatter claims. McCartney still held out, but he feuded with Norris regularly over liquor sales and poor service. Norris even tried forcibly to evict the "pioneer proprietor" at one point by locking him out of his hotel — the first instance, but certainly not the last, of conflict between government administrators and commercial interests. Eventually the two arrived at a tense truce; McCartney spent the summers, when Norris was in residence at Mammoth, at another of his establishments to the north in the "Montana strip," a disputed section of land near the mouth of the Gardner River. By 1881 he had established a post office, and within months the town site of Gardiner arose around McCartney's liquor and livery businesses. The granting of government postal contracts led to the construction of two additional hotels. In 1880 George Marshall erected a frame structure near the junction of Nez Perce Creek and the Firehole River, easily accessible by trail from Virginia City. East of Mammoth, on the plain above the mouth of the Lamar River, John F. Yancey also constructed a small building catering to tourists. His Pleasant Valley Hotel, a fifty-by-thirty-foot log structure, was most famous for the host's whiskey, served in one dirty glass that he boasted had never been touched by water. In addition to the hotels, small tent stores sprouted throughout the park, selling photographs, renting horses and wagons, providing guides, and offering other amenities. Capital was unnecessary; to embark on a commercial venture in Yellowstone, an individual need only offer a service or a product, ideally one that played upon visitors' preconceived ideas and expectations. Despite the enabling act provision that required leases to conduct commerce, none of these small operators possessed them before 1884, and park superintendents lacked any budget with which to enforce the rules.[20]

More changes were imminent for the park businesses, but meanwhile excursionists continued trekking to the reservation. In the summer of 1882, General Philip H. Sheridan enjoyed his second and most eventful vacation tour of Yellowstone. He had been in the park in 1877, leaving only days before the Nez Perces' arrival. This time, leading a party of 150 men with three hundred horses and mules and employing Baronett as guide, he cut the first trail along the Snake River from Jackson Hole to the West Thumb of Yellowstone Lake. Exiting the park to the northeast, Sheridan and his party followed Soda Butte Creek to Clark's Fork and then downstream fifty miles to the mouth near present-day Laurel, Montana, proving that route feasible. They soon encountered construction parties of the Northern Pacific Railroad, at which time Sheridan elected to complete his journey in a more leisurely fashion, returning in the caboose of a work train to Billings, Montana. Within a few weeks, the line had reached the base of Bozeman Pass, due north of the park, and the company announced plans to construct a spur up the valley to Wonderland. To assure sufficient accommodations for the anticipated flood of tourists, the Northern Pacific decided to acquire exclusive lodging privileges in the park.[21]

It seemed a natural step. Since the completion of the first transcontinental line in 1869, railroad companies had emerged as the primary promoters of the American West. Actually, they became promoters of two distinct Wests, two separate images constructed from two different narrative threads in the American mythology. One, the "Old West," was based on the so-called development myth, the tale that western resources — timber, minerals, grazing lands — could generate enough wealth if properly utilized to create a more perfect society. It was a West that offered economic opportunity along with the ability to demonstrate those uniquely American qualities that allowed the frontier to be conquered. Another separate construct, the "New West," appeared in the American consciousness during the latter part of the nineteenth century as a reimagining of the past; Yellowstone and later national parks became important symbols of this emerging image. The New West offered something other than economic opportunity; it promised spiritual revitalization through an appreciation of nature and reliving the frontier experience. The New West image was designed to appeal not to farmers, ranchers, miners, or town builders. Rather, it called to Americans eager to experience life in a mythological past, a romantic version of the frontier process of conquest that others were still chasing.

Railroads and other western boosters marketed these two distinct Wests with different stories. To sell the Old West, companies like the Union Pacific hired immigration agents to distribute samples of potatoes and apples grown along its route to entice potential farmers. The Northern Pacific fervently promoted the riches that awaited the adventurous in Idaho's Coeur d'Alene mountains, where gold and silver promised the American Dream. James J. Hill of the Great Northern convinced thousands of European immigrants that North Dakota was the Garden of Eden — no mean feat of salesmanship. At world's fairs like the Philadelphia Centennial Exposition in 1876, the New Orleans Cotton Centennial and Exposition of 1885, the St. Louis World's Fair of 1904, and the Chicago World's Columbian Exposition of 1892, railroads and western states' boosters passionately sold the Old West. Idaho built cavernous structures featuring all the varieties of lumber available for harvest in that state. California constructed towers of oranges to lure investment in irrigation projects; the one in Chicago measured fourteen feet around at the base and stood thirty-two feet tall. Montana displayed sugar beets larger than horses, proof that the West offered a plethora of resources awaiting extraction. In St. Louis, all western states displayed statues representing those images that boosters most desired visitors to take with them. The statues of Iowa, Nebraska, and Kansas all featured corn; those from the Dakotas, wheat. Boosters from Montana and Wyoming portrayed their states with female figures caressing chunks of silver ore. Smaller regional expositions, such as that held in Spokane in 1890, also attracted promoters eager to show off the bounty of the land.[22]

The New West was marketed to different audiences holding different ideas about what the West really was. Northen Pacific passenger agent Charles Fee wrote a guidebook to attractions entitled *Northern Pacific Railroad: The Wonderland Route to the Pacific Coast, 1885*. Fee's publication was so popular that the railroad published such brochures annually for decades thereafter; these brochures broadened the awareness of Yellowstone National Park and stimulated visitation. Yellowstone received even more promotional attention after 1900, when other railroads, including the Union Pacific, the Chicago, Burlington, and Quincy, and the Chicago, Milwaukee, St. Paul and Pacific, expanded service to the park. In 1898 the passenger division of the Southern Pacific Railroad published its first edition of *Sunset* magazine, which promoted the natural and historic attractions of the American Southwest. Beginning in 1903, the Atchison, Topeka, and Santa Fe started purchasing artworks depicting these same sites — the Grand Canyon and Arizona's petrified forest, for example — to use in promotional displays.

Within a few years the Great Northern Railway focused its promotional efforts on Glacier National Park, eventually adopting a mountain goat, "Rocky," as its corporate logo. The Union Pacific added Zion and Bryce Canyon parks to its marketing campaign. These railroads spared no effort to sell this new, postfrontier West to eastern tourists seeking to experience a mythological past connection with nature.[23]

Despite the boosterism and stories of prosperity and new attractions that characterized the day, business for many western railroads during the 1870s was a struggle. The Northern Pacific had weathered difficult times since Jay Cooke had so actively urged that Yellowstone be designated a national park, but it had recovered admirably to become the primary promoter of park travel. Widespread financial disaster in 1873 had forced Cooke into bankruptcy, and for years the railroad terminus languished in North Dakota, with no cash to complete its transcontinental route. The outbreak of Indian hostilities on the northern plains shortly thereafter discouraged any further construction even when money became available. But by 1878 the U.S. Army had defeated the Indians, and after five years of stagnation the national economy had rebounded. Late in the 1870s, financier Frederick Billings became company president, and the railroad resumed laying track. In 1882 another management coup brought in Henry Villard, a German-born public relations genius, as president. By the time Sheridan met the crews at Laurel, the Northern Pacific was little over a year removed from pounding the last spike in its ocean-to-ocean line. Villard promoted Yellowstone as a main attraction along the route, and with the West once again safe for tourism, he was confident that the park would prove a profitable lure.[24]

Because Yellowstone was a national park, many believed that the government should provide such accommodations necessary for visitors to enjoy this public pleasuring ground. Congress had already decided that private operators would supply visitor services through a system of park leases. But for the first decade of the park's existence, from 1872 to 1882, such concessions — businesses allowed to operate in Yellowstone under government license — were regulated in a haphazard manner. That situation changed with the entry of a group of investors backed by the Northern Pacific. While fly-by-night operators like McCartney, Marshall, and Yancey conducted their trade without sanction, the Interior Department had rejected many others who applied for leases during those first ten years.

Authorities reasoned that proposals for hotels, lunch counters, and liveries were superfluous, as existing freelance operators already served those needs. They dismissed other propositions that did not comply with the act's provision to maintain park features "in their natural condition," such as a landscape gardening plan, a racecourse with grandstands, and a waterfront village on the south shore of Yellowstone Lake. In 1881, Secretary of the Interior Carl Schurz denied an application from two North Dakota men for a hotel monopoly in the park, stating that no exclusive privileges would be granted. Just a year later, however, another group, this one loosely affiliated with the Northern Pacific, filed a similar application. Now government officials hesitated. As the railroad had moved closer to the park, Interior Department administrators became increasingly aware that the existing Yellowstone facilities were inadequate to meet the demands of significant numbers of visitors. Only three options seemed available: the government would either have to operate the businesses itself, which Congress had no interest in doing; it would have to grant leases to small independent operators like Marshall, McCartney, and Yancey, which posed regulatory problems; or it would have to reverse earlier policy and grant monopolistic privileges. Faced with the prospect of angry tourists and public criticism over poor accommodations, the Interior Department decided to accept the only well-financed proposal it had received, that from the Northern Pacific group.[25]

The new investors, prominent men all, submitted a plan intended to control all business in Yellowstone. Superintendent of the Northern Pacific Carroll T. Hobart and Henry M. Douglas of Fort Yates, Dakota Territory, filed the application in July 1882. Senator William Windom of Minnesota was also involved, as were "Uncle" Rufus Hatch, a well-known Wall Street financier, and former senator Roscoe Conkling of New York. The plan included ten-year leases for over forty-four hundred acres of parklands distributed over seven different sites and surrounding the most popular attractions. It also allowed the company to cut timber, mine coal, and extract other resources as needed and prohibited any competitors from acquiring leases — however, Yancey, Marshall, and McCartney retained their small concessions, as did Baronett, operator of the only bridge across the Yellowstone. Magnanimously, the applicants agreed to submit annual fee schedules for approval — the Interior Department would at least have oversight on charges to visitors. Assistant Interior Secretary Merritt Joslyn forwarded a copy to Yellowstone superintendent Patrick Conger on August 10 for his comments, which were extremely negative. Conger informed the secretary that the proposal threatened to lock up too much land in the hands of the investors, that park visitors would be at the mercy of private concerns if they desired to see the wonders of the park. But his resistance — had his reply reached Washington in time — would have mattered little. On September 1, 1882, Joslyn signed the proposal on behalf of the Interior Department; Hobart and Douglas signed for the company. The following year the two men assigned their interest to a new entity, the Yellowstone National Park Improvement Company (YNPIC), which brought Hatch and Conkling officially into the business as their partners.[26]

Members of the new group quickly began to develop their leases. Hatch committed $112,000 cash and an additional $30,000 in credit to construct a hotel at Mammoth Hot Springs that began operations early in the summer of 1883. Soon thereafter, tent camps at Norris Geyser Basin, the Upper Geyser Basin, and the Lower Falls sprang up under YNPIC auspices. All were equipped with solid-wall tents, carpeted and furnished with beds, mattresses, chairs, and other conveniences. Kitchen tents at each location contained large cookstoves. Unlike the previous independent camps operated by unsanctioned parties, these quarters were intended to be replaced by hotels as soon as possible; consequently, their rates were identical to the later, more substantial lodgings. Workers completed about one-half of the Mammoth edifice, known as the National Hotel, in time to house and entertain distinguished guests with amenities that included a Steinway grand piano. Two French chefs and a German baker provided world-class cuisine to complement the luxurious accommodations. Such facilities were perfectly in keeping with popular perceptions of the day, beliefs that only individuals of a certain class had the ability to appreciate the wonders of American nature.[27]

The summer of 1883 was by far the busiest in the short history of the park, with many physical changes taking place. Five years earlier, Superintendent Norris had blazed a primitive road from Mammoth to Madison Junction and the Upper Geyser Basin. Now, using long-awaited congressional appropriations, members of the U.S. Army Corps of Engineers improved and expanded the rudimentary transportation network. They surveyed routes for a 223-mile system of roads and in September began constructing a new route south from Mammoth toward the geyser basins. Most significantly, the Northern Pacific had completed its Park Branch line south from Livingston to Cinnabar, only seven miles north of Mammoth, early in 1883, allowing visitors easier access via stagecoach to the new National Hotel. And the YNPIC solidified its control over park business by contracting with a Bozeman transportation company, Wakefield and Hoffman, to convey visitors on an exclusive basis. Tourists could still come into the park in their own wagons, but no other company could offer transport for hire. Thus, with the exception of a few small, independent hotels, two companies in league with the Northern Pacific controlled the lodging and transportation concessions, and thus access to those attractions most desirable to visitors.[28]

During that summer of 1883, in addition to the usual excursionists from Helena, Virginia City, and Bozeman, three notable parties from the East visited the park. Their presence further advertised Yellowstone as a national symbol. In August, President Chester A. Arthur embarked on an extensive Yellowstone tour, entering the park from the south along the trail General Sheridan had blazed the year before. The president's small party included Secretary of War Robert Lincoln, Senator George G. Vest of Missouri, Montana territorial governor John S. Crosby, General Sheridan, a few journalists, and F. Jay Haynes, recently appointed official YNPIC photographer and destined to become a fixture in Yellowstone. They traveled directly to Mammoth Hot Springs before doubling back to the geyser basins. Returning to Mammoth via Baronett's bridge, the president and his companions refused to stay at the National Hotel, instead "roughing it" as they had throughout the trip, with their own china, crystal, and linens carried on 150 pack mules. On their last night in the park at Mammoth, they encountered Rufus Hatch of the YNPIC, who was himself entertaining an impressive group of VIPs celebrating the opening of the National Hotel. Sixty-one invited guests from the United States, Great Britain, Germany, and France, many of whom traveled with servants, enjoyed Hatch's hospitality, choking on the dust raised by teams of stagecoaches, sleeping twenty to a tent at the outlying camps, and ushering in a new era of Yellowstone tourism. Their experiences, well chronicled by the accompanying international press, typified later modes of park travel; individual visitors, wandering in solitude around the "national pleasuring ground," would soon disappear in favor of large groups moving from attraction to attraction, as defined by popular images of the park. A third group, organized in September by Northern Pacific president Henry

Villard, celebrated the completion of the railroad's transcontinental line, as well as the new branch line to Yellowstone. Like the Hatch excursionists, Villard and his friends toured the park en masse, utilizing parades of stagecoaches and overwhelming the staffs at hotel and camp alike. As the accompanying journalists filed their stories that summer and autumn, Yellowstone National Park seemed to be the center of activity in America.[29]

While the YNPIC busily developed its vast lease acreage, all of which was situated to control access to the park's major natural attractions — the canyon, falls, and geysers, those images that appeared on the covers of railroad brochures and alongside magazine articles — others sought to undermine the company's privileged position. Superintendent Conger, believing that his authority had been usurped by the YNPIC, wrote to friends in Washington, describing the devastation that the company was inflicting on areas surrounding its construction projects. George Bird Grinnell, the outspoken editor of *Forest and Stream* and a prominent advocate of the national park, asserted that the company charged exorbitant rates for contemptible accommodations, the lack of competition allowing greed to set prices. But the most powerful critic was George Graham Vest, U.S. senator from Missouri, who accompanied President Arthur on his Yellowstone excursion; he argued that the YNPIC was taking liberties with public lands.[30]

Vest rallied Senate support for legislation to limit the Interior Department's authority to grant leases for park services. He was outraged that Secretary Henry Teller, who was conveniently absent from Washington while the contracts were being signed, sanctioned the YNPIC "steal" and allowed the attractions of Yellowstone to be surrounded by commercial development. On December 7, 1882, Vest introduced a Senate resolution requiring the Interior Department to submit all contracts involving national park concession leases to the Senate for approval. An amendment drafted by Senator Benjamin Harrison of Indiana, who had himself toured the park the previous year, restricted holdings to ten acres and prohibited the leasing of land within a quarter mile of the Yellowstone River falls or any geyser. The amended bill passed on March 3, 1883, just prior to adjournment, thus reducing the acreage of YNPIC holdings from forty-four hundred to ten.[31]

For the next two years the chief park concession company, its takeover plans stymied by Vest and its finances in disarray, nonetheless attempted to conduct business as usual. Although the 1883 season was a success if measured in numbers of visitors, with the still-unfinished National Hotel at Mammoth and all the outlying tent camps remaining fully occupied throughout the summer, the company was almost destitute. No one — not even Rufus Hatch — would invest more money in a business whose main assets, the park leases surrounding those features that were being promoted as the only things worth seeing, had been taken away. After a falling-out with partners Hobart and Douglas, Hatch filed for bankruptcy protection, and on March 10, 1884, the YNPIC began operating under a series of court-appointed trustees. Hobart, who remained general manager, struggled to continue operations. The shortage of cash prevented construction of the planned hotel at Norris Geyser Basin, where guests still slept in tents, as they did at the Canyon encampment. At the Lower Basin, a "shanty" of raw pine served as inn; and at the Upper Basin, only a single three-bedroom cabin accommodated each stageload of visitors. To compound the problem, many of these way stations rested on land not covered by the revised leases; the Upper Basin shack was too close to Old Faithful, the tents at Canyon too close to the rim.[32]

During this same period, while the YNPIC suffered through financial turmoil, other, smaller leaseholders also served many Yellowstone visitors in various capacities. Although technically the YNPIC held exclusive rights to park lodging and transportation, a succession of superintendents did little to enforce the rule, and the Interior Department continued to grant leases to others. Several old park hands finally received formal contracts from the Interior Department in 1884, legitimizing their existing enterprises. In January, George Marshall signed a lease for four acres in the Lower Geyser Basin, with the stipulation that he expand his hotel to at least sixty rooms. The ten-year term cost Marshall and his new partner, G. G. Henderson, two dollars per year, per acre, which became a standard fee. In April, John Yancey also received a ten-year lease for ten acres in Pleasant Valley surrounding his hotel and tavern. In response to demands from the miners at Cooke City, the Interior Department contracted for a telegraph line between Cinnabar and the Clark's Fork district. In March 1885 Helen and Walter Henderson received a ten-acre lease at Mammoth upon which to construct the Cottage Hotel, two years later enlarging it to hold 100 guests. The Interior Department approved plans for other hotels at the Upper Geyser Basin near Old Faithful, the Lower Geyser Basin, and the Grand Canyon of the Yellowstone, as well as for a livery and blacksmith shop at Mammoth. Secretary Teller granted one other application in 1884, to F. Jay Haynes, the Northern Pacific photographer who had arrived in the area three years earlier. Haynes received approval to build studios on two four-acre sites, one at Mammoth and one in the Upper Geyser Basin near Old Faithful.[33]

Alongside these licensed concessions, numerous profit seekers, taking advantage of lax enforcement and YNPIC financial problems, still operated without sanction of any kind. Some opened saloons near company hotels; others constructed blacksmith shops or livery stables. General stores appeared overnight, typically arrayed within the walls of a tent. Hunting camps occupied the outlying areas despite new laws against shooting game, and local tour guides — "Knights of the oily tongue," according to one visitor — peddled their questionable abilities both at the Cinnabar railroad terminus and at Mammoth. The colony at Mammoth was rapidly becoming a city and attracting squatters who built houses, barns, and bathhouses at the mineral pools. Nearly all these entrepreneurs lacked the necessary capital to improve their enterprises; hence the main Yellowstone settlement resembled a ramshackle, rundown village.

Despite the obstacles facing the YNPIC from competition both legal and illegal, Hobart persevered until 1886, when yet another group of investors, led by Charles Gibson of St. Louis and former Northern Pacific president Frederick Billings, purchased the company assets and negotiated new leases. Gibson and his associates assumed control, organized as the Yellowstone Park Association (YPA), and, with Northern Pacific financial backing, tried to reestablish a monopoly of services. The new company fundamentally changed the character of park services. It was financed almost wholly by the Northern Pacific Railroad and for the first years of its tenure possessed sufficient money to develop its properties. The company assumed responsibility for most of the old YNPIC locations, including those at Mammoth, Norris, and Canyon, and leased a new site on the north shore of Yellowstone Lake. By the terms of its agreement with Interior Secretary L. Q. C. Lamar, most hotels were to be completed by October 1, 1886, and the others within two or three years. The new company retained Wakefield and Hoffman as transportation contractors, convinced park officials to enforce the stagecoach monopoly, and generally cleaned up the worst of the concessions problems. The reorganization was well publicized and well received; public outrage over the shoddy level of services had been common before the

change of management. Americans were being told a story, through commercial advertising and popular media, that suggested nature, represented
in its ideal form in Yellowstone, was incomplete and somehow "unnatural"
without certain services and accommodations.[34]

The YPA wasted little time proving up on its leases. The combination of
adequate lodging, regular transportation routes over improved roads, and
increased security soon encouraged park visitors to follow a uniform itinerary and visit those attractions deemed significant. By May 1886 a hotel
capable of housing 100 guests replaced the tent camp at the Grand Canyon
of the Yellowstone. In August the YPA erected the first of a series of ill-fated
inns at the Norris Geyser Basin; the inn soon burned down and was rebuilt
before the end of the next season. In 1887 the company also constructed a
temporary structure at the Lake site where it later built another new hotel.
The U.S. Army, after taking over park administration in 1886 and replacing
the series of ineffectual Interior Department appointees, evicted many of
the squatters, hunters, and ne'er-do-wells who had cluttered up the scattered settlements. Regular appropriations for roads since 1883 also allowed
the Corps of Engineers to carve out most of the modern-day park routes.
By 1889, although tourist numbers were still a relatively small five thousand
annually, most visitors entered via the Northern Pacific, boarded a Wakefield
stage at Cinnabar, and spent their tour of the park at YPA hotels, riding from
Mammoth to Norris, then the Lower Basin, Canyon, and back, exiting north
to the NP line.[35]

The arrival of the YPA changed the nature of park tourism, but the shift
was subtle. Some visitors, mostly locals who had come for years, still brought
their own wagons and teams, camped where they wished, and avoided the
concessions. Even a guidebook sanctioned by the railroad reflected idyllic
scenes already becoming part of the past. It included photos of solitary individuals sitting around a small cookfire deep in the woods or small parties
clambering through downed timber without benefit of any visible trails. In
reality, such experiences were becoming rare, even as they formed an
increasingly important component in the constructed image of the park.
Park photographer F. Jay Haynes began selling pictures of YPA hotels alongside more traditional views of geysers, hot springs, and the canyon, documenting the assimilation of cultural attractions into the natural features of
the park. Animals, too, appeared in Haynes's photos in greater numbers

now. Hunting had been banned in the park in 1883, to preserve yet another part of the popular image of what nature should look like. Before long, potential visitors would be lured to Yellowstone to see not only geysers, canyons, and waterfalls but also the hotels that started appearing in promotional materials and the bears that begged alongside roads.[36]

While implementing its plans to reshape Yellowstone into a place in keeping with ideas about what such parks should look like, the new company seemed to have reformed the slipshod operation of the YNPIC. Behind the scenes, however, problems persisted. Most concerned political or legal questions over who controlled access to the attractions of the park. For example, the YNPIC leases from 1883 still existed, with some overlapping the new ones of the YPA. Carroll Hobart continually pestered the new concessioners over his ouster and attempted to organize competition at several locations. Another former YNPIC manager, Eli C. Waters, did the same. Both men possessed political connections in Washington and used them regularly to harass Gibson and the YPA. In addition, a split had developed between Gibson and the Northern Pacific managers over price reductions, which the railroad — but not the YPA — could afford. The discounted rates reduced the amount of cash available for park operations. Yet another difficulty arose over the transportation agreement that Gibson had inherited from the YNPIC. Because Interior Department officials were unclear about the legality of granting concessions for transportation only, Wakefield and Hoffman had instead signed an exclusive agreement with the YNPIC in 1883. When Gibson took over in 1886, his company assumed the contract, and the stagecoach operators retained their rights. But by 1890 this agreement presented a political opening for YPA adversaries to exploit.[37]

This controversy began over a common occurrence but eventually cost the Wakefield firm its lucrative concession. In the autumn of 1890, U.S. Postmaster General John Wanamaker became stranded, along with 100 other park visitors, at the small hotel in the Lower Geyser Basin. He and one of his companions, a prominent Chicago judge, protested the lack of stages to carry at least a portion of the group onward. Their complaints reached Washington, as did a report that another stagecoach passenger had died of a heart attack while walking up a steep grade at Mary Mountain to spell the horses. Such events, while not everyday occurrences, were nonetheless not unusual, and ordinarily they were no cause for government scrutiny. But a

Montana rancher and Republican, Silas S. Huntley, had been lobbying powerful acquaintances in an attempt to take over the transportation concession. Wakefield, a Democrat, discovered that politics played an important role in the awarding of park contracts. In October 1890, upon being called to Washington, D.C., to answer the complaints, he discovered that the Interior Department was preparing to reopen the transportation concession for bids, and that his contract with Gibson and the YPA was no longer valid. On March 30, 1891, Interior Secretary John Noble, of the Republican Harrison administration, awarded Huntley a new monopoly franchise.[38]

Huntley had utilized his political connections, including his friendship with President Harrison's son Russell, to land the concession. He then employed the generous contract terms and his family connections to make the business a success. Huntley offered Wakefield $70,000 for his stagecoaches, stock, and miscellaneous equipment, using his exclusive contract to purchase the assets at fire sale prices. A standard clause in the lease agreement, used since 1883, allowed the Interior Department oversight on pricing but for the first time also guaranteed Huntley a profit. The new stagecoach mogul had everything but the money to prosper in his endeavor. He solved this problem by bringing in partners, Harry W. Child and Edmund Bach, both brothers-in-law to Huntley, and the three proceeded to run their transportation enterprise in an impeccable manner.[39]

In the twenty years since its establishment, Yellowstone had undergone a dramatic transformation, both physically and, perhaps more important, in the public imagination. In 1871 Hayden and his survey party explored territory all but unknown to Americans, but by 1892 the forgotten corner of Wyoming was perhaps the most promoted, familiar, and visited part of the West. "Wonderland," as it was still commonly called, was as accessible as the nearest Northern Pacific station. Those wishing to see for themselves the geysers, hot springs, falls, and canyons no longer had to outfit wagons and teams or even pack tents. The most striking change was in the way that visitors toured the park. Instead of independently wandering among natural attractions, strolling through the woods toward a particularly promising overlook, or investigating an unfamiliar wildflower, most tourists now spent much of their time in stagecoaches, hotels, or saloons. They visited those features convenient to lodgings or lunch counters — Mammoth Terrace, Norris Basin,

Apolinaris Spring, Old Faithful, and others highlighted in the Northern Pacific publicity literature. Institutionalization of tourism to maximize profit, the obvious goal of railroad-funded concessions, was slowly transforming Yellowstone. New parks like Mount Rainier, where the Northern Pacific financed facilities as well, would shortly undergo similar changes. National parks were being altered, shaped, designed to fit existing beliefs about which parts of the natural world held value. Already Yellowstone had, in some important ways, been reduced to a series of curiosities seen from passing stagecoaches. But these first twenty years barely hinted at the future, for Harry Child, the man most responsible for making the park what it was to become and for setting a pattern of concessions development in other national parks, had discovered Yellowstone.

2

Harry's Grand Tour

Yellowstone experienced many growing pains between 1872 and 1892. Most of the problems stemmed from the difficulties of shaping the landscape into a marketable product. Many Americans, in fact many people around the world, embrace national parks as the best remaining examples of wilderness preserved, but that was never anyone's plan for Yellowstone or the other national parks in the early days. Indeed, the idea of wilderness was about to undergo significant revision and itself become a commodity. But through the final decades of the nineteenth century, wilderness remained an idea unattractive to a majority of American travelers, still encumbered by images of danger and a lack of order or control. Even in Nathaniel Pitt Langford's re-creation of the so-called campfire conversation of 1870, the Langford-Washburn-Doane party members wished only to preserve specific attractions like geysers and canyons, much as the initial Yosemite grant to California included only the valley and Mariposa grove of giant sequoias. They, like most other citizens of the day, certainly had no interest in wilderness — unorganized, underutilized, savage-inhabited landscape, in the stories of the day — that being perhaps the most common feature of the nineteenth-century American West. When surveyor Hayden proposed in 1872 that an astounding two million acres be reserved in the Yellowstone country, he did so only because he feared other curiosities, yet undiscovered, would be left without protection. Compounding the problem of selling Yellowstone to politicians and potential tourists was the fact that most of the intended park differed little in flora and fauna from the surrounding Rockies; therefore, most visitors, especially in the early years when they came predominantly from Montana, had minimal interest in its meadows, forests, or other such commonplace scenery. They came, as they had been coming to Yosemite since the 1850s, to see oddities. Value could be extracted, wealth generated, only by marketing the parks as "wonderlands," open-air museums displaying strange and intriguing natural phenomena.

With the arrival of railroads in the American West, visitors began traveling to national parks from more distant locales, carrying with them different ideas and preconceptions. Throughout the nineteenth century, influential authors and artists linked nature appreciation with American nationalism. Novelist James Fenimore Cooper, poet William Cullen Bryant, and painter Thomas Cole epitomized this movement with their work in the 1820s and 1830s. Ralph Waldo Emerson's seminal 1835 essay, "Nature," and his disciple Henry David Thoreau's later writings popularized nature as something other than threatening, as a place of respite and spiritual rejuvenation. The accelerating pace of industrialization in post–Civil War America provided citizens with a dramatic contrast between city and country, between natural and unnatural places. Nature became an attraction in and of itself—not wilderness, but orderly landscapes like those in Cole's paintings. Tourists were drawn by promotions and advertisements that constructed images of national parks as places of natural curiosities and nationalist vistas of canyons and waterfalls—uniquely American "wonderlands"—but also by those that portrayed the parks as ideal representations of spiritually uplifting nature preserved, protected from the corrupting effects of development.

More and more, as these romantic ideas about nature spread, tourists were inclined to separate cultural landscapes from those deemed natural, and railroads, concessioners, and administrators began encouraging the repackaging of national parks as the quintessential natural places. At the same time, these groups intensified their efforts to shape the parks to fit collective ideas about how exactly natural landscapes should look. Their interests were always clear; the parks should be resorts, places where railroad patrons could appreciate nature in relative comfort. Implied in this belief was the idea that nature could be treasured only by those of a certain class, those able to afford—and thus appreciate—such spiritual regeneration. To this end, railroad companies funded hotels in the parks whose locations offered views of features deemed valuable by the accepted standards of the time. National park officials pragmatically catered to tourists by helping reshape the landscape to meet expectations, building and improving roads, sanctioning competing concessioners, and generally aiding businessmen in trying to create an accessible natural landscape. From the very beginning, national parks were managed as museums; at first the displays were curiosities, then they were expanded to include scenery and vistas classified as natural. After the first few years of widespread hunting in the parks, even the wildlife was off-limits to sportsmen, becoming yet another attraction in a romanticized, mythological, natural image of the American West.[1]

Few groups contributed more to this process, this growing sense of separation between humans and their environment, than did concessioners, and no concessioner did as much as Harry W. Child, the primary architect of Yellowstone's landscape and the foremost caretaker of its mythology. He was a man of many talents, foremost among them making money. Born in 1857 in San Francisco, he was sent east, to West Newton, Massachusetts, to prepare for Harvard but quickly tired of academic life. Boarding a steamer and returning home via Panama, in 1882 he helped found the San Francisco Stock Exchange and made his first fortune in the process. While still a young man he moved to Montana, where, together with his uncle, he became involved in the lucrative mining industry. By the age of thirty he was general manager of the Gregory Mine southwest of Helena and owned a large home on that city's fashionable Madison Avenue, two doors from the residence of territorial governor and Washburn party excursionist Samuel T. Hauser. He then directed the construction of a $2 million smelter at Great Falls, bringing the project in on time and under budget. Child later turned to banking, first in Helena and later in Salesville (now Gallatin Gateway), Montana, yet another successful venture. In 1911 he partnered with area rancher Charles Anceney to form a land company and to found the famous Flying D Ranch on Spanish Creek, a concern encompassing over five hundred thousand acres and supporting at times twenty thousand head of cattle, one of the largest ranches in the country. He had monetary interests in gold mines, poultry farms, and literally dozens of other regional ventures, financially backing dozens of young men — his "partners" — who owned little besides their capacity for hard work. His financial acumen served him well; Child was a millionaire before reaching the age of fifty. Nevertheless, he was widely known as "Harry Hardup" because, as one acquaintance put it, "he owned only a young empire of land and 30,000 head of stock."[2]

Coming to Montana in the days of the vigilantes, Child fit comfortably into his adopted home, developing a reputation for being both brave and intelligent — if somewhat devious. In 1887 the owners of the Gregory mine, J. W. Seligman and Company, received a frantic telegram at their headquarters in New York. Albert J. Seligman, a young mining engineer and scion of the wealthy clan who had been sent to Helena six years earlier to look after the family's interests, had been taken captive by disgruntled workers in a dispute over back pay. Locked in the mine with him was Harry Child, who negotiated a compromise. Child talked his way out of the mine, rode to Helena, contacted Governor Hauser to forestall police involvement, and wired New York. Within twenty-four hours he had the necessary $250,000 committed. He then gathered the money from local banks and started back for the Gregory. Fearing bandits along the way, he left the trail and slipped around a half dozen highwaymen who were waiting "to waylay him and decamp with the treasure." The miners were paid, Seligman released, and operations returned to normal. Only later did suspicions arise that Child had orchestrated the whole event to cover a management error of his own making.[3]

Child entered the Yellowstone concession business in a manner that became characteristic for him — a family partnership. But upon taking over the YPA's transportation business in Yellowstone, he and his brothers-in-law Huntley and Bach only added yet another company to the confusing array of park enterprises already established. There were two hotels at Mammoth and six others arranged around the park near various attractions. At Norris, the Yellowstone Park Association structure that had burned in 1887 had been replaced by another, itself lost to fire in May 1892. In the Lower Geyser Basin the YPA had taken over the Marshall House in 1886, renamed it the Firehole Hotel, then vacated it in 1891 in favor of a new hotel, the Fountain, erected nearby. The company built another primitive structure in the Upper Geyser Basin near Old Faithful, and others on the north shore of Yellowstone Lake and at the head of the canyon. In addition, John Yancey still held his lease and operated the Pleasant Valley Hotel north of Tower Falls. Lunch stations accompanied nearly all hotels, and additional ones remained scattered throughout the park. Semipermanent tent camps, constructed to accommodate those visitors wishing to tour independent of the YPA hotels, also began appearing in 1892. Eli C. Waters, a manager of YPA properties, operated a sightseeing steamer called the *Zillah* on Yellowstone Lake, and F. Jay Haynes continued to sell photographs from his studios at Mammoth and Old Faithful. In short, business in the park was a model of capitalist competition, notwithstanding Interior Department concerns about an over-abundance of independent concessioners.[4]

The liberal granting of licenses for park services continued throughout the decade. In 1893 the Interior Department approved permits allowing several Bozeman and Livingston guides to conduct parties through the park. William Wylie received a lease to operate several sites in conjunction with a camping business and to transport his customers. George Wakefield, whose YPA contract had been lost to Huntley, protested his treatment vigorously and was pacified with an agreement to bring visitors in from the Union Pacific system terminus at Monida, west of the park. Such a concession was of limited value, however, since that company's tracks ended ninety-five miles short of Yellowstone. Two years later Wakefield launched an independent camping business, equipped with large Concord coaches with room for ten passengers and baggage. Total cost for a ten-day trip was $40 per person, an attractive alternative to the YPA hotel charges. By 1897 the number of independent guides licensed to carry parties through the park had grown to eleven, operating forty-eight wagons and teams. Included among these was the husband-and-wife team of David and Jennie Curry, residents of Ogden, Utah, who later founded one of the most enduring concessions operations in Yosemite National Park. During this same period Mammoth Hot Springs had acquired two new general store franchises, and Eli Waters's Yellowstone Lake Boat Company had expanded its operations as well, leasing acreage on three islands and installing a game corral with bison, mountain sheep, and other animals for visitors to admire. The following year, park photographer F. Jay Haynes and a partner took over the transportation of Union Pacific guests, acquiring a concession for their Monida and Western Stage Company.[5]

Despite this complex array of franchises, the Northern Pacific remained intent on cornering the tourist market for its YPA subsidiary. Huntley, Child, and Bach, whose Yellowstone Park Transportation Company held the exclusive contract to carry Northern Pacific customers, profited greatly from railroad promotions. Park tour tickets sold by NP ticket agents nationwide allowed visitors to book complete Yellowstone vacation trips. The standard package consisted of transportation from St. Paul and five and one-half days in the park at YPA hotels, all for approximately $130. In 1895, to stimulate business, the company reduced rates for round-trip St. Paul–to–Mammoth Hot

Springs tickets to $47.50 and hotel charges to between $3 and $5 per night. It also reduced the prices of park tickets purchased at Livingston from $12.50 to $5. At the same time, the NP offered special fares to entice group travel; in 1896, during the Grand Army of the Republic encampment at St. Paul, the railroad announced a complete five-day Yellowstone package for only $65. All trips were prepaid, requiring customers to stay at YPA hotels and travel on the yellow coaches of the Yellowstone Park Transportation Company. The rail-road issued promotional brochures each year, touting the wonders of the park and asserting that the tour was equal to any in the world.[6]

Although the Northern Pacific successfully courted tourists, Charles Gibson and his partners in the YPA resented the railroad's majority interest in the hotel business, and soon another change in management occurred. Through most of the 1890s, the YPA paid no dividends to stockholders, instead reinvesting its profits. An unhappy Gibson filed suit, then settled with the railroad and quit the park in 1898. His partners, who held little stock, became irrelevant. In need of a strong administrator, the NP in 1901 turned to its transportation contractors: Huntley, Child, and Bach. The three men thus purchased the YPA with a loan from the railroad, and Child was elected president of the company. Shortly thereafter, Huntley died, and Bach became entangled in political scandals; their stock reverted to the railroad. By 1905 Child had purchased enough additional shares to own one-half of the YPA. Two years later, with Northern Pacific management wary about charges of monopoly after the Northern Securities investigation, he acquired all remaining interest in the concessions, again borrowing most of the purchase price from the Northern Pacific. In 1909 Child dissolved the YPA and formed the Yellowstone Park Hotel Company, with his son Huntley Child as treasurer and son-in-law William (Billie) Nichols as secretary. Although technically no longer involved in park business, the railroad would for decades be the family's chief source of funds.[7]

The Northern Pacific was not alone among western railroads in utilizing the American fascination with nature to promote tourism. In the four decades immediately following the establishment of Yellowstone, Congress created several other national parks after intensive lobbying by railroad interests. The Northern Pacific was instrumental in convincing Congress to establish Mount Rainier National Park in 1899 as a companion attraction to Yellowstone. Over the strenuous objections of Senator George Graham Vest of Missouri, the railroad received ample rights-of-way and concessions privileges in the new park. Later, the Tacoma Eastern, a Milwaukee Road subsidiary, also provided access and financed concessions facilities. Not to be outdone, Louis Hill of the Great Northern Railway lobbied heavily for a national park of his own; the resultant Glacier National Park, established in 1910, became one of the most popular of the government reservations. Hill and the Great Northern owned and operated hotels in Glacier for decades. The Southern Pacific Railroad helped create Sequoia National Park in 1890; in Oregon it succeeded in its efforts to add another park to the list of western attractions in 1902 with the dedication of Crater Lake National Park. Farther south, the Atchison, Topeka, and Santa Fe provided access to the South Rim of the Grand Canyon, designated a national monument by President Theodore Roosevelt in 1908 and converted by Congress to national park status in 1919. Yosemite National Park, encompassing the land previously granted to the state of California in 1890, received rail service in 1907 with the construction of the Yosemite Valley Railroad, a short-line road running from the town of Merced to El Portal on the western edge of the park.[8]

Railroad capital allowed national parks to be designed more thoroughly than ever, nature to be constructed in a preconceived image. Combining Northern Pacific capital and Harry Child's management skills, the Yellowstone hotel and transportation companies flourished. Between 1901 and 1910, Child constructed or remodeled three major hotels, those at Lake, Canyon, and Old Faithful. Served by an expanded fleet of specially made Abbott-Downing Concord stagecoaches, the new hotels allowed Child to offer service comparable to that of the finest old-world resorts. Similar facilities in other national parks mirrored Yellowstone's development. At Mount Rainier, the Tacoma Eastern built the National Park Inn in 1906, providing visitors pleasant accommodations and superlative views of the park's namesake feature. Yosemite's Sentinel Hotel, a rickety structure erected in 1876, was overshadowed by the Del Portal in 1907, an extravagant four-story structure financed by the Yosemite Valley Railroad that was later destroyed by fire. The Santa Fe Railroad completed the magnificent El Tovar, hugging the South Rim of the Grand Canyon, in 1905. This structure became an immediate favorite of southwestern travelers and a perennial feature of promotional brochures soon thereafter. In Glacier, the Great Northern constructed its own majestic facility, the Many Glaciers Hotel, in 1915, at a cost of $500,000, twice as much as El Tovar and more than three times as much as Yellowstone's Old Faithful Inn. These hotels, all of which were constructed of rough logs, hand-sawn lumber, or fieldstone, reflected popular beliefs about what was and was not appropriate in areas still largely considered wild, and serve as the best example of how concessioners successfully integrated cultural features into landscapes perceived as natural. They soon became symbols of the various parks as much as El Capitan represented Yosemite, the peak Mount Rainier National Park, or Old Faithful geyser Yellowstone.[9]

Travelers, most of whom fit into one of four categories with distinct social hierarchies, flocked to the national parks during these years. Their time in Yellowstone, which despite all the recent additions remained the most-visited national park in the American West, was typical of the national park experience. Most visitors to the parks were of a class who could afford such vacations, the cost of the trip and time off work a not inconsiderable investment in those days. Concessioners, especially those backed by railroad money, were uniquely positioned to relieve the tourists of some of their funds. Nearly all of those who came to Yellowstone, regardless of their financial standing, left at least part of their vacation budget in Harry Child's pocket. Lowest on the list were the "sagebrushers," those individuals who came in wagons, on horseback, or astride bicycles — Child saw little of their money. Next were those who toured the park via the scattered tent camps typically owned by local guides. These people spent a comparatively small amount of money for basic services — transport on small, independently operated stagecoaches, lodging in canvas tents, and plain fare at meals. Such low-priced tours appealed especially to schoolteachers and other less affluent folk, whose numbers remained limited until the arrival of auto transportation. The third and most numerous group were the "couponers," those who bought the packaged railroad tours and spent a tightly scheduled five and one-half days enjoying opulent lodgings, gourmet meals, and roomy coaches. The fourth and final group consisted of the well-to-do vacationers who traditionally spent upwards of two weeks in the park, idly moving from the spacious lobby of the Old Faithful Inn to the hotels at Canyon, Mammoth, or Lake at their leisure. Again, like the couponers, these individuals spent their money with Child. As business increased, the value of both hotel and transportation companies soared, their estimated worth in 1913 exceeding $2.25 million.[10]

Under Harry Child, touring Yellowstone and experiencing nature became a comfortable, civilized adventure. Visitors from eastern cities typically arrived in the park via the Northern Pacific, and the service was first-class. Boarding morning trains in St. Paul or Duluth, guests discovered luxurious accommodations. Many enjoyed sitting in the bubblelike windowed excursion cars, marveling at the scenery of the northern plains and Dakota Badlands. Others preferred relaxing in the accompanying lounge cars or lingering over a meal in the formal dining car. Whichever their pastime, travelers eventually retired for the night to splendidly outfitted Pullman Palace Sleeper cars. The next evening the train arrived at the Livingston depot, an outwardly rustic structure with strikingly modern furnishings inside, and the following morning passengers rode southward through Paradise Valley to Gardiner, the northern gateway to Yellowstone.[11]

The middle-class couponers that the Northern Pacific delivered to the Gardiner station provided Child his most dependable source of income. Their experiences in Yellowstone illustrated how smoothly the companies operated under his direction and how the park was being displayed, certain features attaining value by virtue of being featured on the tour. During a typical pre-1915 trip, a Yellowstone Park Transportation Company agent and a string of large, six-horse "tallyho" stagecoaches, all bearing the famous yellow colors, met tourists arriving at the station in Gardiner (the tracks having been extended south from Cinnabar in 1902). The agent then loaded both baggage and passengers aboard the coaches, and the string moved from the station through the stone arch marking the northern entrance to the park. "For the benefit and enjoyment of the people," read the inscription above their heads as the newly arrived guests cheered their way into Yellowstone. Equally apt would have been "For the benefit and profit of Harry Child." The short five-mile trip terminated at the Mammoth Hotel porte cochere, where, again, transportation agents unloaded trunks and bags and turned the visitors over to the hotel staff. After rooms were assigned and lunches eaten, the tourists were free to explore Mammoth Hot Springs for the afternoon. In the evening, orchestra music followed dinner; guests often dressed as they would in the city and waltzed into the night. Always, employees from Child's company were on hand to assist visitors with whatever they might need.[12]

Arising early the next morning, the tourists embarked on the first leg of their park adventure. They discovered smaller four-horse stagecoaches, each designed to carry up to eight passengers, lined up along the loading porch of the hotel. Transportation company agents assigned each guest a place in one of the coaches, which was their permanent seat throughout the duration of the tour. Each also received a white linen duster to protect clothes from the clouds of dirt that accompanied the stagecoach caravans and, in cool weather, buffalo-skin lap robes. The stages pulled up one by one along the porch, and guests and baggage — no more than twenty-five pounds per person — were loaded; when all were ready, the line slowly moved out, the stagecoaches keeping about one hundred yards apart to minimize dust. Heading south from the Mammoth Hotel, the groups traveled to the Norris Geyser Basin and lunched at the transportation company's station. After an hour or so investigating the area, they again boarded the coaches for the remainder of the day's forty-mile trip to the Lower Geyser Basin and the Fountain Hotel.[13]

By 1915 the Fountain was one of the oldest hotels on the tour and offered guests numerous diversions beyond the natural attractions of the area. Built in 1891 at a cost of $100,000, it housed 350 tourists comfortably, having steam heat, electric lights, and the only baths featuring natural hot-spring water. The social life at the Fountain was a highlight for many; formal balls, attended by the soldiers stationed nearby at Nez Perce Creek camp, occurred with regularity throughout the season. If dancing was not to a visitor's liking, he or she could step outside and witness a spectacle that soon became a tradition at all Yellowstone hotels — the feeding of the bears. The Fountain staff originated this practice during the 1890s, and innumerable trips were remembered not for geysers or canyons but for the garbage-hungry bruins that surrounded the dump each evening.[14]

Such attractions were common at many national parks. Scenery, while ostensibly one of the reasons for visiting, could only be appreciated so much. Concessioners soon learned that guests expected more than access to scenic vistas and natural phenomena. Often, wildlife added to the attractiveness of park tours. Yosemite, Rocky Mountain, and Sequoia, in addition to Yellowstone, promoted so-called bear shows, nightly events for which these heretofore wild animals would be lured to garbage dumps and gorge themselves for the amusement of visitors. Other popular attractions included Yosemite's famous firefall, in which a burning bundle of logs was launched over the brink of Glacier Point each evening during the season for the enjoyment of tourists encamped in the valley below.[15]

The next stop on the Yellowstone tour was nine miles farther along at the Upper Geyser Basin, where a general store, swimming pool, and photo shop complemented the Old Faithful Inn, which earned a reputation for rustic grandeur soon after its opening in 1904. A monumental edifice that dominated the landscape in the flat Upper Geyser Basin, the inn seemed to overshadow the nearby geysers. A stone foundation supported a rough log exterior. Dormers studded the massive wood-shingled roof, and a viewing balcony atop the structure allowed tourists to see the entire Upper Basin; at night a searchlight illuminated the famous Old Faithful geyser. Inside, an immense lobby housed an eighty-five-foot-tall stone chimney with eight fireplaces cut into the sides. Interior balconies on each of the six floors overlooked the lobby, creating the effect of entering onto a stage. The interior walls were also made of logs, and the door hardware and copper ceiling lights had been hand-forged on-site. Furnishings mirrored the rustic design—bedsteads, rocking chairs, and dining tables were all fashioned from local materials.[16]

The Old Faithful Inn, as well as several later buildings, resulted from an unusually successful partnership. To design and supervise its construction, Child had hired Seattle architect Robert Reamer, and together the two collaborated to provide the park environs many distinctive structures. They had met while wintering in La Jolla, California, Child's preferred off-season locale, and immediately forged a close personal relationship that was reflected in their buildings. Child desired eye-catching hotels; Reamer insisted on compatibility with natural surroundings. The combination resulted in some of the most impressive guest accommodations in the world and some of the most enduring cultural symbols of the park. An acquaintance once commented, "When Harry Child builds a house, or even a barn, on a mountain side, it always looks as if the Lord had placed it there." In addition to the Old Faithful Inn, Reamer was instrumental in constructing the Canyon Hotel, remodeling the Lake Hotel, and erecting Child's summer home at Mammoth Hot Springs, all of which reflected quite clearly a desire not to alter landscapes but to frame nature for visitors, to present it as they expected it to be.[17]

The Child-Reamer partnership was more than a simple business relationship; indeed, its legacy extended beyond park boundaries. Reamer became a part of the Child family, living with the concessioner during the years he worked in the park and known familiarly as "Robert" to Child's children and grandchildren. Assisted by Child's wife, Adelaide, he selected all furnishings for both the Old Faithful Inn and the Canyon Hotel and later designed the family's ranch house outside Helena. Child (or perhaps Adelaide — she and Robert were the best of friends) also persuaded the Northern Pacific to hire Reamer when the company constructed a new depot in Gardiner and likely helped the architect acquire the contract to design the entry itself, the famous "Roosevelt Arch" at the northern boundary. Reamer became so much a part of the family that he even accompanied the Childs on a European vacation in 1909.[18]

On the third day of the tour, visitors journeyed from the Old Faithful Inn to the West Thumb, or bay, of the lake, where they lunched at another transportation company facility built near a small thermal area. Travelers then had two options: continue on around the shoreline in their coaches to the Lake Hotel or board a ship of the Yellowstone Park Boat Company, yet another of Child's companies, and cruise in a more leisurely fashion. The boat company was a small but profitable operation with a colorful history. Eli C. Waters, a former YNPIC manager, began the practice of ferrying passengers across the lake in 1889 aboard a salvaged Great Lakes steel-hulled steamer, the *Zillah*. He later built a larger, wooden vessel, modestly christened the *E. C. Waters*, to expand his fleet. Disagreements with park superintendents over safety, however, kept it from ever being used, so it sat at anchorage for twenty years and became a tourist attraction in its own right. Waters was one of the few park concessioners who seemed to attract the enmity of others. Whether due to his unscrupulous use of political connections against park administrators or his wide-ranging — sometimes bordering on the bizarre — gimmicks to attract more customers, the disdain of his colleagues was unmistakable. "Everyone here and west who knows Waters," wrote one railroad official, "represents him as utterly unreliable." In 1894, to augment his boat service, Waters established an island menagerie containing bison (the Yellowstone herd, the last sizable one in the country, consisted of only a few hundred animals by this time), mountain sheep, and elk. He wanted to add Indians to the display as well, but those plans fell through. Despite being ridiculed as cheap and tawdry, the display attracted tourists, especially when Waters offered stagecoach drivers a fifty-cent commission for each customer who chose to sail across the lake instead of ride around. He later rescinded the offer, and the drivers cut deeply into his cash flow by discouraging the use of his service. By 1907 these constant battles caused Waters to lose interest in his business. The animals, uncared for, were released into the park by order of the superintendent. The same year a competitor, Thomas E. Hofer, gained a license to operate power launches on the lake, and Waters was effectively finished. After years of conflict with almost everyone in the park, Waters retreated to his home in Fond du Lac, Wisconsin, and sold his boating concession. When Hofer failed to locate sufficient funds for the purchase, Harry Child and his son-in-law William (Billie) Nichols used Northern Pacific financial backing to buy the company and incorporate as the Yellowstone Park Boat Company in 1910.[19, 20]

All these maneuverings further concentrated Yellowstone business in the hands of the Child family. But the couponers on the grand tour remained unaware and uninterested. Those who chose to sail the lake and those who chose to ride the stagecoaches both eventually arrived at the Lake Hotel, another of Child's grand achievements. In 1903, Child assigned Reamer to renovate the structure, which had been built in 1891 as a plain, clapboard-sided hostelry. The remodeling transformed the old fisherman's retreat into an elegant resort. Two massive gables protruded from the old plain front, supported by eight fifty-foot Ionic columns. False balconies added style to the facade, and the odd, canary yellow paint Reamer chose for the exterior, trimmed in gleaming white, created a unique look. Inside, California redwood highlighted the spacious lobby. The pace was slower here than the social whirl at Fountain or the bustle of souvenir hunters at Old Faithful. Not surprisingly, the Lake Hotel soon became a favorite of those visitors who could afford extended stays in the park, as well as a restful break for the busy five-and-one-half-day couponers.[21]

One of the most attractive features of the coupon tour was its inclusiveness. Rooms, transportation, and meals were all part of the package. The relaxing atmosphere of the Lake Hotel especially encouraged visitors to partake of the typically hearty fare. Child never skimped on food for his guests. A herd of milch cows grazed in the park all through the season, occasionally being mistaken for bison or elk by city-bred visitors, to provide fresh milk and cream. Other herds of cattle and sheep supplied the hotels with beef and mutton from a slaughterhouse on Indian Creek, just south of Mammoth. While obviously not native to the region, these animals were nonetheless accepted by tourists unquestioningly as part of a natural, unaltered landscape. Menus were not extensive — most supplies still had to come long distances — but chefs offered diners ample choices. Upon being seated in the dining room for breakfast, each guest discovered a menu on the table; selections were then circled, as many as each diner desired. A typical breakfast included such choices as stewed prunes, broiled Yellowstone trout (caught fresh from the lake, where native cutthroats swarmed so thickly that the supply seemed inexhaustible), veal kidney sauté on toast, ham and eggs, bacon, potatoes, Philadelphia scrapple, hotcakes, corn muffins, coffee, tea, milk, and cocoa. If, after such a meal, anyone wanted lunch, he or she could choose to eat trout, steak, cold assorted meats, potatoes, salads, various cheeses, and dessert. Dinner presented yet another variety of selections, ranging from mutton to mincemeat pies.[22]

From the lake the coaches loaded once again for the fourth-day run to the Grand Canyon of the Yellowstone. The rustic, vaulted charm of the Old Faithful Inn and the tranquil airs of the Lake Hotel yielded to elegance and, above all, sheer size at the Canyon Hotel. Another collaboration between Child and Reamer, this structure was exactly a mile around at the foundation, its immense girth making it appear low-slung even at four stories tall. The interior featured a lounge, described as having "no counterpart in America for size, magnificence, spectacular impressiveness and practical comfort combined," measuring two hundred feet long and one hundred feet wide. French plate glass windows ran the length of the room, and an orchestra stage occupied the north end. A vaulted ceiling supported by finished beams made the lounge appear even larger than it was, especially with two thousand electric lights providing illumination at night. When the orchestra played, according to one visitor, "the spectacle of the dancers and promenaders, the stir and interest of the summer-night throng, will become unobtrusive, impersonal, an impression rather than an interruption, in the bigness, the roominess" of the lounge. Two curved staircases on either side of the stage led to an equally spacious lobby. Every space in the hotel was oversized; the dining room measured 175 feet long by 60 feet wide, with an additional bay alcove 50 feet in diameter. The kitchen was larger yet, 190 by 50 feet. In the basement, bowling lanes, billiard rooms, and convention facilities, all impressively modern, accompanied perhaps the best wine cellar in the Rockies.[23]

The construction of the Canyon Hotel was itself a spectacular accomplishment for Child and Reamer, as well as the workers themselves. To open the hotel for the season of 1911, crews worked throughout the winter hauling sledloads of materials — lumber, hardware, cement, machinery, and supplies — from the railhead at Gardiner, forty miles distant. Temperatures as low as forty degrees below zero and winds upwards of thirty miles per hour hampered their efforts. Snowdrifts of twenty feet often foundered the six-horse teams en route to the site, almost eight thousand feet above sea level. As many as fifty drivers and two hundred horses ferried the freight over the mountain passes and across windswept winter meadows each day. More than one hundred men lived in bunkhouses at the site and worked seven days a week. A medical staff treated the frequent cases of frostbite, and the kitchen, completed first to provide workers with hot nails needed for construction, became a refuge from the brutal climate. Reamer spent most of the winter on-site as well, propelling himself around the huge foundation on skis and occasionally participating in a game of snow baseball — also on skis — during a rare day of rest.[24]

The evening at Canyon highlighted the final night of the standard park tour, the end of which was as smooth and practiced as all that came before. The next morning visitors, once again boarding the stages, donning dusters, and settling themselves in their assigned seats, traveled from the canyon back to the Norris Basin, lunched, and returned to the Mammoth Hot Springs Hotel late in the afternoon. After having their coupons punched — as required at every stop — they reclaimed excess baggage from the hotel staff, switched from the park coaches back to the six-horse tallyhos, and made the five-mile return trip to Gardiner in time for the evening train.

With his Yellowstone Park Hotel Company, Yellowstone Park Transportation Company, and, after 1911, Yellowstone Park Boat Company, Child served the most — and the most affluent — travelers and dominated park concessions during the "golden age" between 1890 and 1916. But other small franchisees profited from the ever-increasing numbers of hotel guests as well, two in particular emerging as significant. F. Jay Haynes, the Northern Pacific photographer who came to Yellowstone in 1881, had established his own small empire. He owned a studio in the Upper Geyser Basin near Old Faithful and one at Mammoth, quite close to the Child home, where he lived with his wife, Lily, and children George, Jack, and Bessie. In the winter he moved to St. Paul, where he also maintained a photo shop, or rode the Northern Pacific rails in his Palace Studio car, providing photographic services to communities throughout the West. In 1898 Haynes diversified his holdings by founding a stage company, the Monida and Yellowstone (later renamed the Yellowstone and Western) to carry passengers from the Union Pacific system into the park from the west entrance, in direct competition with Child and his Northern Pacific partners. After losing out to Child in a bid to construct the Old Faithful Inn in 1902, he leased space at the new hotel and sold his park views from that location. Haynes and Child enjoyed a competitive yet amicable relationship; their children grew up together in the park, and the two families socialized frequently.

In 1915 yet another empire builder, Charles Ashworth Hamilton, began purchasing many of the small souvenir and sundry stores that complemented each hotel. His Hamilton Stores soon became, along with Haynes, Incorporated, and Child's Yellowstone Park companies, the third of the great Yellowstone family concessions dynasties. Again, the business connections included strong personal ties — Child financed Hamilton, who had been his secretary, on his initial venture into the park stores, and the two remained close personally and professionally for the rest of their lives.[25]

The Northern Pacific couponers, as well as those carried by the Union Pacific and Burlington lines — whose agents also sold the packaged tours by 1915— provided the three main concessioners, as well as the few independent holdovers, a steady, dependable source of income. During the 1890s, however, the number of tourists utilizing the small, franchised tent camps scattered around the park had increased enough to draw Child's attention; he therefore embarked on a twenty-year quest to corner this segment of the concession market as well. Several local guides operated camps in the park, but one in particular, William Wylie, who owned the largest of the companies, resisted all approaches. A Bozeman resident with profitable ranches in the Gallatin Valley, he had been leading parties through Yellowstone since the 1880s. He had managed his camping business under a series of one-year contracts with the Interior Department from 1892 until 1896, when he acquired a long-term lease. He then replaced his tents with solid, wood-and-canvas structures, and his locations became permanent settlements. Camp guests paid low prices for spartan accommodations and dust-plagued, jostling stagecoach tours, the vehicles not on a par with Child's sparkling yellow Concords. Despite regular solicitations, Wylie strenuously resisted all attempts to be driven out of business, even when the Northern Pacific and the hotel company together undercut prices to force his withdrawal. In 1905 he won this fight over unfair practices in a hearing before the Interstate Commerce Commission and seemingly was in Yellowstone to stay.[26]

Nevertheless, Child remained quietly determined to acquire the Wylie camps, a goal he accomplished later that year. After making repeated but unsuccessful appeals to his Washington political contacts, and wary of both the antimonopoly sentiment then in vogue and the Northern Pacific, to which he already owed hundreds of thousands of dollars borrowed to build the hotels, Child approached familiar, local allies to dispose of his competition. One such man was A. W. Miles, who owned a large, profitable dry goods establishment and a grocery store in Livingston, Montana. He was also Wylie's main supplier, having extended generous credit to the camping company for many years, and thus could exert pressure. Another was A. L. Smith of Helena, an officer of the State Bank of Montana, who was always willing to finance a promising venture. In 1905, shortly after the Interstate Commerce Commission ruled for Wylie, these three purchased the camping company. Child, not wanting railroad officials to know that he was using profits from the hotel and transportation companies for this purpose, remained a silent partner. To further the subterfuge, he had Smith purchase the stock for him, paying cash for a two-thirds share. Miles bought the other one-third by calling in Wylie's outstanding bill for supplies. The new partners incorporated in West Virginia, well out of Northern Pacific territory, as the Wylie Permanent Camping Company, taking advantage of the well-known "Wylie Way" advertising slogan by retaining the former owner's name.[27]

Over the next several years the company became immensely successful, largely due to the injection of new capital, the fortuitousness of good timing, and the business acumen (and railroad connections) of Child and Miles. In 1906, the first summer after the new owners assumed control, travel to Yellowstone increased nearly 100 percent, from 13,727 visitors in 1904 to 26,188. The Portland Industrial Exposition and Trade Fair attracted people from Chicago and points east over the Northern Pacific rails to Oregon, many of whom took advantage of specially priced tickets and stopped off at Yellowstone on the way. That summer, 3,668 guests stayed in the camps. At the same time the company added to its four existing locations by constructing Camp Roosevelt near Tower Falls and establishing a site on Swan Lake Flat, about five miles south of Mammoth Hot Springs. Two years later, the Union Pacific Railroad completed a branch line to West Yellowstone, Montana; Child and Miles took advantage of the new revenue source by building a camp at Riverside, five miles inside the west entrance. In 1909 another exposition, this one in Seattle, again drew large crowds to the park; a record 5,024 people visited the "Wylie" camps.[28]

The Yellowstone camps soon became famous as an inexpensive, more relaxing, and less formal means of seeing the park. They catered to those who wished to avoid the social niceties — and the "tip-conscious bowing and scraping" — of the hotel tour and soon developed their own subculture. Campers, like poor cousins who prided themselves in being independent, seemingly set out to prove to the hotel couponers that their economical method of sightseeing was much more entertaining. Many became regulars, visiting each summer, and at each camp they joined with the staff in providing campfire entertainment, ranging from amateur talent contests to group songfests. They wrote their own songs that became fixtures at every location, rewriting the lyrics to popular tunes to celebrate the "Wylie Way" style of touring. Eventually, the camping company collected the compositions and provided guests with a songbook so that newcomers could participate — loudly, so the hotel porch-sitters could hear what they were missing. To some young vacationers, this campfire entertainment paled in comparison to the possibilities afforded by ample dark forests and inattentive chaperones. The young men and women who preferred each other's company to that of the camp crowd were known as "rotten-loggers," and many later discovered themselves featured in the evening fireside stories.[29]

The increasing popularity of camp-type accommodations signaled the beginnings of a fundamental shift in, a democratization of, national park tourism, one that would be completed only with the later widespread use of automobiles to tour the West. But even before auto tourism boomed, the camps proved immensely successful not only in Yellowstone but also in other parks. Perhaps the most famous of the camps were those in Yosemite, especially Camp Curry. Founded in 1899 by former Yellowstone guides David A. and Jennie Curry, the valley camp, positioned so as to provide majestic views of Glacier Point, immediately attracted guests eager to experience nature. The Currys were promoters on the same scale as Harry Child, and within a little more than seven years were hosting almost 320 people per night during the season. By 1915 Camp Curry, with its enviable location in the valley, boasted not only nature but, like the Yellowstone hotels, other attractions as well. Groceries could be purchased; dancing was available each evening, for a nominal fee; guests could use the camp's bowling alley or play on one of its billiard tables in the game room. A motion picture projector offered nightly features, and a photo shop provided custom souvenirs. Curry and park officials were often at odds, however, and in 1915 a competitor, the Desmond Park Service Company, was offered a chance to serve park visitors as well. Owner D. J. Desmond converted an old army barracks into the Yosemite Lodge and provided a slightly less complete list of services but nonetheless attracted significant numbers of campers. The Desmond Park Company originated bear-feeding shows like those in Yellowstone and in 1916 revived Indian Field Days to compete with the Currys. All in all, the Yosemite camps provided those less well-off the opportunity to appreciate nature, or at least the version of nature constructed by promotional campaigns, nationalist narratives, architecture, and other means, that they had come to expect. Their nature was more intellectually accessible — available to be felt, heard, and smelled, unlike that experienced by hotel- and stagecoach-bound visitors. It was also affordable, and it soon became representative of a new ideal in the national park experience.

Mount Rainier National Park offered tourists camping facilities as well. Mount Rainier, in fact, led the way in the democratization of national park tourism. Guests could choose their preference from among several competing camps' operations, all of which offered a variety of services. George Hall's Wigwam House, while technically a hotel, was in reality a lodge and camp, the forerunner of many later such facilities in all of the western parks. It represented a transition of sorts, furnishing less costly accommodations than more traditional hotels but offering a higher level of service than the typical camp. More primitive — or rustic, to those who were busily romanticizing their park experiences — were Indian Henry's camp and John Reese's Camp of the Clouds. Reese's operation boasted sixty tents and provided cafeteria-style meal service; by 1911 it also offered auto rentals, photo shop services, and groceries. In 1916 William Wylie himself returned to the business, establishing camps at Zion National Park and along the North Rim of the Grand Canyon.[30]

Touring the parks via the camps became increasingly popular in the first decades of the twentieth century, as more and more middle-class Americans decided to see for themselves all the wonders of the West so often described in newspapers and magazines. In Yellowstone the many satisfied customers provided steady income for Child and Miles. By 1909 their Wylie Permanent Camping Company had expanded greatly, having accumulated 27 large passenger coaches, 63 mountain spring wagons, 4 surreys, and 378 horses, while repaying its owners handsomely. But circumstances forced Child to relinquish his majority control — reluctantly — that same year. With the arrival of the Union Pacific in West Yellowstone, F. Jay Haynes, who held the transportation franchise for that railroad, threatened Child's burgeoning empire. The Union Pacific backed Haynes in a bid to operate competing hotels within the park, a move that, if successful, would inflict serious financial trauma on Child, since he had borrowed heavily from the Northern Pacific to build the Old Faithful Inn and was even then negotiating for a further $100,000 for the Canyon Hotel. To maintain his exclusive hold on park hotels, Child agreed to sell Haynes half his interest, or one-third of the camping company. On May 14, 1909, the two signed a contract, subject to Interior Department approval, to exchange 333⅓ shares of Wylie Permanent Camping Company stock for $60,000. Interior Secretary Richard Ballinger approved the deal on July 10; on September 22, the two principals signed final papers transferring the stock.[31]

Despite losing majority control of the camping company, Harry Child continued to profit enormously from his far-flung business ventures. In 1910 alone, he collected dividends of $16,666 from his remaining one-third share of the Wylie Permanent Camping Company, $60,000 from his hotel company stock, and approximately $58,000 from the transportation company. Interest on money he had loaned to his companies added over $28,000 to that total. In addition, Child maintained banking offices in Helena, providing further investment opportunities such as his partnership with Charles Anceney in the Flying D Ranch and an interest in a poultry operation in Helena called Green Meadow Farms. He also owned a considerable amount of real estate in Gardiner and Salesville, Montana, as well as homes in Helena and La Jolla, California.[32]

Regardless of his other commitments, Child spent most of the summer in the park with his family, and the Yellowstone Park Companies obviously occupied a privileged position in his varied portfolio. Yet, as much as he would have liked to, he could not operate this empire alone. To fill most jobs he relied on a successful system begun in the early days of the YPA and later emulated by most national park concessioners in the West. As early as the 1880s, each summer, hordes of seasonal employees recruited from nearby towns such as Livingston, Bozeman, or Helena hired on as park help. By 1900, as railroad promotion brought more tourists, the company's need for workers increased, and recruiters extended their efforts to St. Paul and the upper Midwest. Every spring, in anticipation of the coming season, company managers from each division traveled to the cities and spoke at schools and colleges — teachers and university students were their favorite targets — about the glorious benefits of a summer spent working in Yellowstone. Those who accepted the challenge received low wages and toiled long hours but enjoyed a unique working environment, a situation that required enthusiasm, persistence, and tolerance. Upon signing a company contract, they officially became "Summer Savages," a term denoting any seasonal park concession worker. By the end of May, Northern Pacific "Savage Specials" arrived in Gardiner with the year's complement of staffers. Like the tourists who would soon follow, they boarded the tallyho stages to Mammoth, where supervisors assigned jobs for the summer. Some became "heavers," or waitresses; others, "sheet-snatchers" (maids), "pearl divers" (dishwashers), "steam queens" (laundresses), or simply "savages" (stagecoach drivers). The arrival of the Savages marked the official start of the tourist season; they contributed much enjoyment to the tour. To the hotels the young workers lent a sense of joyful enthusiasm; in the camps they typically led the singing or told the bawdiest stories; aboard the stagecoaches they narrated trips with tales of fur trappers, bears, or, sometimes, previous hapless passengers. The tradition of employing Savages, begun as an economic necessity in a locale with a short three- or four-month season, remained one of the most useful ways of promoting the park, as each fall many returned to college as ambassadors for Yellowstone and the various park companies.[33]

The stagecoach drivers were, without a doubt, the most colorful group among the Savages. They were typically a bit older than the others, more often locals with coarse frontier manners, who spent more time with the tourists than did any other park personnel. The challenge of driving sometimes skittish teams over narrow mountain roads, combined with the generally unsophisticated nature of the drivers, caused some apprehension among travelers; frightened guests frequently walked to the next hotel, camp, or lunch station rather than ride in terror. Those whose nerves allowed them to remain aboard often received a language lesson, as the drivers were all famous for their inventive use of profanity. One teamster, after a particularly creative outburst, inspired a pair of passengers to commission and send him a bronze medallion recognizing his prowess. Others, particularly first-year drivers, regularly frustrated guests by misidentifying features, misstating distances, or — particularly annoying — falling asleep, hungover, atop their seats.[34]

The majority of stage drivers performed admirably, even though guiding a coach through Yellowstone could be extremely dangerous to the Savages and passengers alike. A few, however, experienced problems. In one instance a driver, after unloading his passengers at the Canyon Hotel, spooked his team by brushing the stage wheels against an iron railing. He tried to recover, but the animals bolted, overturning the coach and dragging it on its side down the road toward another incoming vehicle. Thrown from his seat, the driver could only watch as a woman on the second stage, riding up front, panicked, grabbed the reins, and steered the incoming team directly into the path of the runaways. The ensuing collision injured four passengers severely. Another time a stagecoach, traveling in the dark at the insistence of hurried passengers, hit a rock and overturned near the west entrance, killing one woman and injuring eight other visitors. Even Harry Child himself, who occasionally drove special guests around the park, was not immune to the dangers of the roads, at one time spilling noted Boston lecturer John L. Stoddard into the swift currents of ice-cold Alum Creek.[35]

Other hazards of the Yellowstone roads were less common but much more exciting to visitors who were anxious for a taste of the Old West. As the population of the American West grew, as cities emerged and the frontier — at least in popular perception — disappeared, more and more tourists arrived in the park anxious to experience a taste of the past. Soon the concessioners would use this frontier anxiety to lure greater numbers of guests. But throughout the period between 1890 and 1910, stagecoach robberies occurred just often enough to provide some frontier ambience without it being invented by park promoters. In one typical case, two men, Charles Switzer and Charles "Morphine Charlie" Reebe, held up a Yellowstone Park Transportation Company stage near Canyon, relieving the passengers of over $800. Both were quickly apprehended by an investigator hired by Child, one Ed Howell, himself a notorious poacher and troublemaker who at times found gainful employment in the park. The men were consequently locked up in the guardhouse at Fort Yellowstone, the army encampment at Mammoth Hot Springs. Several years later, in 1908, a lone man perpetrated another, more ingenious heist on the road between the Old Faithful Inn and the lake. At a certain point in the road, a sharp curve kept stage drivers from seeing far ahead, since they typically allowed one hundred yards between coaches. That was all the robber needed. Armed with a Winchester rifle and a sidearm, he positioned himself beyond the curve; as each stage appeared, he halted it and gave the driver a bag and orders to collect from the passengers. In this fashion the "desperado," as he was described in dispatches, looted seventeen coaches belonging to Child, Haynes, and Wylie and carrying 174 tourists — the greatest stagecoach robbery of the twentieth century.[36]

The ensuing manhunt, although ultimately unsuccessful, typified how thoroughly the concessioners had become part of Yellowstone National Park management. Hotel telegraph operators relayed the information to Child's headquarters at Mammoth, and company personnel immediately began guiding search parties of soldiers seeking the gunman, since most of the soldiers stationed at the park knew little about the terrain away from the roads. By the next morning a soldier reported to Child that the search party had found a white bag full of "empty pocketbooks with the exception of one which contained 11 cents." A query of concession workers soon identified a possible suspect, one D. M. Ferguson. Over the next several days, reports from various company employees flooded in, allowing authorities to reconstruct Ferguson's every move since he had entered the park. "Friday night August 21st stayed at Wylie camp, Riverside and gave an entertainment. Saturday he proceeded to Upper Basin, . . . slept at Wylie camp, Upper Basin and gave an entertainment with his fiddle." By collecting the information and interviewing workers, Child proved to the authorities that Ferguson was not their man, but he was unable to locate the actual robber, who was never caught. Nevertheless, the concessions personnel had proved themselves invaluable in the administration of the park.[37]

Between 1886, when the U.S. Army assumed responsibility for Yellowstone, and 1916, when the National Park Service took over, the Child, Haynes, and Hamilton executives and employees, as well as park administrators and their families, fraternized, socialized, and even intermarried to such an extent that any divisions became almost meaningless. They all certainly shared a common vision of what the park should be, a basic philosophy that the natural landscape should conform to expectations. Harry Child's sister-in-law — the widow Huntley — married park superintendent S. B. M. Young; his daughter, Ellen Dean Child, married Lieutenant William M. (Billie) Nichols, a former West Pointer stationed at Yellowstone who, after resigning his commission, became the eventual successor to the company presidency. Other concessioners participated in this intermingling as well: Bessie Haynes married Lieutenant Frederick T. Arnold; Jennie Henderson, park postmistress and daughter of G. L. Henderson of the Cottage Hotel, married George Ash, superintendent of the Yellowstone Park Transportation Company. Elizabeth Trischman and her sister, Anna Pryor, daughters of army carpenter George Trischman, operated a successful souvenir store and later a cafeteria at Mammoth Hot Springs. Their brother, Harry, later became assistant chief ranger in the park. An active social calendar, highlighted by frequent VIP visits — such eminent persons as William Jennings Bryan, Theodore Roosevelt, and Mark Hanna all called at Yellowstone at the height of their celebrity — allowed government officials and concessions personnel frequent opportunities for fraternization. The two groups were, in fact, a team, both having the same goal — creating a landscape that would attract increased attendance. Within this mix of administrators and entrepreneurs, protectors and profiteers, the park superintendent reigned as official chieftain — but those who lived in Yellowstone knew, as did anyone who spent time among them, that Harry Child was the true power behind the throne.[38]

By 1916 Child had firmly established himself as the predominant concession operator and the main force behind the regimented style of touring that ascribed value to those portions of the park deemed suitable for appreciation. His Yellowstone Park Hotel Company and Yellowstone Park Transportation Company provided the railroads a stable, predictable service for their passengers. His boats on Yellowstone Lake and brightly striped tents in the permanent camps all operated on a definite schedule within an established, polished system. Child's vision of world-class tours at grand hotels such as those at Canyon, Old Faithful, and the Lake had become a reality. He had upgraded and expanded the transportation system until it was the largest of its kind in the world. He had ruthlessly assumed control over the boat company and had driven several smaller operators out of business, in the process improving the levels of service. All the while, Child was reinventing the park for his guests, assuming for them the responsibility for deciding what nature should be and how it should be experienced. Few wandered where they wished any longer; instead, they followed a printed schedule. Few but the wealthy tarried for weeks in the park as many had in previous times; trips of five and one half days limited most visits. Even those who attempted to travel in the old style, with personal conveyances and private campsites, usually ended up in one of the permanent camps, which dotted the landscape around all major park features. Child even managed to eliminate — for a time — the most serious threat to his system of packaged tourism, the automobile. But in 1916 the era of stagecoach tours, grand hotels, and romantic nostalgia ended in Yellowstone; despite Child's best efforts, the automobile would complete the democratization of tourism and dramatically alter the landscape that he had so purposefully constructed during the glory days of Harry's grand tour.

During the last portion of the nineteenth century, Yellowstone tourism, like national park tourism in general, was dependent on an upper-class clientele whose ideas about nature largely determined how park landscapes were designed for viewing. Scenic vistas, sublime features, natural curiosities — all appealed to those educated or perceptive enough to appreciate such things. Economic necessity started to break down many class barriers to park travel early in the twentieth century, and the growth of camp accommodations in Yosemite, Mount Rainier, and Yellowstone demonstrated that new groups were becoming important to concessioner profits and administrative appropriations. These new tourists, however, arrived with different ideas about how nature should look. They came seeking the spiritual and emotional renewal, the nationalist pride, that the stories told by previous travelers had brought them to expect. But they also came seeking the Old West, the mythological frontier experience, the national past. Soon they would arrive expecting parks to be places of recreation as well as locations housing scenery and history. The growth of middle-class America combined with the accessibility provided by automobiles forced Harry Child into a drastic repackaging of Yellowstone, an attempt to market the park as all the things visitors expected it to be.

3

Transitions

National parks often seemed to be anachronisms. During the period between 1820 and 1860, when trappers, miners, and settlers were invading the American West, these most isolated regions remained relatively untouched by any but the bands of Native Americans who frequented the areas. After the Civil War, when expansion entered its most dynamic phase and pioneers transformed the West from a frontier to a settled land, places like the Yellowstone plateau, the Yosemite Valley, and the Grand Canyon still maintained a sense of mystery and an image as places of nature. In 1883 Yellowstone presented a singular opportunity for President Chester A. Arthur to escape civilization; in 1903 it offered the same chance to President Theodore Roosevelt. National Parks were among the few places that Americans believed retained their natural characteristics, devoid of raucous urban centers, agricultural development, or landscape-altering mining claims; they represented idealized examples of what "nature" was supposed to be. Even during the early years of the twentieth century, when technology rapidly transformed United States society into a fast-paced urban maelstrom, many parks, including Yellowstone, held fast to the old ways — lazy afternoons at grand hotels, travel in horse-drawn coaches, dashing cavalry officers strolling along the grounds in front of admiring crowds on hotel verandas. At the same time, the parks were becoming symbols of a disappearing Old West, remnants of frontier times and thus repositories of our national heritage. Whether guests expected a natural, unaltered landscape or the last vestiges of the western frontier, entering a national park was almost like stepping back in time.

The anachronistic character of the parks survived through the early years of the twentieth century. The soldiers stationed throughout Yellowstone and

Yosemite — brought to both after repeated complaints about ineffective administration on the part of Interior Department officials — combined with the systematic method of sightseeing that concessioners encouraged, created an atmosphere conducive to an orderly, predictable routine. Despite the reduced cost of packaged tours offered by railroads, most visitors remained upper- or middle-class, producing an ambience of exclusiveness. This air of privilege was enhanced by the luxurious hotels and attendant services enjoyed by those seeking nature. Even the raucous character of the camps housing those who had come to "rough it" in the style of the Old West could not dispel the general feeling of immunity from outside problems.

Concessions operators all participated in the creation of environments befitting "wonderlands," and increasingly promoted national parks — through bows and arrows, feathered headdresses, and cowboy hats sold in gift shops, for example — as frontier experiences. But they also competed with one another strenuously for tourist dollars. In Yosemite, camp operators David and Jennie Curry expanded their operations despite competition from the Yosemite Park Company. At the South Rim of the Grand Canyon, which would not become a national park until 1919, Ralph Henry Cameron battled the Atchison, Topeka, and Santa Fe Railroad and its partner, the Fred Harvey Company, for control of facilities. And in Yellowstone, despite monopolistic government policies and Harry Child's best efforts to control everything, he and the Northern Pacific had continually encountered new challenges to their dominance.

Child's Yellowstone Park Transportation Company retained exclusive rights to carry visitors into the park from the Northern Pacific tracks at Gardiner, but the arrival of other railroads launched a heated competition for tourist dollars. Beginning in 1908, F. Jay Haynes's Yellowstone and Western firm provided service from the new Union Pacific terminus at West Yellowstone. In 1909 another railroad, the Chicago, Burlington, and Quincy, established a park entry from Cody, Wyoming, which was served by a third franchisee, Holm Transportation. Child controlled the hotels, but other concessions were in a constant state of flux. He shared ownership of the Wylie Permanent Camping Company with Haynes and A. W. Miles. Two other camping concerns, the Shaw and Powell Company and Hefferlin's Old Faithful Camps, also vied for business. General stores owned by George Whittaker, Anna Pryor and Elizabeth Trischman, and C. A. Hamilton offered souvenirs, supplies, and trinkets.[1]

Many different Yellowstones emerged in the public consciousness when Harry Child began collecting concessions. The first, public park was the idyllic "pleasuring ground" created by an act of Congress and the concessioners: the hotels, the stagecoaches, the nightly entertainment; even the original attractions, geysers, waterfalls, and canyons, remained relatively unchanged and accessible, albeit often for the price of a packaged tour. Americans remained free to enter and wander as they wished, but the increasing level of accommodations made that option less attractive in a society discovering the advantages of modern convenience. Another constructed image of the park was that of the frontier. In addition to the trinkets sold in gift shops and the general stores, rental stables appeared near the hotels, and trail rides became common add-ons to the price of a park tour, and evening campfires at all park settlements evoked images of the old days in the West. But there was yet another Yellowstone, an Oz-like place where, like the famous wizard, those pulling the strings remained out of sight, hidden behind the imposing facade of the Mammoth Hotel, where Child maintained offices, or atop the Haynes Studio across the parade ground. The concessioners' internal struggle for profits, their relationship with a confused array of administrators — although the army dictated day-to-day operations, the Interior Department maintained nominal jurisdiction — and their efforts to design the park and manage tourism for maximum return on investment created an atmosphere less serene than outward appearances indicated.[2]

Both of these parks — the public places of nature and frontier, as well as the more private commercial Yellowstone — experienced tremendous change between 1916 and 1931. Three factors dramatically altered both the tourist experience and the concessions landscape. First, automobiles required park operators to adapt, to meet changing public demands for accommodations that fit a new, mobile lifestyle. Grand hotels and public transportation, the mainstays of Yellowstone business, relinquished their position to the more egalitarian camps, transforming the outward appearance of the park. Second, the National Park Service, the first government agency with both the power and the interest to challenge concessioners as the preeminent force in Yellowstone affairs, altered the private park by forcing consolidation and eliminating competition. Finally, in 1917 and 1918, during World War I, restrictions on rail travel and a consequent reduction in visitor numbers placed an added burden on park businesses; for the first time in the national parks' history, tourist volume decreased, and Yellowstone's business owners suffered as dearly as any park operators in the nation. The decline of tourism forced a contraction of concessions operations and required further adaptation. Through these many changes, Harry Child again proved the most flexible, most inventive, and most successful of all park concessioners.[3]

In 1915 the Yellowstone landscape changed dramatically when progress arrived with the roar of internal combustion. The automobile, by this time no longer a curiosity in most of the country, had nevertheless remained excluded from the outwardly serene environment of national parks. Public pressure to allow cars had been building for years, only to be rebuffed by park administrators citing unfit roads. Indeed, most national park roads were destined to challenge even the most adept drivers. But the automobiles carried with them a sense of inevitability, and even those concessioners who were closely allied with railroads could not oppose their entry forever. Mount Rainier was first to admit autos in 1908, followed, in rapid succession, by General Grant National Park (one of the Southern Pacific's creations) in 1910, Crater Lake in 1911, Glacier in 1912, both Yosemite and Sequoia in 1913. None of these parks possessed road networks as extensive or well maintained as that in Yellowstone. But Harry Child, who had large sums tied up in livestock and stagecoaches, had lobbied the Interior Department successfully for years to keep cars out of Yellowstone. The Northern Pacific, Burlington, and Union Pacific Railroads, which had equally large sums tied up in concessions facilities and whose spur lines serviced the park, joined the cause. In 1915, despite these efforts, the first autos passed through the north entrance at Gardiner, bringing with them a new era. By 1916 the number of private automobiles entering the park had reached 13,500; by 1917 there were more than 19,000.[4]

The advent of motorized public transportation promised to ignite another wave of commercial warfare among concessioners. None of the transportation providers — Child, Haynes, or Holm — wanted to switch from stagecoaches to motorized conveyances, but none wanted to be excluded from the potential profits. Unable to change from stagecoaches to buses quickly, and while vehemently protesting to Washington officials about the incompatibility of cars and the traditional horse-drawn stages on the narrow park roads, Child and the other concessioners began preparing for the inevitable. In 1916 a coalition of operators formed the Cody–Sylvan

Pass Motor Company, the first to offer motorized park tours and a rare cooperative effort by several major park franchisees. But this company, beset by internal squabbles, existed only through the summer of 1916.[5]

Shortly after the season ended, as Child, Haynes, and the others counted profits amid the snow squalls of autumn, another catalyst for change arrived, spawned by a long-running controversy at another national park. In 1901 a proposal to construct a dam in Yosemite's Hetch Hetchy Valley had created a public debate about the administration of the public preserves. San Francisco municipal authorities wanted to create an impoundment to provide water for the city, but national parks were specifically protected from any such development. Interior Secretary Ethan Hitchcock staunchly resisted this project until leaving office in 1906. His successor, James R. Garfield, approved plans for the dam immediately after assuming the post, despite massive protests in the press by John Muir and the Sierra Club. The election of William Howard Taft as president in 1908 delayed congressional approval because he and the project's lead advocate, forester Gifford Pinchot, were avowed enemies. In 1913, however, during the Wilson administration, Interior Secretary Franklin K. Lane, a former San Francisco city attorney, pushed the plan through to final approval over renewed protests from the small group of preservationists. The Hetch Hetchy Valley soon disappeared under a reservoir, but the massive amount of publicity created a new awareness of the status of national parks and a renewed call for a strong agency to protect them against any further encroachment.[6]

Eventually, the debate generated enough criticism to force congressional action. One of the most vocal proponents of stronger regulation was businessman Stephen T. Mather, whose interest soon led him directly into park management. In a 1914 letter to Lane, he complained about the wretched conditions in Yosemite. Trails, he wrote, were impassable; trespassing cattle roamed freely; and, worst of all, commercial timber interests had encroached upon park lands. Since Mather and Lane had been classmates at the University of California, the secretary offered a short and poignant reply: "Dear Steve, If you don't like the way the national parks are being run, come on down to Washington and run them yourself." Mather did just that. In January 1915 he became Lane's assistant in charge of national parks. On August 25, 1916, President Woodrow Wilson established the National Park Service, and Stephen Mather became its first director.[7]

Mather, a millionaire entrepreneur who had made his fortune in the borax business, brought a businessman's perspective to the new agency. His authority extended to all aspects of park services, from the location of buildings to the prices of rooms, tours, and sandwiches. He believed that concessions should be afforded "a large measure of protection" and that competition should be discouraged if the needs of the public were being met. He further asserted that the policy of granting exclusive franchises in national parks "has been thoroughly tested out by the Department and is in accord with good, sound business practices." He then argued that competition "destroys opportunity for proper earnings on investments and brings higher rates and decidedly poor service to the public." Mather considered Yellowstone and its multitude of concessioners the perfect opportunity to demonstrate.[8]

Mather attracted an accomplished group of administrators to the new agency, including Horace Marden Albright. Together, the two men formed the nucleus of NPS administration, functioning as the inspiration for the rest of the organization and forming a relationship that provided smooth leadership. Albright, like Mather and Lane, was an alumnus of the University of California at Berkeley, first arriving at Washington, D.C., in 1913 as a young attorney specializing in land law. When Congress created the NPS, he became assistant director, and he and Mather together had complete control over all national park operations. Foremost on their agenda was a consolidation of Yellowstone concessions, which remained ungovernable and disorganized despite Child's efforts at monopoly. Both believed that the competition among franchisees was detrimental to the traveling public and that monopolies for each major facet of the operation — hotels, transportation, and camping — would simplify administration and increase visitation. Mather and Albright focused their attention on Child, who, despite his continued protests about automobiles, nonetheless remained the most capable and financially solvent of the concessioners. And the two NPS officials were completely committed to motorize the transportation concession.[9]

After the Yellowstone business owners abandoned the cooperative Cody–Sylvan Pass Motor Company in 1916, Mather and Albright tried and failed to convince the park operators to agree on a permanent plan for motorization; eventually, frustrated, they imposed one of their own design. In November 1916 Albright met in Chicago with the main Yellowstone concessioners and their attorneys. During the four-and-one-half-hour session, the group debated four separate proposals, ranging from individual motorization by each business, a solution unacceptable to the NPS, to organizing a single company, like the temporary Cody–Sylvan Pass Lines, with ownership proportionate to current investment in the park. While none of these proposals was approved, all parties agreed, in principle, to a single transportation operation, with NPS director Mather deciding which of the park operators would acquire this valuable franchise. Thus, in December, Mather called the concessioners to Washington and presented them with a sweeping and uncompromising plan for reorganization.[10]

Through his program for consolidation, Mather simplified ownership and operations of all concessions. He allowed the Yellowstone Park Hotel Company to keep its lodgings and awarded the hotly contested transportation monopoly to the Yellowstone Park Transportation Company. Child thus had a solid hold on the two most profitable businesses in the park. Using threats of franchise cancellation as leverage, Mather instructed Haynes to surrender his one-third interest in the Wylie company, sell his Yellowstone and Western Stage Lines to Child, and retire from all but his photographic business. In the most complex part of the proposal, Mather demanded that Child, like Haynes, forfeit his interest in the camping business and transfer his and Haynes's holdings, along with $5,000 in Transportation Company stock, to an escrow account. The stock was to be used by Child's former partner A. W. Miles, J. D. Powell of the Shaw and Powell Company, and an assortment of minority investors to finance a new camping monopoly. In return, this group conceded all rights to transportation.[11]

Mather imposed his will on concessioners in other parks as well. In a July 1915 visit to Mount Rainier, the future NPS director discovered forty-two different companies operating in that park. Accommodations, unlike in Yellowstone, were limited to camping facilities and rustic lodges such as Reese's Camp of the Clouds and Longmire's National Park Hotel, neither of which boasted anything close to luxury facilities. Mather desired both to consolidate concessions operations and to have a flagship hotel constructed. In March 1916 he and Albright convinced a group of Tacoma businessmen to invest in the Rainier National Park Company. Other concessioners had their charters revoked or were refused renewal. By the time the 1917 season opened, a new luxury hotel, the Paradise Inn, awaited guests, and the Rainier National Park Company had a regulated monopoly on services in the park.[12]

The concessioners and NPS officials Mather and Albright shared one fundamental belief—the more tourists the better. Child, although resisting the arrival of automobiles for years and resentful at being cut out of the camping business, began promoting the new, motorized method of seeing the park with a vengeance. He led a motor tour from California to Yellowstone that demonstrated the adequacy of the approach roads; he lobbied Congress for a national park-to-park highway linking Yellowstone with Rocky Mountain and Glacier parks; and he personally chauffeured government officials around the loop roads of the park, indicating the points at which repairs or modifications were in order. The NPS officials, believing that the only way to justify their continued existence was to increase the number of park visitors, assisted in popularizing tourism. Mather, described by his biographer as "pathologically fraternal," maintained close ties with groups such as the American Automobile Association and individuals at national publications, both of which he recruited to help publicize national park tourism. A nationwide campaign to "See America first," aimed at capturing those Americans disillusioned with the conflict in Europe, bolstered his cause further. He recruited his good friend Robert Sterling Yard, Sunday magazine editor of the *New York Herald* and former editor of *Century* magazine, to lead the charge on NPS publicity, paying Yard $5,000 a year out of his own pocket to publicize the parks. Popular journals regularly published accounts of visits to the national parks, often praising the Park Service's management of Yellowstone: "A tourist must be blind and deaf," insisted one such editorial, "not to realize that the whole spirit of the park management is to place everything at his service." Rangers stationed at points of interest offered information on geology, wildlife, and history; they also warned tourists of penalties for breaking the rules; but visitors encountered "no officious supervision, no parade of authority; if there are infractions the rangers are taught not to bluster and to threaten, but to argue quietly and explain the reasons for the regulation."[13]

Child adapted well to the new conditions that motorization brought to Yellowstone tourism. His absolute control of transportation allowed expansion opportunities previously unavailable, and he pursued them with vigor as the 1917 season approached. With the demise of competitors Haynes and Holm, he inherited the passengers, goodwill, and loan capital of the Union Pacific and Burlington Railroads. Borrowing heavily from these two companies—

as well as from his traditional source of financing, the Northern Pacific—Child contracted with the White Motor Company of Cleveland to build a fleet of custom touring buses. He then formed a separate company, Yellowstone Park Lines, to ferry visitors from more distant park gateways—initially Cody and Moran, Wyoming, later expanding the service to Gallatin Gateway and Red Lodge, Montana—to the borders of the reservation, where they would transfer to park buses. In keeping with the tradition of elegance established by his grand hotels, Child also commissioned several seven-passenger White touring cars, available for hire on a daily basis for those who shunned the more egalitarian buses.[14]

The switch from stagecoaches to buses or touring cars altered tourism patterns once again and was perhaps the most significant transformation yet experienced. Greater numbers of guests, along with their increased mobility, changed the standard park tour and rendered some facilities obsolete. Lunch stations between hotels were closed, no longer needed because of the ease with which buses covered the distances. The Fountain Hotel, the oldest in the park, also became superfluous when Child switched from the five-and-one-half-day tour to a shorter, now manageable four and one-half days. Because trips between hotels were quicker, visitors regained some of the freedom of past years, before the regimentation of tours. Now, however, instead of wandering aimlessly among geysers or springs, they typically signed up for a two- or three-hour scheduled side excursion to nearby attractions, chauffeured by one of Child's yellow buses.[15]

Motorized transportation, along with a single concessioner serving all railroad passengers, allowed the couponers—those purchasing packaged railroad trips—greater flexibility in scheduling their trips. Child designed several standard tours to accommodate every possible desire. Tourists could now choose to enter via Gardiner (on Northern Pacific tracks), Cody (on the Chicago, Burlington, and Quincy line), West Yellowstone (Union Pacific), or Moran, Wyoming (Chicago and Northwestern). If they arrived in Gardiner, little had changed since stagecoach days; instead of the six-horse tallyhos, guests now rode buses. The standard tour still proceeded counterclockwise around the loop roads of the park, stopping at Mammoth Hotel and the Old Faithful Inn, then to the Lake and Canyon Hotels before returning to Gardiner on the fifth day. But visitors could now purchase packages allowing their exit from any of the park gateways, on any railroad, thus shortening their visit as they wished. Or, if coming from the west, guests could enter at West Yellowstone, travel the park, and exit via Cody and continue on eastward.[16]

While in the park, tourists no longer suffered the discomforts of stagecoach travel — dust, long hours spent in close quarters — but instead enjoyed a new level of comfort and safety. Child's buses were specially designed for Yellowstone and later adopted in Glacier and Rocky Mountain National Parks as well. The 1917-model Whites (as well as the 1920 models later added to the fleet) resembled stretched roadsters more than conventional buses. They featured removable canvas covers to allow unfettered viewing by passengers, seating for eleven (two up front with the driver and three across each of the three rear seats), and a canvas boot on board the back for luggage. Seats were made of leather, and all the doors opened only on the right to minimize the possibility of a passenger stepping out into traffic. Four blankets in each vehicle kept guests warm on chill mornings and doubled as a driver's bedroll. Acetylene headlights, lit by a spark from a Prest-O-Lite key, illuminated roads during hours early or late. The traditional Yellowstone Park Transportation Company colors, bright yellow with black trim, covered all exterior surfaces.[17]

The Summer Savages adapted equally well to the coming of motorization. Young men well versed in the mechanical and operational aspects of the new technology replaced stagecoach drivers as the most colorful of Yellowstone's characters. The buses, although state-of-the-art, required constant maintenance, especially after traveling the steep grades of the park. Brakes needed regular service; tires needed special attention; and, after long downhill stretches with the transmission in low gear to reduce speed, spark plugs frequently fouled and had to be cleaned. The bus drivers became, in Savage dialect, "gearjammers." With the demise of the stagecoach and the new, modern look of buses, Child adopted a uniform for his drivers. He replaced the traditional western garb of the stagehands with brown corduroy ensembles — jackets, pegged trousers, and flat-billed touring caps — accessorized with brown leather puttees, or knee-high boots. The gearjammers, whose jobs required special skill and training, assumed the role of the departed stagecoach drivers at the top of the Savage social scale.[18]

Motorization accelerated the pace of park life for both tourists and concessions personnel, creating a less personal atmosphere. Stagecoach drivers had typically retained the same passengers for an entire tour, becoming well acquainted with them in the process. Gearjammers, on the other hand, because of the new technology, completed their assigned routes much quicker—most legs of the park tour required only half a day, with guests deposited at the next hotel en route in time for lunch. The drivers then reported to the transportation office at each location—only four major developed areas remained, at Mammoth, Old Faithful, Lake, and Canyon—for a new afternoon assignment. Only those with enough seniority to operate the touring cars served the same group for entire trips. Unlike the stagecoach hands of previous years, most gearjammers were college men who worked in the park for only a season or two, often unable to add the colorful stories and asides that had entertained coach travelers during the era of the grand tour.[19]

The third and final factor changing the unseen, private Yellowstone—simply because it made some operations financially untenable—was the nation's entry into World War I in 1917. Railroads, primary carriers of tourists for the park businesses, were subjected to government control through the U.S. Railroad Administration and no longer scheduled special excursions to Yellowstone. The consequent reduction in travel caused the hotel company to close down most of its facilities during 1917 and 1918. The camps of the newly formed Yellowstone Park Camping Company remained open (under NPS orders) but lost money. All park operators suffered; even Child, who had borrowed heavily from the railroads to purchase his White Motor Company buses in 1917, missed note payments during this time. His companies, however, stayed solvent. But the camping business did not have this cushion, and when tourists returned after the armistice of November 1918, its previously tenuous financial problems soon became irreversible, offering Child another opportunity to add it to his portfolio.[20]

The camping concession had gained importance rapidly. Railroad tourists entering Yellowstone before 1915 had stayed at the camps in significant numbers, but the hotels remained preeminent. The coming of the automobile, the evolution of a more mobile society, and a larger, broader middle-class encouraged independence in vacationing and threatened to shift the emphasis away from the standard loop tour and back toward less rigidity. Such an occurrence would be disastrous for Child and the railroads, which had invested heavily in the hotels and whose future profits depended on mass utilization of the newly motorized transportation fleet. As rail traffic decreased, automobile numbers increased, and the nature of park tourism experienced yet another fundamental shift, creating direct competition between hotels and camps.[21]

The Yellowstone Park Camping Company, formed early in 1917 under orders from NPS director Mather and plagued with difficulties from its inception, was on the verge of collapse after the summer of 1918. The war limited visitation, negating the expected increase because of automobile traffic. The ownership was fragmented. Majority stockholders Miles and Powell, both experienced in camp operations, were losing interest as profits lagged. The NPS established free campgrounds for auto visitors, cutting into the company share of business. And Child never delivered the agreed-upon $5,000 in YPTC stock to the new owners. Worse yet, he had also failed to surrender half the Wylie shares bought back from Haynes at Mather's direction, further confusing the ownership situation. Only the efforts of one man — general manager Ed Moorman — kept the company operating through the 1918 season. He had been an employee of William Wylie and had remained the hands-on manager of the camps throughout its many permutations, lending a much-needed sense of continuity. Despite his struggles to keep the business viable, changes were inevitable after the disastrous war years.[22]

Another longtime company employee, Howard Hays, was himself becoming restless and desirous of change. He had started selling camp tours as a travel agent in Salt Lake City in 1905 and had risen through the ranks to become general agent and traffic manager by 1916. After eleven years of promoting the "Wylie Way" in newspapers, at trade shows, and even at world's fairs, Hays joined the Chicago and Northwestern Railway and Union Pacific Railway, managing their combined Department of Tours for a brief period. Then, during the war, he worked for the U.S. Railway Administration's Bureau of Service, again in Chicago. Now, after his service ended, he wanted to become involved in Yellowstone again.[23]

Hays could not have had better timing. By 1918 Harry Child was in ill health, a combination of diabetes and other chronic disorders making his continued survival uncertain. His son Huntley had recently run afoul of NPS director Mather and had been banished from all park businesses. The war had been profitable to many in the United States, and investment capital was abundant. Moreover, Mather and Albright were not happy with the consolidation that they had effected and were interested in facilitating a change; they were concerned with the financial condition of the camping company and with the future of the other concessions if Child should die.[24]

Hays originally planned to return to Yellowstone concessions, but his goal soon became more ambitious and involved many men experienced in western tourism. In December 1918 he learned that his close friend Roe Emery was on the verge of acquiring a transportation monopoly in Colorado's Rocky Mountain National Park. The two men concocted a grand scheme to form one corporation, with sufficient capital and expertise to monopolize tourist services in three of the major western national parks — Yellowstone, Glacier, and Rocky Mountain. But, while their experience was adequate, neither possessed such capital. So Hays, through Emery, met with Walter White of the White Motor Company in Cleveland, a young industrialist who had made millions building vehicles for the armed forces. White was already involved in the parks — he supplied Child his buses — through his deals with various transportation concessions and would be the financial partner in the fast-forming organization. Hays next broached the subject with Gerrit Fort, who was an official with the U.S. Railroad Administration and, like himself, ready for new adventures; Fort expressed a cautious interest in the idea. The men then contacted NPS assistant director Albright, who would become superintendent of Yellowstone by 1919; he assured Hays that the Park Service would be receptive to any such proposal. The group, with the full knowledge and support of the NPS, was plotting no less than a complete takeover of concessions in three of the largest national parks.[25]

Encouraged by the interest, Hays proceeded to work on his ambitious scheme while keeping other options open. On January 5, 1919, he traveled to San Diego, where Child lived during the winter months, to inquire if the assets of the hotel and transportation companies might be for sale. He wrote to Emery and stated that, if the news was positive, he would communicate by telegram using a prearranged code. He also met with A. W. Miles and established a backup position for himself, learning that, if he partnered with longtime company man Moorman in a purchase, the camping company could be had for $150,000 on generous terms.[26]

The backup plan was a wise maneuver because the more ambitious strategy of a complete takeover came together quickly but, lacking money, just as quickly lost momentum. Early in January, Hays received a positive response from Child, who insisted that for ten years he had wanted out, but no one had ever made him an acceptable offer. Even now, neither man truly believed that a deal could be struck; Child did not think that Hays could muster the capital necessary to buy his Yellowstone businesses (Walter White, because he supplied Child buses, had insisted that Hays keep his involvement secret), and Hays was skeptical of ever agreeing on a price. By the end of the month Hays learned that White had been unable to interest any bankers in backing the potential deal. He then turned to James Hannaford of the Northern Pacific, which currently held an $800,000 mortgage on the park hotels, to inquire about bypassing Child altogether, but Hannaford refused to betray his longtime client. So Hays, while still hoping somehow to finance the entire purchase, turned his attention to his fallback position with the camps.[27]

The Yellowstone Park Camping Company thus became the focus of much attention, even competition, in the spring of 1919, and as a consequence Harry Child discovered that his position as the preeminent Yellowstone deal maker was in jeopardy. Unstable financially, the company attracted several potential buyers. Child wanted the business in the worst way; he still seethed about the imposed restructuring that had forced him to relinquish control, though most would argue that he received the best of the deal. No one believed that he, even now with failing health, would ever quit Yellowstone, despite his remonstrations to the contrary. But he wanted the camping company at a bargain and, knowing that Hays was interested but believing him unable to acquire financing, mistakenly waited for the owners to lower their asking price. He even sent an encouraging, if patronizing, note to Hays, advising him not to "be discouraged, little boy, but stand up to the dough dish." Hays, however, had managed to interest Emery and White in this smaller acquisition by promoting it as a possible springboard to complete concessions control. He had also persuaded Mather and Albright to restructure the franchise contract so that the government would take a smaller percentage of the profits. This deal White could finance on his own; by April 10, 1919, Hays was riding a Northern Pacific train east from Forsyth, Montana, with an option to purchase the Yellowstone Park Camping Company.

The buyout proceeded smoothly. Hays, Emery, and silent partner White gave the stockholders of the company approximately $70,000 in cash and notes payable for another $70,000. They cut Moorman in on the deal (at Miles's insistence), changed the name slightly (from Yellowstone Park Camping Company to Yellowstone Park Camps Company), and by June had complete operational control. Child fumed; they had stolen it from under his nose, and the camping business he wanted so badly had again eluded him.[28]

With the assistance of Moorman, Hays quickly began rebuilding the rundown company. They added more substantial facilities to compete with the NPS free campgrounds, catering to tourist demands for a level of service somewhere between that at the lavish hotels and the primitive camps. Instead of the traditional tent camps, the two men designed lodges, large communal structures housing dining, entertainment, and meeting facilities, as centerpieces for expanded permanent developments. In 1919 they constructed a new lodge at Camp Roosevelt, providing offices and a dining room, and later added an "assembly house." They erected frame cabins at several locations to replace some long-standing canvas-walled structures. In 1920 they built Lake Lodge, then "delicatessens" at Old Faithful and Fishing Bridge, two of the most heavily visited sites. Old Faithful also received a "large dance hall" for tourist amusement. At Mammoth, Hays and Moorman expanded the existing camp and added both a swimming pool and a laundry for tourist use. By 1923 the Mammoth Lodge was open for business, and the following year the lodge at Sylvan Pass became operational. The two men also promoted the business admirably, increasing both visitation and profits annually.[29]

Other interested parties — including Emery, White, Albright, and Child — observed this progress with varying levels of interest and concern. Emery was least involved because his interest in the camps was purely financial; the transportation franchise in Rocky Mountain National Park occupied most of his attention. White concealed his stake in the company by having his stock issued in Hays's name and keeping it, along with a deed of trust for his wife, in a Cleveland safe deposit box. In this way, whenever Child came east to purchase more buses for his transportation business, White could deny holding stock in the camping company — Child would not likely do business with a competitor. Albright actively supported Hays, still believing that the goal of a consolidated concessions operation, encompassing several parks, was feasible. But the other principals had abandoned the idea of ever taking the hotels and transportation away from Child. Instead, buoyed by the success of Hays, Emery and White began investigating opportunities at other parks and contented themselves with the growing amount of money taken in by the camps.[30]

Child maintained control of two vital concessions, hotels and transportation, yet his satisfaction was tempered because the camping concession, the one aspect of Yellowstone tourism that had long evaded his control, had been awarded to others — and with the entrance of private automobiles into the park, the camps flourished. By the spring of 1924, the Yellowstone Park Camps Company had evolved into a solid, profitable, well-run operation. Then because of a fortunate set of circumstances, Child finally got another chance to own the monopoly that had eluded his control for so many years. Restored health had renewed his interest in park business; after battling chronic illness since 1918, he was reinvigorated by the discovery of insulin in 1921. And now Hays himself was ill, hospitalized with pleurisy in Livingston. In addition, Emery and White had discovered opportunities to invest in Glacier and Sequoia National Parks, and they wanted Hays to participate. Using Hays's illness as a pretext (so as not to give the impression of profit taking to Mather and Albright), the three partners, through Hays, made Child aware that they were interested in selling the camping company.[31]

Having missed one opportunity in 1919, Child did not hesitate this time. Mindful of his ever-increasing indebtedness to the railroads, he recruited California hotelier Vernon Goodwin to share the financial burden. In April 1924 Goodwin and Billie Nichols, by now firmly ensconced as Child's second-in-command, arrived at the Park County Hospital in Livingston and, after further lengthy negotiations, purchased the camping company for $660,000. Goodwin, a former managing director of the Los Angeles–based Alexandria Hotel Company and president of the California State Hotel Association, brought considerable expertise to his new role as president of the camping company. The omnipresent A. L. Smith, Child's Helena banker and front man in the deal, served as secretary and treasurer. The new owners changed the name of the company again, to the Yellowstone Park Lodge and Camps Company, to reflect more accurately the new focus of the business. Within a year Child traveled to Cleveland to sign a purchase order for another eighty White buses, but even then he would not admit to owning the company, much as White had denied his own role to Child.[32]

So, as of 1925, Harry Child finally secured what he had coveted for years, a practical monopoly of all Yellowstone concessions, but he paid dearly for the privilege. He spent $660,000 for a business that he could have bought for $150,000 five years earlier. However, the chronic frugality of "Harry

Hardup" and a rare miscalculation of the competition's ability delayed his ultimate success. Child took his beating with unusually good humor, probably because he truly liked Hays. Upon hearing of Hays's later business venture in Sequoia National Park, he wrote: "I note with pleasure that you are going to promote a sanitarium for knocked-out National Park officials. Please reserve rooms there for the writer, W. M. Nichols. . . . also I presume you have already engaged accommodations for Director Mather and Superintendent Albright. This whole bunch of artists is on the way."[33]

Child had proved remarkably adaptable when confronted with upheaval. He used his past record and financial acumen to acquire the motorized transportation franchise, enabling him to maintain control of railroad tourism. He had, after some delay, absorbed the camping concession, which, when combined with his hotels, captured the vast majority of the private auto travelers. He transformed the Yellowstone Park Boat Company, which had long ferried passengers across Lake Yellowstone, into a diverse operation of rental boats and tackle shops scattered throughout the park, usually headquartered at the new lodges to glean auto tourist dollars. Child also adjusted well to the arrival of the NPS in Yellowstone, using his political skills to great advantage by forming an uneasy alliance with Mather and Albright. The NPS eventually went so far as to subsidize Child's development, asking Congress for $492,300 in fiscal year 1922 for "roads, sanitary facilities, camping grounds, and electric lighting plants for the public camps and hotels." In addition, NPS rangers at park gates prohibited motorists in rental cars from entering and charged tourists in private vehicles a $7.50 toll. Child thus found himself having to answer only to an agency that actually promoted his monopolizing park lodging and transportation in an effort to simplify its regulatory job.[34]

Such commonality of purpose characterized the relationships between Mather and Albright and other prominent national park concessioners as well. Mather encouraged concessioners to mold parks to suit public expectations, and those who did not share his vision soon discovered themselves seeking new opportunities. For over a decade he and the Currys, first David and after his death his widow, Jennie, had fought over how Yosemite National Park should look. The Currys wanted to expand services, but in ways that would attract groups less desirable than those Mather most wanted, those with whom he could most easily identify, the well-to-do California vacationers. In 1915 Mather had brought in D. J. Desmond to compete with Camp

Curry, and Desmond's successor operation, the Yosemite Park Company, offered limited lodging and services in the valley. But Yosemite lacked a flagship hotel, an edifice that would appropriately reflect the grandeur Mather and others saw in the mountain retreat. So as he had in Yellowstone and Mount Rainier before, Mather forcibly consolidated concessions operations in Yosemite in 1925 to assure that his conception of the park became reality. The Yosemite Park and Curry Company, as Mather's invention was named, consisted of the two main competitors and acquired a regulated monopoly over park concessions. With Donald Tresidder, son-in-law of David and Jennie Curry, as president, the company signed its first contract in 1926; at Mather's insistence, the contract stipulated that a luxury hotel would be built. In July of the following year, the $1.5 million Ahwahnee was dedicated, providing extravagant accommodations to Yosemite visitors for the first time. The grounds were designed by Frederick Law Olmsted Jr. and featured a putting green; inside, guests were greeted by an English butler in the grand foyer. Ironically, although the Ahwahnee remained popular for decades, at about this same time such lavish facilities were losing favor in other parks as guests flocked in ever-greater numbers to the more egalitarian lodges and camps.[35]

At about this same time, Mather was busily encouraging the creation of new national park attractions. In 1923 he actively lobbied Union Pacific Railroad officials to spin off a subsidiary company, the Utah Parks Company, to provide concessions services at Zion, Bryce Canyon, Cedar Breaks, and the North Rim of the Grand Canyon. The next year Zion Lodge was completed; in 1925 Bryce Canyon Lodge joined the growing list of lodge-and-cabin developments that were attracting more rail as well as automobile tourists. That same year the Union Pacific instituted the Loop Tour of these canyonlands parks, attracting 1,847 riders. In 1928 the Grand Canyon Lodge opened, expanding the Utah Parks Company operations and drawing more guests. Even greater numbers of visitors rode the Atchison, Topeka, and Santa Fe line to the South Rim, which had been developed as a tourist destination long before the canyon acquired national park status in 1919. The Santa Fe, along with its partner, the Fred Harvey Company, had arrived in the park a full decade before Mather and the NPS, built the phenomenal El Tovar Hotel, and effectively managed the place as they saw fit. The U.S. Forest Service, under whose administration the canyon fell before 1919, never had established a significant government presence. As in the other parks, numerous smaller concessioners vied for their pieces of the tourist business. At the Grand Canyon, however, many of the commercial interests also had land claims that predated federal protection. Nevertheless, Mather once again pressured business interests into streamlining operations. In 1920, the Harvey Company and the NPS signed a twenty-year contract granting the company exclusive concession privileges on the South Rim.[36]

Another attraction Mather promoted was wildlife. After 1894 most national parks prohibited hunting, and wildlife became a premier draw for eastern tourists looking for a piece of the Old West. Visitors wanted to see animals, especially the elk, bison, and bears that evoked Old West images. Predators were hunted, poisoned, and trapped, some to extinction, in an effort to protect elk, antelope, and deer. Hired hunters used packs of hounds to eliminate mountain lions from Rocky Mountain, Yosemite, and Yellowstone. Strychnine and steel leghold traps reduced populations of coyotes, lynx, and bobcats in those and other parks. Wolves were gone from Yellowstone before 1920. Yet, ironically, bear-feeding shows remained popular in many places, and tule elk gazed at tourists from behind fences in Yosemite.

Many tourists associated wildlife with Yellowstone more than any other national park, and with Horace Albright's appointment as superintendent there in 1919, wildlife management was geared even more toward visitor enjoyment. Albright was a promoter of the first order, and under his administration the tradition of using wildlife as part of constructed nature scenes took on greater prominence. National Park Service officials authorized the construction of bleachers near some dumps, like the Canyon dump in Yellowstone, for visitors' comfort. Park rangers killed otters that were eating trout; others destroyed pelican eggs to protect the parks valuable sport fish, many of which were nonnative species introduced by park officials earlier and harvested by concessioners for years to feed their guests. In 1922 a hatchery was built to provide trout for park waters; other such facilities would later appear in Glacier, Mount Rainier, and Yosemite. But bison, or buffalo, were the big draw, and Albright made sure visitors enjoyed these creatures so associated with the Old West. The Lamar Valley was home to a buffalo ranch, where bison had been bred for many years to help the species recover from near extinction. Under Albright, the ranch became a popular tourist spot; by the mid-1920s, busloads of Yellowstone

Park Transportation Company customers would picnic in the valley and thrill to buffalo roundups and stampedes instigated for their pleasure. Park officials built fences at boundaries to prevent elk from migrating out of the park in winter. The Lamar Valley bison were rounded up and corralled in winter, fed with hay from fields plowed and planted along the river nearby.[37]

Director Mather, like his former assistant Albright, remained deeply interested in promoting the parks, and together their policies led to remarkable stability and profitability in commercial operations. Harry Child and the other two Yellowstone notables, C. A. Hamilton, himself in the process of consolidating the general store concessions, and Jack Ellis Haynes, who had taken over operation of the photo shops from his father in 1916, used the lax federal regulatory practices to entrench themselves. Operators were to have twenty-year contracts, but these three often arranged for early renewals, both to secure financing for expansion and to limit the chances of encroachment by outsiders. Child's twenty-year agreement of 1917 was canceled and a new one granted in 1923. Hamilton renegotiated a twenty-year pact in 1930, two years before his old contract expired, and promptly floated a $100,000 bond issue to cover costs of improvements. Haynes received contract extensions in both 1921 and 1926; he prompted the NPS in 1930 to assign him the exclusive right to market photo images of Yellowstone, which required Hamilton to refrain from selling postcards. With Mather's blessing, Child, Hamilton, and store owner Anna Pryor (whose businesses Hamilton later purchased) became partners in Yellowstone Park Service Stations, giving them control of gasoline sales and automobile repairs in the park. With the NPS taking a minimum franchise fee and each partner's respective role — and increasingly the NPS officials and park concessioners were thinking themselves to be partners in promotion and packaging — carefully delineated, all three concessioners made money throughout the 1920s and 1930s except in the worst of the depression years.[38]

Following a disastrous 1925 fire at Mammoth in which Child lost much of his bus fleet, park businesses settled down into a routine more like that of the tourists. Child upgraded his buses with 1925 models designed to carry more passengers, and business resumed virtually uninterrupted. By the end of the decade, visitation increased, and Child's companies became more profitable than ever. In 1925 alone, the Yellowstone Park Hotel Company earned over $400,000 net on gross sales of almost $835,000, and its balance sheet showed a net worth of almost $6 million. That same year, net income from the Yellowstone Park Transportation Company added over $718,000 to Child's coffers, and the new Lodge and Camps Company over $250,000. The Yellowstone Park Boat Company contributed roughly $30,000 to the total net income of nearly $1.4 million. In 1928, after spending $235,000 on a new wing and lobby improvements for the Old Faithful Inn, the hotel company still reported net profits of over $275,000, the transportation company nearly $600,000. The Camps and Lodge Company, even after spending over $300,000 on new buildings at Canyon, Lake, and Old Faithful, still brought in almost $345,000— total profits of over $1.2 million. Net income for the combined companies exceeded $1.5 million in 1929.[39]

Little of the money generated by the various companies ever left the family. Only one outsider, Vernon Goodwin, a trusted friend and partner in the Lodge and Camps Company, held any stock. The four railroads serving the park by the end of the 1920s — the Union Pacific; Chicago, Burlington and Quincy; Chicago, Milwaukee, St. Paul and Pacific; and the Northern Pacific — still held hotel mortgages and notes on transportation equipment, but payments on those were almost always made promptly and had little effect on the bottom line. Harry Child remained the majority owner of all the companies, with his wife, Adelaide, daughter Ellen, and son-in-law Billie Nichols holding minority interests. Other family members received pieces of one company or another — grandson Dean Nichols, for example, held a small percentage of the Lodge and Camps Company, as did grandson Huntley Child Jr., the son of Harry's exiled eldest. Even the United States government benefited little from Child's successes in the park — franchise fees, originally intended to fund government operations in Yellowstone, had become a mere nuisance. Over the last half of the 1920s, Child paid less than $275,000 in total fees, an average of under 1 percent of net income per year.[40]

Between 1925 and 1931, as Yellowstone experienced tremendous popularity with American vacationers and business boomed, Child and Billie Nichols, who had become the day-to-day general manager of all operations, spent much of their time fending off challenges to the now-established empire. Late in the 1920s, the Denver and Rio Grande Western Railroad Company announced a special "five-fare rule" intended to recapture some of the business lost to private cars. The plan would allow passengers to transport two persons and a private automobile for the price of five tickets.

Child and Nichols, annoyed at a promotion that they believed would invite Californians to bring their cars into Yellowstone, protested loudly that the program seemed to "encourage the very thing that most railroads are fighting against," the use of private autos for vacation travel. Railroad couponers, whether buying expensive hotel packages or more moderately priced lodge-based tours, remained the mainstay of Child's business, and any promotion to increase the numbers of independent visitors threatened his profits. In another case, Nichols instructed company employees to record the names and addresses of all Yellowstone visitors who arrived on tour buses belonging to educational or church groups. In most cases, these vehicles were allowed to enter the park without transferring to the concessioner's vehicles, as commercial tour groups were required to do. He then asked railroad officials to verify whether the school and church exemptions were legitimate or simply an attempt by travel agents to circumvent the transportation monopoly. Nichols at one point even hired a private detective firm in Salt Lake City to assure that railroad ticket agents were offering customers every possible service.[41]

Most of these threats to family profits were minor — were, in fact, more likely perceived than real. Nichols may have been extremely vigilant simply to prove to Child that he was committed to maintaining the strength of the family business. In one case, however, the threat was genuine, and its resolution demonstrated both how staunchly Child and Nichols defended their interests and how much support they enjoyed from Mather and Albright of the NPS. In May 1926 Arthur K. Lee, U.S. senator from Wyoming, applied to the Chicago-based Hertz Drivurself System for a franchise to rent automobiles at Gardiner, West Yellowstone, and Cody. He intended to provide Yellowstone tourists an alternative to the buses of the park transportation company. John Hertz, president of the rental car firm, wrote Mather asking about Rule 2 of the park motorist manual: "The park is open to automobiles operated for pleasure, but not to those carrying passengers who are paying, either directly or indirectly, for the use of machines." Preliminary inquiries to NPS staffers had suggested that Hertz rental cars might be exempt from this provision, and General Motors, which was subsidizing the effort, dearly wished to make inroads into the White Motor Company domination of national park markets. In June, Mather held a hearing at Mammoth Hot Springs at which Child's attorney, Taylor B. Weir, filed a brief strongly protesting the Hertz plan, as did attorneys for Rainier concessions operators and the Glacier Park Transportation Company, both faced with similar threats. Mather made no decision but scheduled further hearings for November in Washington, D.C., at which both he and Albright demonstrated support for the concessioners and reiterated their total authority over park matters. A transcript from that hearing revealed how wise Child had been to forge strong personal ties to both officials:

> MR. ALBRIGHT: As I understand it, from your reasoning so far, we really have not any power to license you at all?
>
> MR. CONDON (attorney for Hertz): My point thus far is that you have no power to deny us the right to rent cars near the park to a person who wants to drive through the park.
>
> MR. ALBRIGHT: It would be a condescension on your part to let us punish you?
>
> MR. CONDON: As a matter of law you have not any power to license us to the exclusion of anybody else.
>
> [Mather then became involved in the exchange:]
>
> MR. CONDON: One of the mistakes frequently made by a man in business is to irritate an official with whom he deals or with whom his customers deal.
>
> MR. MATHER: Some remember the amenities which result in good favor, one of which is to see that the police officer gets a five dollar gold piece at Christmas time.

In June 1927, after lengthy deliberations, Mather refused the Hertz application, and Child retained his transportation monopoly.[42]

By 1930, widespread change was again in the offing for Yellowstone concessions. Economic conditions across the country indicated difficult times ahead for the tourism industry. Equally important, a generational transition was taking place in the park. F. Jay Haynes had been succeeded by son Jack in 1916, and the Haynes Picture Shops had prospered along with the larger businesses of Child. Horace Albright, superintendent since 1919, departed in 1929 to assume the NPS directorship following Mather's retirement; his replacement, Roger Toll, was an unknown quantity, perhaps not as closely allied with the concessioners as Albright had been. And Harry Child, frequently in poor health since 1925, had increasingly relied on Billie Nichols to manage park affairs and spent more of his time in California.[43]

Such a decision had to be difficult, for no one had enjoyed Yellowstone more than Child. Each September, shortly before the season ended, he gathered a group of friends — who were legion in the area — and embarked on a whirlwind camping excursion. He "has the same yearning to go camping that a letter carrier has to take a walk," one participant recalled. Commandeering three or four supply trucks from the Mammoth garage, he traveled from hotel to hotel, closing up each and outfitting himself for a grand adventure. He gathered surplus food from Mammoth; cooks and waiters from Old Faithful; ice, vegetables, and fruit from the Lake Hotel; then horses, tents, and camping equipment from the various lodges. "Von Hindenburg going through Belgium," the storyteller insisted, "was nothing compared with Harry Child raiding his system for camping paraphernalia." This grand trip highlighted the season for those lucky enough to be invited. Fishing was another of Child's pleasures. "He had a passion for running water; a nose for trout and grayling; a sort of sixth sense that enabled him to drop a fly in the right place," a companion remembered. But his most distinguishing characteristic was his restlessness; Child was never content with the status quo, a trait that served him well in business but aggravated his friends. "His whole idea of camp life is to get away from the spot where he happens to be," said Robert Davis, a writer, sportsman, and frequent guest of Child. "When Harry Hardup is finally tucked away into the mold and a large marble slab is erected over him, a voice will roll forth exclaiming: 'I know a better place; let's move.' "[44]

Early in 1931, before the Summer Savages arrived to open the park for another year, before Yellowstone awakened yet again to greet the hordes of raucous vacationers, Harry Child died at his home in La Jolla, California. For seventy-four years he had lived at a breakneck pace. His legacy would endure for decades, both in the businesses he built and in the legend that grew up around his memory. A dedicated Republican in a Republican age, he had been a friend to Presidents Roosevelt, Harding, Coolidge, and Hoover, entertaining each at one time or another on visits to Yellowstone. In fact, some say that Harry Child first interested Roosevelt in big-game hunting. He always accommodated important visitors; the king of Sweden conferred a knighthood upon

Child following a personally conducted trip through the park. His business associates, who numbered in the dozens across the West, and his competitors as well — men such as Howard Hays and Jack Haynes — considered him a close personal friend, a man they respected for his character as much as for his success. His companies would endure, less prosperous at times, without his dynamic leadership, but unchanged to most tourists. In fact, few were probably ever aware that their host in Yellowstone — "the noblest host in the world," according to one friend — one of the truly visionary park architects, was gone. One Yellowstone — the public park he had designed and built — remained unaltered by his death. The other Yellowstone — the private one, the park of cramped offices and convoluted business deals — would never be the same.[45]

Defending the Empire

Harry Child's death ushered in yet another era for Yellowstone concessions. The generational transition that had begun with Jack Haynes taking over from his father in 1916 became more pronounced when Billie Nichols assumed control of the various Yellowstone Park companies. Within a few years John Q. Nichols, who was the son of Billie and Ellen, and Huntley Child Jr., a nephew, became officers in the family business. Like junior executives when the boss leaves town, the younger generation experienced a sense of freedom, a broadening of possibilities, and the Yellowstone Park companies assumed a new, more expansive character that reflected the change in leadership. The same shift was occurring in the ranks of the National Park Service — Mather had retired in 1929, and Albright remained as director only until 1933 — as younger men rose to positions of authority. This new generation of leaders, among both the concessioners and the NPS, had been schooled in the methods of their legendary predecessors and steeped in the stories about the places national parks occupied in the national consciousness. In the tumultuous era of the Great Depression, New Deal, and war, however, they discovered that they needed to adapt their marketing practices to reflect a new mythology, to reshape the landscape to fit new ideas, and once again to confront new challenges facing Yellowstone.[1]

Child had left an estate configured to provide his widow, Adelaide, Billie Nichols, and the other family members a solid basis for future financial success. Early in his Yellowstone venture he had hired one of Montana's most respected accountants, Hugh D. Galusha, and in the 1920s the two men had constructed a complex financial structure to limit tax exposure. They established the H. W. Child Trust, a holding company owned by family members, including Adelaide, daughter Ellen and her husband, Billie Nichols, their children (John, Dean, and Adelaide Nichols), and another grandchild, Huntley Child Jr. The trust retained forty thousand shares of the H. W. Child Corporation, which owned the Yellowstone Park companies. The family trust also owned nearly two-thirds of the Vernon Goodwin Company, still nominal proprietor of the Lodge and Camps Company. Outside Yellowstone, assets included majority interest in Flying D Ranges, real estate in Montana (including most land in the towns of Gallatin Gateway and Gardiner), and personal property valued at approximately $100,000.[2]

Despite the complex structure of the estate, Billie Nichols comfortably assumed control of all commercial enterprises. His background of privilege and accomplishment prepared him well for such responsibility. The son of William Ford Nichols, Episcopalian bishop of California, he had graduated from West Point alongside classmate and friend Douglas MacArthur. After serving under General S. B. M. Young (another Child brother-in-law) for a short time in Yellowstone, he fell in love with Ellen Dean Child, Harry and Adelaide's only daughter. In 1905 he resigned his commission, and the two were married, after which he became involved in the family business. By 1931 he was assistant to the president and was the obvious heir to the presidency. Adelaide Child had only rarely been involved, preferring to rear her children and occasionally assist architect Reamer in decorating the hotels. She now spent most of her time in Helena and La Jolla. Since eldest son Huntley had been banished after a confrontation with Mather years before, and daughter Ellen was, like Adelaide, more attuned to family concerns, Nichols became the undisputed head of the wide-ranging family businesses.[3]

He received help from many quarters. California hotelier Vernon Goodwin, a longtime associate of Child and a man Nichols respected, became a vice president of the Child companies and regularly offered advice. Although spending little time in Yellowstone, Goodwin nonetheless possessed both the experience and the knowledge of park conditions that made him extremely useful as Nichols acclimated himself to the role of leader. More important was Galusha, the Helena accountant, the one person who knew as much about the various enterprises as had Child himself. For years, when the tourist season arrived, Galusha moved his office to Mammoth and acted as company comptroller, personally dealing with daily financial matters. During the 1920s, when business increased dramatically, he expanded his staff accordingly and allowed Child to avoid the expense of an in-house financial department. Nichols relied heavily on Galusha — and later on his son, Hugh Jr., or "Bud," who inherited the family business much as Nichols had. In addition, concessioners Jack Haynes and Charles "Ham" Hamilton advised Nichols in certain situations, particularly those concerning NPS contracts and regulations. Both had considerable experience in such matters, having learned much of what they knew from working with, and competing against, Harry Child. Even NPS director Horace Albright became a valued counselor.[4]

Out of the myriad Yellowstone franchisees that had existed early in the 1900s, only four had survived until 1930, thereby strengthening the sense of community. The Child family enterprises, far and away the largest, coexisted with Haynes Picture Shops and general stores owned either by Hamilton or by Anna Pryor and Elizabeth Trischman. Jack Haynes had expanded his father's operations with studios at all major developments and, after Hamilton refused an NPS request to build a store of questionable profitability at Tower Junction, had himself received permission to diversify at that location. There were seven service stations in the park, co-owned by Child, Hamilton, and Pryor, cafeterias at the several automobile campgrounds that had been constructed in the 1920s, and scattered tackle shops, riding stables, and swimming pools. The extended family feeling that had long existed in Yellowstone became more intense as the number of operators decreased and, after Harry Child died, became the single most important characteristic of park life.[5]

Child had run his empire alone, a benevolent dictator who answered all challenges. But Nichols could not sustain such a role. With Galusha, Goodwin, and the others providing assistance, he ran the companies almost by committee, allowing managers much leeway in their daily operations. Fortunately, Child had left him capable individuals in these positions. As head of transportation, F. E. Kammermeyer had long been a pivotal part of the business, acting as a coordinator to operate the buses in a systematic fashion and as a consultant to design the special vehicles. Ed Moorman, who had begun working with Wylie in the 1890s, supervised the lodges and camps; his experience proved invaluable during the early years of Nichols's tenure, when that company became the most dynamic of the four. Howard Brown, a longtime employee who also provided solid leadership, headed the hotel company. Nichols acted as general manager for all companies, with Galusha as his second-in-command. All were part of the Yellowstone family, and all were intensely loyal.[6]

Nichols assumed control of the companies at a difficult time, but by delegating responsibility he was able to react to the ever-fluid conditions of park tourism. Shortly after Child died, the impact of the Great Depression struck Yellowstone. Travel during the 1931 season dropped only slightly from the previous year, but in 1932 the economic bottom fell out — only 136,000 visitors as compared with 275,000 in 1929. Most ominously for Nichols, a scant 8,500 of them arrived by rail, which was the staple of the hotel and transportation companies. Yet through intensive promotion, reduced fares, and imaginative tour packages, Nichols and the railroads were able to increase the numbers significantly by middecade. The effort, however, required Nichols to spend much of his time on promotional schemes and repelling competitors, leaving day-to-day operations in the hands of his managers.[7]

The crisis facing both hotel and transportation companies was perhaps the most serious threat to continued profits. Child had invested millions in both concerns, only to lose business steadily to the lodges and camps — which provided a smaller return on investment — as auto travel became predominant. By the 1930s this trend had accelerated. In 1932 the Canyon Hotel, with the capacity to house eight hundred guests per night, remained between 5 and 10 percent full throughout the season. The Mammoth Hotel, able to entertain five hundred at a time, had fewer than thirty-five hundred people all year — an occupancy rate of approximately 17 percent. The situations at the Lake Hotel and the Old Faithful Inn were even worse. House counts dropped so low that Nichols — after asking permission from the NPS and the railroads — closed both hotels before the end of summer and kept them out of service through the 1933 season. In 1934, with business recovering only slightly, he shuttered the Lake and Mammoth Hotels for the summer. The cost of maintaining a serviceable transportation fleet was also prohibitive in the face of dwindling business. At the height of travel, the company operated 270 buses and twenty-five touring cars in addition to numerous two- and five-ton trucks used for carrying supplies and several Ford automobiles driven by supervisory personnel. Only a fraction of this fleet remained in service. A massive garage and repair facility in Gardiner and ten smaller shops scattered throughout the park, all with considerable inventories, drained profits as visitation lagged.[8]

The railroads serving Yellowstone joined Nichols in attempting to boost tourism. Northern Pacific passenger agent Max Goodsill contacted Congressman Fiorello LaGuardia of New York, asking him to organize low-cost Yellowstone tours from the eastern seaboard. He also produced a short film, *The Yellowstone on Parade,* to court convention business; the hotels at Mammoth and Canyon, renovated between 1927 and 1930, boasted large meeting rooms for this purpose. For the first time ever, Nichols offered railroad ticket agents a small commission for selling tour packages and marketed Yellowstone trips through independent travel agents. To increase the percentage of guests utilizing the hotels, the railroad managers agreed to omit any mention of lodge and camp operations in their promotional brochures, although tourists could purchase packages for such accommodations at a slightly lower cost. The one contentious issue was the duration of park tours: Nichols wished to maintain the four-and-one-half-day trip, while the railroad executives pressured him to offer shorter, less-expensive tours. Concessioners in other parks — most successfully Howard Hays, who had taken over the Glacier Park Transportation Company from Roe Emery shortly after leaving Yellowstone — were offering excursions as brief as a single day. But Nichols, whose hotel investment precluded such a program, resisted any drastic reductions; he even experimented with longer trips of seven and one-half days, which failed miserably, and eventually compromised by instituting a three-and-one-half-day tour. Despite these efforts, rail travel to Yellowstone sagged to a woeful 6,700 people in 1933. That year, Nichols closed the Lake and Mammoth Hotels. Other parks faced similar circumstances. Hotels in Glacier National Park were shuttered for the season, as were some facilities in Grand Canyon, Yosemite, Mount Rainier, and Rocky Mountain National Parks.[9]

By 1936 the worst years in Yellowstone appeared to be over. Albright's successor as NPS director, Arno Cammerer, proposed that Nichols consolidate the four companies — hotels, transportation, boats, and lodges and camps — into a single entity to simplify financial oversight. So in 1936 a new corporation, the Yellowstone Park (YP) Company, absorbed the assets of the four. Nichols incorporated in Delaware and received a new twenty-year contract assuring continued monopoly rights. Business also recovered slightly:

the first financial report of the new company revealed a net profit of almost $400,000—less than the boom days of the 1920s, but a significant amount during the Great Depression.[10]

The only component of the new conglomerate that had successfully weathered the difficult years of 1932 and 1933 was the Yellowstone Park Lodge and Camps Company. Increased auto travel had boosted its business, and managerial foresight had established the enterprise as the mainstay of Nichols's business. It had virtually carried the hotel and transportation divisions through the rough years, earning net profits of approximately $100,000 in both 1932 and 1933 and then $200,000 in 1934 and nearly $275,000 in 1935. Much of this income derived from the new lodge-centered camps that had been constructed at Roosevelt, Lake, and Mammoth by Howard Hays and Ed Moorman since 1919. By the time Child purchased the company in 1924, these new lodges were central to the profitability of the camps company. Increasingly, automobile tourists preferred substantial lodgings during their travels — motels dotted highways across the nation — yet remained reluctant to patronize the hotels, which were perceived as snobbish and as limiting their newfound mobility. Park tourism had become thoroughly democratized, and motorists demanded comfortable, affordable rooms and services. Since most also desired accommodations more private than those in typical motel-type structures, Child had embarked on a program of cabin construction to satisfy their demands.[11]

By the time Nichols consolidated the businesses in 1936, the growth of the lodge and camps division had once again transformed the built landscape of Yellowstone. The great hotels at Mammoth, Canyon, Lake, and Old Faithful had existed in relative isolation — the single souvenir store or, in later years, service station often their only accompanying services. They were self-contained, holding everything their well-heeled visitors needed, from barber shops to laundries. But the expansion of the lodges created a new, more diverse form of park development. Automobile tourists wanted many of the same services but in a different form. Hence, the small hotel-centered settlements gave way to larger, more expansive developments, with more buildings and more services, that further concentrated the tourists in small areas and again reduced the utilized area of the park. The expansion of developed areas leading to a concentration of tourists may seem contradictory, but because of the increased variety of accommodations offered at a limited number of locations, visitors tended to remain closer to settlements than they had previously. In addition, the increase in mobility created by automobiles allowed guests to arrive at their chosen location earlier in the day, generating a need for auxiliary services, such as ice cream shops, snack bars, and other income-producing services. Tourists tended to congregate at the developed sites, and as in the old days when Yellowstone was thought to be a collection of oddities, developments focused on those attractions believed to hold value — value that Nichols was determined to extract.[12]

The lodges themselves occupied the center of these new, sprawling developments. The largest rivaled the hotels in size, if not splendor. The decor was universally rustic — much like that of the Old Faithful Inn. Advertised as offering "a unique adventure in mountain accommodations," the lodge buildings housed vast dining rooms, spacious lobbies or "recreation halls," and curio shops tucked away in the corners. By 1936 such establishments had been located at Mammoth, Lake, Old Faithful, and Canyon, near the hotels. At each site, housekeeping cabins accompanied the main buildings, each furnished with wood-burning stoves, full-size beds, and electric lights. Communal baths served each group of cabins. Public automobile camps — also operated by the YP Company and offering sparsely furnished cabins for rent — usually were constructed nearby so guests could take advantage of the lodge services.

At most of these new developments several peripheral enterprises existed as well. Pryor and Trischman operated a souvenir store and a cafeteria at Mammoth, and a swimming pool abutted the lodge and cabins, which numbered 383. At Old Faithful, 560 cabins, a public bathhouse, two general stores owned by Charles Hamilton, and a cafeteria accompanied the lodge. At Lake, the developed area had expanded to include the Yellowstone River outlet and famed Fishing Bridge a mile up the shore from the hotel. Scattered along the shoreline were the lodge, 550 cabins, cafeteria, service station and garage, store, and bathhouse, in addition to two NPS public campgrounds. The Canyon area, with over 450 cabins and a spacious main building, offered most of the amenities found elsewhere around the lodges. Haynes Picture Shops provided photo services at each location, and service stations accompanied every lodge and campground. The main structures formed the heart of these settlements and became increasingly popular with organized tour groups that required meeting space for large numbers of people. Other, smaller developments at West Thumb (tourist cabins, Hamilton's Store, Haynes Picture Shop, and service station), near Tower Falls (Roosevelt Lodge, cabins, and store), and Sylvan Pass (lodge, cabins, and cafeteria) lacked the large-scale construction of the others but were also popular with automobile tourists. As one railroad brochure touted, the lodge experience was "camping par excellence."[13]

The old tent camps had earned a reputation for casual pleasure, and the new lodge developments retained that quality. Unlike in the hotels, where dining remained a relatively stodgy affair, eating at the lodges was a communal event, with meals served family style at long tables. In keeping with tradition — and the park promoters were, by this time, marketing park traditions as heavily as any other attraction — evening campfires around which guests sang, ate popcorn, and participated in talent shows or storytelling remained fixtures at the lodge settlements. Nightly dances entertained visitors and Savages alike; the latter, barred by company policy from spending their off hours in the hotels, were always welcomed at the lodges. The mixture of organized tour groups (largely railroad travelers, since after 1924 ticket agents could sell park tours via either hotels or lodges) and auto tourists created a lively combination. After an especially boisterous fraternity group visited one location, camp managers requested that the railroads divert such business — "organized whoopee parties" — elsewhere in the future, since their "regular customers didn't enjoy 'Sweet Adeline' at three o'clock in the morning."[14]

Because Child had invested so heavily in the hotels, Nichols desperately tried to maintain respectable levels of occupancy. The lodges prevented him from doing so. Despite the occasional problem, their informal atmosphere created overflow conditions at several locations. During one season in the mid-1930s, park superintendent Roger Toll requested that the company restrict booking conventions at Old Faithful and Canyon lodges to free up space for individual vacationers — this while the hotels remained less than one-half full. Nichols repeatedly raised the price of lodge accommodations to induce travelers to use the hotels, but to little avail. The cost of a park tour via the lodges had been eleven dollars cheaper than via the hotels in the 1920s, but by 1936 Nichols had shrunk the difference to only a single dollar. Still, despite a brief revival of rail travel in middecade, the lodges remained full, the hotels relatively empty.[15]

The success of the lodge and camps division of the Yellowstone Park Company spurred a general recovery by park businesses late in the 1930s. Nichols altered the character of other company divisions as well by appealing to the new mix of auto and rail customers. Since motorization in 1917, the transportation fleet had grown steadily, with new models of buses added each year between 1920 and 1924 and a wholesale replacement following the fire of 1925. The disastrous years of the early 1930s and a steady decline in rail business had rendered much of the huge fleet useless. Nichols therefore decided to transform the composition of the transportation company dramatically. In 1937 he upgraded his buses with new White Motor Company models. Like the older versions, these were custom-made, but without the open styling of the previous years. The new buses carried fourteen passengers instead of eleven and were designed with a canvas roof panel that could be rolled back to allow open-air viewing of park attractions. The following year, with the new buses in service, he attempted to sell two hundred of the obsolete models at fire-sale prices: $100 each for the 1917 models, $300 apiece for the 1920s versions. He generated little interest at first, but eventually a Mexico City businessman purchased most of the oldest models, and the remainder were bought by nostalgia buffs as keepsakes.[16]

During this same time Nichols overhauled the boat division, originally purchased to transport stagecoach passengers from West Thumb to the Lake Hotel. Motorization, however, had also altered the character of this enterprise. During the 1920s Child had abandoned the ferry service and concentrated on developing a fleet of rental boats and a chain of tackle stores. Nichols further diversified the operation in the 1930s to increase business. Between 1931 and 1934 he commissioned three sightseeing craft — the *Adelaide,* the *Adelaide II,* and the *Marion,* all named after family members. During the 1933 season, after he closed the Lake Hotel due to lack of business, the boat company faced a serious crisis, since the majority of its customers came from there. Nichols devised a plan to bus tourists from Canyon to Yellowstone Lake and conduct fish fries on Stevenson Island. An almost immediate success, these outings became regular features of the park tour in later years. He also expanded the company fleet of rental craft, adding speedboats for hire.[17]

The constant adaptation to changing conditions and public demands proved successful, as the Yellowstone Park Company recovered from the slack years of the early 1930s admirably. Another impetus to recovery appeared courtesy of the federal government, which had long considered the concessioners "partners" in park management. Since 1916, when Congress created the NPS, Yellowstone concessioners had developed a close relationship with the leaders of that agency. Mather and Albright, who tirelessly promoted national parks, were partly responsible for the boom times of the 1920s. They nearly always supported the concessioners and favored government expenditures to construct an accessible park, one that would attract visitors drawn by the mythology of nature, history, and, by the 1930s, the tradition of park tourism itself. Their program of promotion and development guided future directors as well. The NPS philosophy, shared by all park concessioners and summed up in a 1935 report, lamented the fact that "during the six days given over to Creation, picnic tables and fireplaces, foot bridges, toilet facilities, and many another of man's requirements even in natural surroundings, were negligently and entirely overlooked." By helping the concessioners construct a park specifically designed to offer the greatest number of visitors a reality reflecting their diverse expectations, the NPS apparently believed that it was rectifying these divine errors.[18]

With the advent of the New Deal recovery programs in the 1930s, Yellowstone — and the concessioners — benefited greatly from newly available emergency funds. The Bureau of Public Roads undertook massive construction projects — costing between $2 and $3 million in peak years — designed to improve visitor access to concessions facilities. By the end of the decade, the federal government had provided Nichols and the other concessioners 348 miles of highway within the park, 49 miles of approaches to the south and east, and a number of service roads for freight and maintenance. Another government agency, the Civilian Conservation Corps, also operated four camps in Yellowstone — at Mammoth, Lake, Canyon, and the Lower Geyser Basin near Nez Perce Creek. The duties of the young enrollees included clearing and marking trails, building boardwalks, and removing dead timber, all of which created a more acceptable version of "nature" for visitors, in keeping with the tradition of constructing an idealized environment.[19]

The program of public awareness pursued by the NPS and the concessioners to improve attendance in the park succeeded: the boom of the 1920s provided enough financial cushion to carry Nichols, Haynes, and the rest of the park operators through the worst years of the Great Depression.

Ironically, however, the publicity also generated criticism. Harry Child had built his empire largely unnoticed, pulling strings from behind the scenes, with most park visitors never fully appreciating the level at which he dictated policy and determined the way they saw the park. Even the antimonopoly sentiment sweeping the nation during the Progressive Era bypassed his exclusive franchise because he operated in a unique environment, sheltered by a mythology that stipulated special treatment for the custodians of national treasures. But with the economic troubles of the 1930s, the end of Republican government, and different ideas about what national parks should be emerging, concessions received more attention.

A hint of the changes that lay in store came from an unexpected source. Secretary of the Interior Harold L. Ickes, in an address to national park superintendents in 1934, announced his desire to limit development in the parks. In his view, Yellowstone and the other reservations should allow citizens "a renewed communion with Nature," something nearly impossible with the existing program of construction and development. Up until this time, most park visitors, and certainly NPS administrators and concessions operators, saw little conflict between the concepts of development and nature. But Ickes was demonstrating that new ideas were taking shape, ideas about the way nature, to be spiritually useful, should look. He recognized, he said, that more and more park visitors "take their nature from the automobile" but insisted that "the parks ought to be for people who love to camp and love to hike . . . and wander about." Ickes's remarks also illustrated the basic contradictions that were appearing in popular ideas about national parks and would soon be reflected in policy, the much-visited debate between preservation and use. Even while chastising the superintendents for allowing too many roads to be built, for catering to public demands for services, Ickes advocated opening the parks to more visitors, claiming that NPS officials and concessioners had created class distinctions that limited access and enjoyment for many Americans. Citing Yosemite as an example, Ickes asserted that the park administrators had "a terrible problem out there." The Ahwahnee, Mather's luxury hotel that attracted mostly California's idle rich, typified much that the secretary believed wrong with national park development. "I did not see why," he said, "the government should spend money in acquiring and maintaining a park in order to permit people to spend one or two or three or four months there. That is special privilege. One thing that I am opposed to is special privilege. Parks are for the reasonable use of all the people, and no one is to have any vested right of interest in any of the parks." Lavish facilities and a broad range of services attracted the wrong crowd, Ickes continued. "If you give them hot and cold running water for shower-baths the next thing they will want will be their breakfasts in bed. Frankly, we don't want that kind of people in the parks." Of course, those were exactly the kind of people that NPS administrators and concessioners had been trying to attract for decades.[20]

Ickes said he suspected that most NPS officials were allowing concessioners to dictate policy, that growing demands among the American public for the parks to be recreational facilities were being reflected in expansion of services and facilities. Most shockingly to the concessioners, Ickes lamented the lack of legislation allowing the federal government to "take over all of these concessions and run them ourselves," an off-the-cuff remark that created instant distrust among park operators, a feeling that lasted throughout his tenure. "We lie awake nights," Ickes told the superintendents, "wondering whether we are giving the customers all of the entertainment and all of the modern improvements that they think they ought to have. But let's keep away from that, because if we once get started there will be no end." What Ickes failed to realize was that the process had begun long ago, and the end was not in sight.

In some ways the NPS itself was responsible for changing ideas about what national parks should be. In 1933 NPS director Horace Albright had convinced President Franklin Roosevelt to give the agency jurisdiction over historic sites as well as more traditional national parks. The executive order transferring responsibility for such sites to the NPS complicated the service's management problems and confused the public. Previously, national parks had been places of nature; of course, they had been marketed as many other things as well, but the core idea, that nature was the primary attraction, never disappeared. Now, with the NPS managing and promoting such places as Civil War battlefields, presidential birthplaces, and even the White House, the agency's public identity became muddled. And since most Americans identified the NPS with the national parks — especially the "crown jewels" of the system like Yellowstone, Glacier, and Yosemite — the parks' images blurred as well. For the first time, contradictory ideas about what the national parks should be appeared in public debate.

The same debate was beginning to occur within the ranks of the NPS itself. The same year the agency assumed responsibility for the monuments and historic sites, a three-person team of wildlife biologists with whom the service had contracted issued *Fauna of the National Parks of the United States: A Preliminary Survey of Faunal Relations in National Parks*, or *Fauna No. 1*, the first in a proposed series. This report marked the beginning of an important ideological thread within the service, a belief that designing the parks to meet visitor expectations was inappropriate. Instead, these scientists argued, the goal should be to replicate as closely as possible those conditions that existed before the parks had been altered. The chief author of the report, George Wright, thus departed from NPS tradition, which viewed visitor desires as paramount. But this was not a battle between science and tradition; rather, it was a struggle between those who believed the parks should reflect popular ideals and those who believed they should construct those ideals. In essence, Wright and his associates, Ben H. Thompson and Joseph F. Dixon, were advocating that the Park Service take the lead in educating tourists regarding what they should value, what they should want their parks to be. It was an idea with little support among much of the agency's personnel, but it would reappear thirty years later as a powerful force and an immense complication for NPS officials and concessioners alike.[21]

While the debate raged within the Interior Department and the NPS, park concessioners quietly went about their business of altering the parks to fit what they believed was the dominant public desire. If recreation was what the public wanted — and it seemed so, judging by the tourist numbers at Hot Springs National Park in Arkansas, the NPS's first foray into such marketing practices — then recreation was what the concessioners would deliver. Paul Sceva, longtime manager of Mount Rainier's Paradise Inn and now general manager of the Rainier National Park Company, had installed a one-thousand-foot toboggan run in 1924 and built a golf course near the hotel in 1931. By the mid-1930s, both Mount Rainier and Rocky Mountain National Parks had become meccas for winter recreation enthusiasts and competed for guests with private developments such as Idaho's Sun Valley. In 1935 the NPS agreed to clear the road to Rainier's Paradise Inn through the winter, and that same year the park hosted the National Ski Championships and the Olympic trials. Other such recreational developments included a proposed tramway from Yosemite Valley to Glacier Point, promoted by the Yosemite Park and Curry Company, that would later be rejected. Similar proposals for cable cars to cross the Grand Canyon had been discussed for years. In 1936 the popular belief that national parks could offer recreational opportunities was codified when Congress passed a law making the NPS responsible for developing recreational opportunities on public lands. Soon most tourists expected such opportunities, and the NPS naturally turned to its longtime partners, the concessioners, to reshape the parks again. Already swimming pools dotted many parks; in Yellowstone, those at Mammoth and Old Faithful, using water from the hot springs nearby, proved most popular. Mountain climbing grew more common in the Yosemite and Rocky Mountain parks, as did calls for NPS rescues; tennis courts, croquet lawns, putting greens, and other such features cropped up in many parks, suiting those who believed recreation was of primary importance but alienating some who thought that nature, as they perceived it, was losing its place in the parks. Some who believed that park policy was moving in the wrong direction founded the Wilderness Society in 1935, evidence that contradictory mythologies were emerging; these competing ideas about how nature should be valued were destined to clash over ownership of the sacred national park landscapes.[22]

The changing nature of the parks spurred a public airing of the concessions situation. In 1936 A. C. McIntosh, a former Yellowstone seasonal ranger, published a scathing indictment of concessioners in the magazine *American Mercury*. He lamented the fact that park visitors discovered "predatory money-changers" in addition to the scenic beauty and insisted that "big business has taken charge." He accurately dismissed the traditional justification for high prices in the park being the result of a short season with the observation that "the season is no shorter than in outside resort centers" and observed that freight costs were comparable as well. Noting that tourists "run the gauntlet of stores, lodges, and hotels in a manner analogous to sheep passing through a shearing pen," and that "the speed with which many visitors glimpse the park reminds one of the auto races at Indianapolis," he stated that the prices were "not set by fair competition" but were arbitrarily fixed by the companies, with only token oversight by the NPS. McIntosh focused public attention on commercial enterprises that previously had been obscure and called for changes: "The people referred to in the first Yellowstone Park Act were the American people, not a small group of concession operators."[23]

Despite the criticism and broadened public awareness of park concessions, business steadily improved after the mid-1930s. Regardless of the increasing profits, the YP Company, in the best tradition of "Harry Hardup," often went to great lengths to collect every dollar it was owed. In July 1939, for example, a guest wrote a check at Canyon Hotel for $5.50, covering his room charges. The signature was illegible, and no name was printed on the check. Helen Conners, the YP Company general cashier, traced the check to a "Captain John Eric Bibby" of California. She then obtained his automobile license number from the NPS rangers (who had recorded it upon his entry into the park) and wrote to the California license bureau for information, stating that the driver of a Rolls-Royce, name unknown, had left a package at the Canyon Hotel. She received an address by return mail and promptly billed Bibby for the delinquent amount. In another instance, the company unsuccessfully employed a private detective, known only as "Investigator G-5," to collect $65.00 in overdue payments from the operator of a New York travel agency.[24]

By the early 1940s, Yellowstone operators — along with the rest of the country — were on the verge of their greatest challenge ever. National park tourism boomed in 1941, with over twenty-one million visitors enjoying NPS sites that season. But after December 1941, World War II devastated the tourism industry, and park concessioners, despite their privileged monopolies and seemingly insular lives within the reservation, suffered a serious decline. In August 1942 Nichols began drastically scaling back operations. He cut executive salaries 25 percent, asked department heads Kammermeyer and Brown, who were too old to serve in the military, to find outside employment, and offered another three hundred vehicles for sale to reduce expenses. He and Goodwin then asked NPS director Newton Drury to close the park for the duration of the conflict, but Drury refused. Consequently, the Yellowstone Park Company failed to make a profit in 1942, losing approximately $38,000 on operations.[25]

Director Drury tried to maintain full operations in all national parks, but he soon realized the futility of such a plan and allowed concessioners to reduce services. Rationing limited the amount of gasoline available to potential visitors; private citizens had little access to tires; and the government pro-hibited railroads from carrying vacationers. With visitation almost nonex-istent and concessioners losing money and unable to staff their facilities, Drury allowed businesses to scale back in 1943. All services at Crater Lake National Park were closed, and two of the three lodges on Isle Royale were shuttered. Lassen Volcanic in California boarded up the few facilities that existed, and even operators at the biggest draws like Great Smoky Mountains, Yosemite, Glacier, the Grand Canyon, and Yellowstone asked Drury for per-mission to shut down. Military officials utilized the largely abandoned parks for training purposes. Mountain warfare training took place at both Mount Rainier and Mount McKinley; desert warfare was practiced at Joshua Tree National Monument. The navy took over Yosemite's Ahwahnee Hotel for a hospital and the Mount McKinley Hotel for a recreation center.[26]

In Yellowstone, Nichols, Haynes, Hamilton, and Anna Pryor cooperated on a plan to serve the few guests who arrived. They consolidated facilities at the largest developments, sharing expenses and employees. Pryor opened her general store at Mammoth as a restaurant; her adjacent coffee shop became a motel. At Old Faithful and Fishing Bridge, Hamilton provided all services within his stores, including meals and lodging. All hotels and lodges remained closed; no buses operated. Government rules even restricted com-pany vehicles used to transport supplies. Wartime regulations rationed meat, sugar, and other staples and required guests to have a ration book. Office of Price Administration ceilings applied also, limiting meal and housing charges. Haynes opened his shops at Mammoth and Old Faithful for a lim-ited time, then moved his stock of postcards, film, and park guidebooks — the already famous *Haynes Guides* — to Hamilton's stores. Telephone service was sharply curtailed, and telegraph lines were disconnected. The small hos-pital at Mammoth funded by the concessioners closed. Laundries lacked employees and shut down. Even the regular church services, held in the lit-tle stone chapel at Mammoth, halted. The park grew silent, the great hotels empty and without maintenance, the buses confined to garages, the lodges devoid of Summer Savages.[27]

Yellowstone remained quiet throughout the seasons of 1943 and 1944. In addition to the almost complete absence of tourists, the departure of family members and friends contributed to an atmosphere of melancholy. John Q. Nichols, Billie's son and assistant, served from 1942 until the end of the conflict, attending officers' training school at Miami Beach, receiving a commission as a first lieutenant in army aviation, then being stationed in California, Arizona, and Nevada. The army utilized his experience in Yellowstone by assigning him to operate officers' clubs. He was sent overseas late in 1945 and was among the last to return to the park. Huntley Child Jr. served as well, entering the army as a first lieutenant in 1943 and being stationed at Rock Island Arsenal. Hamilton's close friend and assistant, Gar Helppie, was drafted in December 1942 and spent the duration of the war away from Yellowstone, as did Joe Bill, longtime manager of the YP Company print shop and one of Jack Haynes's closest friends. But no sons died; no close friends failed to return. With the sparse tourist numbers and the absence of so many family members, however, Yellowstone concessioners endured the worst years in their history.[28]

Although the war devastated business in the park, the concessions families suffered comparatively little economic disruption. Billie and Ellen Nichols, wealthy enough to weather the temporary lull in their cash flow, spent much of their time either at their home on Spanish Creek, on the Flying D Ranch property north of the park, or in La Jolla. Unlike the YP Company, which lost so much income that the company defaulted on note payments during the war, Haynes, Hamilton, and Pryor actually profited from the reduced levels of service. Haynes shuttled between his main store in Bozeman, Montana, and the park, acting as liaison between Nichols and superintendent Edmund Rogers. Hamilton remained in Yellowstone during the summers, personally overseeing operations at Old Faithful and reportedly doing a brisk business in bootleg liquor. And Pryor, having a virtual monopoly at Mammoth Hot Springs without competition from hotel and lodge facilities, experienced only minor hardships.[29]

Nor did family members encounter any financial difficulty during the war years. The H. W. Child Corporation earned a net income of over $120,000 in 1942; the Flying D Ranch added $165,000; and Nichols, as president of the trust that wielded majority control of these two entities, distributed the proceeds regularly. In addition, YP Company assets included a cash surplus of more than $3 million, so Adelaide lived comfortably in La Jolla, with a chauffeur and domestic staff; all her children, grandchildren, and great-grandchildren received income from the trust. The family had become quite extensive: the Nichols side included Billie and Ellen Dean Child Nichols, their children John (and wife Betty), Dean (whose wife, Martha, was, like him, a doctor), and Adelaide (who had married Californian Michael Casserly), as well as four grandchildren — Peter and John Q., Nichols Jr., and Marianna and Joan Casserly. The Child side included Emilie Child (Huntley Sr.'s widow); her daughters, Marion Child Sanger and Margot Child Pomeroy; their brother, Huntley Child Jr.; and his wife, Emily, daughter, Jane, and son, Harry W. Child II. Annual dividend checks amounting in 1942 to $28,672 for Billie and $275 for each other family member were supplemented by monthly allowances of approximately $125. As effective head of the family, Billie — even his children and grandchildren called him by his nickname — also doled out funds for emergencies or special occasions. When son John entered the Army Air Corps in 1942, Nichols instructed Galusha to purchase the mortgage on his La Jolla home to avoid any possible inconvenience.[30]

Despite the lack of hardship endured by the Child and Nichols families, most Americans still faced difficult times. In the spring of 1945 business in Yellowstone remained poor, but Interior Secretary Ickes and NPS director Drury once again refused Nichols's request to close the park entirely, so the concessioners began preparing for another slow season. Before the end of June, however, a noticeable shift occurred. Park travel increased by 35 percent; cabins at Fishing Bridge and Old Faithful opened and were filled with guests; inventories that had been allowed to dwindle over the past few seasons became troublesome; and Savages began returning to work serving tourists. By July business had grown even more, with income already exceeding the previous year's total. Before much longer, Nichols and the rest of the concessioners realized that a massive recovery was under way.

The tourist rush soon overwhelmed the ill-prepared park companies. Americans wanted to return to normal, and visiting national parks was a part of everyday life. On August 13 the government discontinued gasoline rationing, and within days visitors flooded into Yellowstone. The few employees on hand attempted to maintain services, but their efforts were futile. Nichols failed to attract emergency workers, since the end of the war had created numerous employment opportunities and high wages. He simply could not convince enough people to come to work. Many of those he did employ — mostly schoolteachers, retirees, and high school students — had to leave by the end of the month, and others quit in favor of higher-paying jobs elsewhere. Meanwhile, the tourists displayed no sign of ending their assault. Nichols even opened the old Cottage Hotel at Mammoth after years of disuse to accommodate the influx. On August 25 the NPS issued a statement announcing that park facilities were limited and understaffed, hoping to dissuade people from embarking on their planned trips. At the same time, the agency requested that Nichols and the others remain open longer into the autumn to accommodate visitors. The combination of inadequate supplies, few workers, and mothballed facilities created havoc — the boom times seemed as difficult as those of the bust.[31]

Throughout the next several seasons, as park travel increased steadily, concessioners struggled daily to accommodate the hordes of tourists. Most YP Company facilities had been closed during the war years; disuse, the harsh Yellowstone climate, and obsolescence — the hotels averaged over forty years old — caused continuous maintenance problems. Many long-time employees had taken lucrative positions elsewhere during the war. Some remained away, and others demanded higher wages to return for seasonal work. Division managers constantly traveled to nearby towns, looking for employees to fill over sixteen hundred positions. Nichols was forced to close cafeterias, cabins, and other facilities regularly, especially late in the season after many workers departed. Hamilton and Pryor, because they required fewer employees than did the YP Company, fared better but still endured demands for higher wages and shorter hours.

Still, the tourists kept coming. In 1947 a record 932,503 people visited Yellowstone, a 60 percent increase over any previous total. During July and August, more than ten thousand persons entered the park daily, even though Nichols could accommodate only seventy-eight hundred in hotels, lodges, and cabins. Railroad travel, although still a dwindling percentage of the total, rebounded in the postwar years as well, with the five lines bringing over sixteen thousand guests to Yellowstone in 1947. Part of this recovery can be attributed to promotion. The Northern Pacific and the Union Pacific tried valiantly to retain their park business, displaying miniature working models of Old Faithful geyser at fairs and travel shows. Northern Pacific passenger agent Max Goodsill even rented four bear cubs from Superintendent Rogers in 1946 to advertise at the Chicago Railroad Fair on Lake Michigan. Good-sill was not content with the miniature geysers: he built a model that spouted forty feet. The next two years set records as well, with over one million visitors in both 1948 and 1949.[32]

The postwar travel explosion that caused hardship for Yellowstone concessioners did the same for operators in other western national parks. Most tourist facilities, having been closed during the war, suffered damage from neglect and the harsh climates prevalent in many western parks. In Yellowstone, conservative estimates to refurbish deteriorated structures ran as much as $2.5 million, even higher if new construction costs were included. At Yosemite, already experiencing chronic overcrowding, the situation was similar. Even smaller parks, such as Lassen Volcanic in California, discovered their concession facilities sadly lacking in the face of increasing postwar travel. To compound the problem, the NPS was demanding that operators upgrade and expand their physical plants to meet rising demand, but most concession contracts were due to expire within five years. Because these agreements represented the only security for outside loans, the operators had little chance of funding new construction.[33]

The national park concessioners shared more than their postwar travel and expansion problems and common ideas about shaping parks to fit market demands. A small clique of closely allied families owned many of the lucrative park enterprises. Some were wealthy, socially prominent Californians who, like Harry Child, had taken advantage of Mather's monopolistic policies during prior decades to dominate all business in the parks. Don and Mary Tresidder — he the president of Stanford University and she a daughter of the famous Curry camping founders — controlled the Yosemite Park and Curry Company. Others were less prominent but equally successful, such as Howard Hays and Roe Emery, who operated in Glacier, Rocky Mountain, and Sequoia National Parks, and Don Hummel of Lassen Volcanic and Mount McKinley National Parks. Yellowstone concessioners Nichols, Jack and Isabel Haynes, together with Charles Hamilton and his heirs, daughter and son-in-law Ellie and Trevor Povah, constituted a significant portion of the group. Paul Sceva in Rainier (the most militant of the assemblage) and the Harvey family in Grand Canyon (the only concessioner widely known to the general public) rounded out the privileged circle. These operators formed the nucleus of the Western Conference of National Parks Concessioners (WCNPC), which became the single most influential body in determining NPS policy in the post–World War II era.[34]

The WCNPC had originated in the 1920s to defend concessions empires against threats, but for decades it encountered little opposition. Throughout the Mather and Albright directorships the NPS stridently avoided confrontations with concessioners, who by the end of World War II had enjoyed thirty years of almost total freedom from government oversight responsibilities. Mather and Albright had routinely supported proposals for park development intended to increase concession profits. Their successors were simply overmatched when infrequent conflict with operators arose. Individual franchisees, like Nichols and Don Tresidder of Yosemite, were intimately involved with the administration of the parks and, in some cases, effectively ran them. The NPS treated the WCNPC, officially the collective lobbying group for the businesses, not as an interest or pressure group but simply as a "partner." The long-standing congenial relationship between concessioners and the agency remained strong throughout the war years.[35]

But soon the concessioners faced challenges to their dominant position. Complaints about poor service, inadequate facilities, and overcrowded conditions began filtering into the NPS and the Interior Department. As Interior Secretary Harold Ickes had demonstrated with his speech to park superintendents in 1934, Interior Department officials sometimes disagreed with the NPS and concessioner ideas about what national parks should be. In 1946 newly appointed Secretary of the Interior Julius Krug, together with Undersecretary Oscar L. Chapman and Assistant Secretary for Public Lands Crow Girard "Jebby" Davidson, attempted to alter the traditional NPS-concessioner "partnership" approach to park management, launching a crusade to reassert authority over both the NPS and concessioner operations. Many of the twenty-year contracts were up for renewal within the next five years, and the officials attempted to reform four troublesome points: preferential rights of renewal, term of contract, rate of franchise fee, and building ownership. Operators had always been assured of preferential treatment in the renewal process; in fact, most contract expirations were never announced or opened for competitive bids. Krug wanted to encourage competition for the lucrative operations. He also wanted to shorten the twenty-year standard contract and raise franchise fees from 3 percent of net income to 5 percent. But the main point of contention was the ownership of concession buildings. The federal government had always held title to the structures — they were on public lands — which precluded concessioners borrowing against their facilities, hence limiting their ability to secure outside financing for expansion. An unwritten agreement between concessioners and the NPS, however, provided reimbursement for improvements upon termination, something that had never before occurred. The revised policy negated that understanding, guaranteeing the outgoing concessioner compensation only from a successor organization and leaving the government without any financial obligation. Krug hoped to instigate a revolt among concessioners, to goad them into refusing new contracts under these terms, and to engineer a government takeover of concession operations, much as Ickes had intimated during the previous decade.[36]

The concessioners and their allies — most prominently NPS officials — immediately began to defend themselves against this assault on their lucrative monopolies. Shortly after hearing of the proposed changes in December 1946, WCNPC attorneys Herman Hoss of the Yosemite and Curry Company and Taylor Weir of Yellowstone advised all members against signing any new contracts under those terms. This moratorium, which affected approximately two-thirds of the total number of concessioners, effectively halted any construction or capital improvements in park facilities and exacerbated the problems of tourist accommodation. Former NPS director Horace Albright openly supported the operators, privately advising some not to sign the new contracts. Current director Drury drafted a thirteen-page memo, asserting that the reforms would devastate visitor services in the parks. The NPS and the concessioners, allies without opposition for many years, now closed ranks and fought the proposed changes, actions that resulted in a three-year standoff. Secretary Krug, through his assistant secretary for public lands, "Jebby" Davidson, insisted on forcing concessioners to sign new contracts; however, NPS director Drury, under constant pressure from the WCNPC, refused to acquiesce, instead granting contract extensions to all operators under the old terms. In addition, the concessioners turned to Congress for legislation that would provide protection from the Interior Department proposal and received favorable responses from many members.[37]

While the NPS and concessioners staunchly held firm, the reform coalition within the Interior Department gradually weakened, then collapsed. The House Appropriations Committee, which had originally supported an eventual buyout of all Yellowstone operations, lost interest due to more pressing monetary concerns. Secretary Krug resigned in 1949 and was succeeded by Chapman, whose commitment to concessions reform was less enthusiastic. Then, during the winter of 1949 and 1950, a series of hearings before the U.S. House Subcommittee on Public Lands dealt the most serious blow to reform efforts. During the course of the hearings, attorney Taylor Weir, who represented all the Yellowstone concessioners, exposed Davidson as a hypocrite and a liar, and the reform movement effectively ended. In 1950, after months of being assailed by concessioners as a "socialist" who wanted to "emasculate the swell NPS officials" and "oust the free-enterprise concessioners," Davidson resigned. With the two main instigators for reform gone, Interior Secretary Chapman surrendered; contract terms remained at twenty years, franchise fees would be small fixed payments, and, most significantly, the concessioners would acquire "possessory interest" in their buildings.[38]

WCNPC attorney Herman Hoss discovered the obscure "possessory interest" phrase and utilized it to strengthen the position of the concessioners. He had lifted the term from the California Tax Code and inserted it into the model standard contract that Chapman eventually approved. In essence, possessory interest meant that concessioners, while not holding title to their buildings, were entitled to direct compensation from the U.S. government if their contracts were canceled or not renewed. Their rights to capital improvements would not expire with their franchises, making the twenty-year contract term irrelevant unless Congress approved a buyout at the conclusion of the agreement. In effect, the adoption of possessory interest legalized what had previously been a "gentleman's agreement" between the concessioners and the NPS and virtually assured park businesses of perpetual monopoly rights. So, even if the parks were by law and tradition not for sale, the concessioners effectively owned the most valuable parts of them, those parts that had long been designed to attract visitors.[39]

While the WCNPC disposed of the government challenge, Nichols endured other difficulties both personal and professional. He lost a steady source of income when the Northern Pacific, discouraged over poor profits, abandoned its Park Branch line in 1948. He had suspended major improvements to his hotel and lodge developments during the battle with Krug, and the physical structures had fallen deeper into disrepair. Although profits had never been greater — in 1951 net income exceeded half a million dollars — Nichols reinvested little money in renovations or repairs. He began drinking heavily and became indifferent. In 1944 he sold the family stake in the Flying D Ranch (although keeping the house at Spanish Creek and a token amount of acreage), and by 1950 he seemed to be losing interest in the YP Company as well.

Nichols was not alone. In 1951 his son John and nephew Huntley Child Jr., both executives in the company, expressed a desire to sell the family holdings. The most obscure of the Yellowstone concessioners, Anna Pryor, decided she had endured enough cycles of boom and bust and prepared to sell her store and coffee shop at Mammoth to Hamilton, who was himself negotiating with the NPS to allow his daughter Ellie and son-in-law Trevor Povah to assume control of his stores. The only operator seemingly unaffected by the turmoil within the park was Jack Haynes, who quietly tended his picture shops while awaiting NPS approval of a new contract.[40]

By 1951, visitors coming to the park expected a certain level of services — long-standing marketing campaigns had created such expectations. But with the degradation of facilities and lack of management interest, most guests departed disappointed. Nichols had not replenished his transportation fleet after the wholesale dismantling of the 1930s and 1940s; in addition, the White Motor Company stopped building buses, and parts became scarce. As a consequence, the precision transportation schedules of earlier years became difficult to maintain. The camps and lodges offered spartan accommodations at high prices; complaints were frequent, but the facilities remained busy due to lack of alternatives. The hotels, higher-priced and without maintenance for years, attracted few customers. Cafeterias and dining rooms lacked experienced help and served inferior food. Rental cabins were often without blankets or even firewood. Some guests, unable to find clean, affordable lodgings, slept in their cars. For over fifty years concessioners and government officials alike had promoted Yellowstone as able to be all things to all people — natural curiosities, sublime landscape, the Old West frontier, recreational site — never imagining that the number of visitors or the diversity of ideas about what the park should be could exceed their capabilities. But it was happening; the challenge in coming years was to choose a solution to the problem, and that decision rested not with Nichols and the YP Company but with the National Park Service and its new director, Conrad L. Wirth.[41]

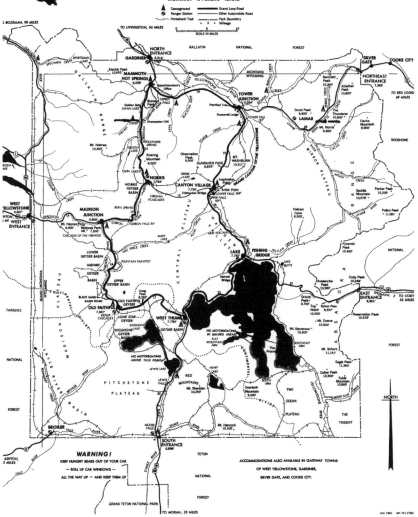

Yellowstone National Park, as shown in the official 1961 NPS tourist brochure provided to all guests upon entering.

Even the immense size of the lobby did not dispel the comfortable ambience of the Canyon Hotel lounge, as pictured in this pre-1914 Haynes postcard.

The contemporary interior of the Canyon Lodge dining room, shown here in 1957, shocked many visitors accustomed to more rustic facilities.

Tourists await their assigned vehicles on the porch of the Mammoth Hotel, c. 1920.

In contrast to the unique architecture and furnishings of the Canyon Hotel, the lounge in the new Canyon Lodge reflects the sterile, homogeneous style prevalent throughout the structure.

Public auto camps operated by the NPS attracted tourists wishing to avoid the more formal tent camps, hotels, and lodges.

Howard Hays of the Yellowstone Park Camps Company leads a procession through Roosevelt Arch at the northern entrance to celebrate the opening of Yellowstone for the 1923 season.

The Mammoth public auto camp, with Mammoth Lodge and Cabins in the background, 1929. Such camps, although operated by the NPS, also included concessions such as groceries, service stations, and lunch counters.

Main Street, Old Faithful auto camp, 1929. Facilities expansion remained a priority in this, one of the last boom years prior to the Great Depression.

Old Canyon Lodge and Cabins, built during the 1920s and typical of the rustic architecture of the day, were scheduled to be replaced by Canyon Village in 1957. The old Canyon Hotel is in the background.

NPS director Conrad Wirth and Yellowstone superintendent Edmund B. Rogers at the annual Campfire Pageant, September 1956. Within weeks, Wirth replaced Rogers with Lon Garrison to accelerate the pace of Mission 66 development in the park.

Yellowstone superintendent Lon Garrison shows Wirth, center, and NPS regional director Howard Baker one of the new interpretive displays created under Mission 66.

William M. (Billie) Nichols (right) and future YP Company transportation superintendent F. E. Kammermeyer with the fleet of 1920 model White Motor Company buses at Mammoth, c. 1923.

This is the home designed for Harry Child and his family by architect Robert Reamer in Mammoth, just across the old army parade grounds from the Mammoth Hotel. This home and the others visible next to it were sold as company assets and remained occupied by concessions executives through the 1990s.

Charles A. Hamilton poses in front of his Old Faithful store, c. 1920. Such building styles, utilizing rough-hewn logs and fieldstone, helped promote the idea of concessions as fitting into a natural environment such as Yellowstone.

*Breaking ground for Canyon Village, 1956. Left to right, J. E. Haynes, Charles A.
Hamilton, Conrad Wirth, and Billie Nichols.*

*General Ulysses S. Grant III, with his hand on the shovel, joins Superintendent Garrison
at the groundbreaking for Grant Village in 1963. This site was one that NPS officials
insisted needed to be made more "natural," in keeping with visitor expectations.*

The magnificent Old Faithful Inn as it looked in 1912. After the park was opened to automobile traffic, a porte cochere and observation deck were added to the front of the structure. Even after being surrounded by parking lots in the 1950s, the inn epitomized visitor expectations of national park architecture.

The Canyon Hotel, which had to be closed in 1957 when guests flocked to the old structure in lieu of staying at the modern Canyon Village Lodge or cabins.

Canyon Village Lodge, c. 1957. Note the harsh lines in contrast with older park structures. Visitors looked upon this concrete-and-glass building in confusion, not expecting such contemporary designs in a place they considered immune from progress.

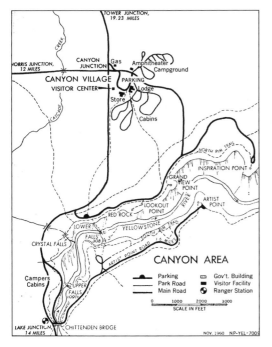

The partitioning of the park into areas of wilderness and areas of public use was by 1960 being reflected in all aspects of park promotion. This map from the 1960 NPS brochure presents Canyon Village not as a part of a larger reservation but as a separate and distinct place.

Guests at one of the Wylie Camps pose for a photo, c. 1900. These popular striped-tent camps were later replaced by cabins and lodges as concessioners tried to satisfy changing visitor desires. Despite all the structural changes, however, the Yellowstone camps remained favorites with tourists seeking a more relaxed park experience than could be had in the hotels.

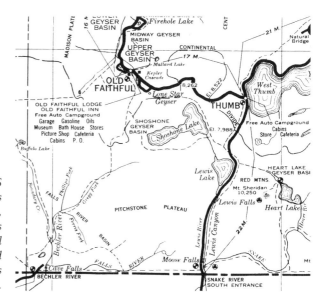

A section of the 1941 NPS map of Yellowstone shows how cultural features, such as the concessions facilities at Old Faithful and West Thumb, had become prominent parts of the park.

A group of tourists enjoy the Grand Canyon of the Yellowstone from the comfort of a 1925 model White Motor Company bus. The canvas tops in these vehicles rolled back to allow sightseers unobstructed views of the scenery without ever leaving their seats, allowing schedules to be maintained.

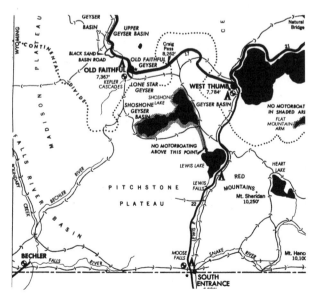

After the widespread criticism of Mission 66, the NPS printed this map for the entrance brochure in 1961. Notice the absence of concessions facilities.

Harry W. Child, the driving force behind many of the concession facilities in Yellowstone.

The Coming Crisis

5

The 1950s began uneventfully in Yellowstone. Despite the crowded conditions, obsolete facilities, and customer complaints, business for all operators remained profitable and the day-to-day problems similar to those of prior years. The nepotistic nature of Yellowstone concessions provided continuity in management. Stockholders elected John Q. Nichols and Huntley Child Jr. as vice presidents of the Yellowstone Park Company, and both men actively participated in administering the business. Hugh Galusha, longtime company accountant, served as auditor and chief adviser to President Billie Nichols; his son, Hugh Jr., trained at Pennsylvania's prestigious Wharton School of Business as both an accountant and an attorney, also assumed an executive position within the concessions firm. Other operators enjoyed the same smooth progression. Trevor Povah, Hamilton's son-in-law, became general manager of the stores and service stations. Jack Ellis Haynes remained content with his photo shops and his general store at Tower Junction. Park superintendent Edmund B. Rogers, theoretically in charge of overseeing business operations for the National Park Service, rarely intruded on company matters and spent most of the year at home in Denver. The same families who had effectively run Yellowstone for decades concentrated on recovering the profits lost during World War II and maintaining their privileged way of life. But tourism was changing; perceptions about value were changing, and with them ideas about national parks. The concessioners failed to see these changes coming.

At first most of the daily problems were little more than nuisances. The decline in numbers of rail passengers, constant since early in the 1920s, continued unabated and in 1951 forced the Milwaukee Road to sell its Gallatin

Gateway Inn, an elegant stopover where guests detrained before transferring to the buses of the Yellowstone Park Lines. New owner Paul Hollenstein attempted to circumvent the YP Company franchise and operate his own park tours. Nichols, ever vigilant in defending against even minor incursions against his exclusive contract, assigned company employees to sabotage the business. Other private tours, from all parts of the country, regularly entered Yellowstone under the guise of nonprofit educational or church excursions; some the company caught and prosecuted, others avoided paying the required fees. The transition to a credit economy, which fueled economic growth throughout the nation, also annoyed company managers. In 1952, when Conoco Oil Company, which supplied Yellowstone's gasoline, requested that park service stations accept credit cards as payment for fuel and repairs, Nichols resisted, believing such a move would damage his cash flow. Eventually, Conoco prevailed, but this episode demonstrated to Nichols that he was losing touch with the realities of commerce in modern America.[1]

Another minor conflict arose when Anna Pryor decided to sell her park businesses. Hamilton, since he owned similar concessions elsewhere in the park, was the logical buyer for Pryor's Mammoth general store and lunch counter. He wanted the YP Company to share in the purchase, but "Ham," as he was affectionately known, had developed a reputation for drunkenness, shady dealings, and greed. He unwisely blamed Galusha for tax difficulties caused by his failure to take inventory for a number of years. He had overextended himself buying California real estate and had run afoul of state tax authorities there, focusing IRS attention on his Yellowstone operations. During the summers, Hamilton and his wife, May, lived in a lavishly appointed apartment above their Old Faithful curio store, surrounded by European antiques and rare works of art. Not wishing to enter into another partnership with such a character — Hamilton already shared the Yellowstone Park Service Station concession — YP Company officials declined to share in the purchase of Pryor's assets. The two parties eventually reached a compromise allowing Hamilton to take over her store and sell the lunch counter to the YP Company, thereby disposing of Pryor, their last — albeit minor — competitor.[2]

None of these routine dealings involved outside parties other than the NPS, which had to approve the Pryor sale. In fact, the operations of the YP Company had remained relatively free from outside control since the 1890s.

Although the Department of the Interior maintained nominal control over transportation, lodging, and other services between 1891, when Harry Child arrived, and 1916, when the NPS was founded, it never enforced oppressive regulatory measures. In 1916 NPS director Mather, by imposing consolidation upon the operators to modernize park businesses, had actually helped Child dominate concessions, and his benign approval of the 1925 takeover of lodges and camps further strengthened the YP Company position. The emergence of the NPS had simplified operations for all Yellowstone concessioners, allowing them to negotiate with a single government entity rather than several, as had been the case in prior years. It also provided them with a sympathetic ally with enforcement powers to defend their monopolies. The agency, particularly under Mather and Albright, had proved to be philosophically compatible with concessioner goals of promotion, development, and expansion.[3]

By the 1950s, however, the situation had changed. Decrepit facilities and overcrowded conditions in many parks led to public complaints about the level of available services. Negative publicity followed, and federal legislators, always sensitive to the whims of public opinion, again focused their attention on the national parks after decades of relative disinterest. Interior Secretary Julius Krug had damaged the relationship between the NPS and its "partners" by attempting to reduce concessioner influence late in the 1940s. During that battle he also split with NPS director Drury, whom the concessioners nonetheless distrusted because of his reputation as a staunch preservationist who opposed further development in the parks. Such beliefs, that modifying landscapes was somehow damaging to the very qualities that had made the parks valuable in the first place, were becoming more widespread. So until personnel changes occurred at both Interior and the NPS, the concessioners proved reluctant to acquiesce in the long-term development program needed to ensure sufficient guest facilities.

By 1951 such changes had taken place, so the NPS and concessioners attempted to repair their fractured alliance. Oscar Chapman succeeded Krug as secretary of the interior in 1949, and the contrary assistant secretary, "Jebby" Davidson, resigned the following year. Dale Doty, a friend to many of the concessioners, replaced him as chief department liaison to the operators. Drury departed in 1951, and Chapman appointed Arthur E. Demaray, a longtime agency employee who had served under Mather and Albright, to a brief, honorary term as director before Demaray retired as well. Then, in December 1951, Chapman promoted Conrad L. Wirth, another of the Mather-Albright traditionalists, to the NPS directorship, and the agency and its concessions partners tried to reestablish the common goals that they had pursued for years. Wirth actively promoted a policy of growth and development that seemed compatible with the desires of concessioners, including the YP Company. But other factors — public opinion and congressional action — intruded upon the heretofore private decisions about park management and forced Wirth to assert his authority over park businesses. By middecade, the relationship between the NPS and the YP Company had been damaged beyond repair. While Wirth desired investment and expansion, the concessioners believed such ideas to be counterproductive; after all, they held virtual monopolies on some of the most valuable commodities — nature, history, tradition — in the country.[4]

Congressional interest in Yellowstone concessions policy also complicated YP Company business enormously, although corporate political contacts tempered early incursions. The first indication of future problems appeared early in 1953, when Senator Guy Cordon of Oregon attached a rider to a Senate appropriations bill that would require the NPS to open concession contracts to competitive bidding upon their expiration, much like the Krug plan of five years earlier. Nichols and his subordinates immediately enlisted the aid of their many congressional allies. Senators Frank Barrett and Lester C. Hunt of Wyoming, whose state received over $250,000 per year in taxes from park business, were certainly sympathetic to company concerns. Senators John C. Stennis of Mississippi, Estes Kefauver of Tennessee, Francis Case of South Dakota, and John Sparkman of Alabama, all of whom had asked company managers to employ the children of prominent constituents over the years, likewise expressed support. Huntley Child Jr. convinced these men that without some assurance of contract renewal, capital improvements — so necessary to accommodate the still-growing numbers of tourists — would be halted. He reminded them of Krug's attempt to allow bids on concessions and blamed that controversy for delaying necessary improvements. He further explained that, if the YP Company contract was opened for bids upon its expiration in 1955, he had no choice but to recommend that Nichols stop investing money in the

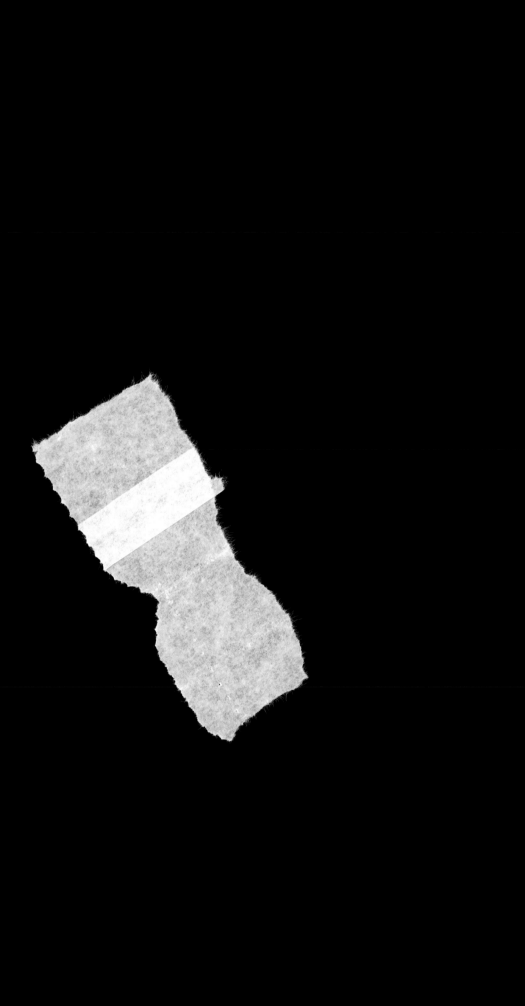

park. In the House of Representatives, where a similar bill had been introduced, Child Jr. convinced Congressmen Wesley D'Ewart of Montana,
George Smathers of Florida, and John P. Saylor of Pennsylvania — who had
recently toured Yellowstone compliments of the YP Company — to oppose
any change in policy. "We went through quite a period of uneasiness when
Krug was secretary," Smathers remembered; he assured Child of his support
by noting that "the policy . . . was satisfactory to both sides and is still in
effect." With Barrett leading the opposition to Cordon's amendment, the
Senate reached a compromise acceptable to the House by which the NPS
would have to submit concessions contracts for review only after they were
negotiated; no competitive bidding would occur, a victory for the company.[5]

Legislative interest in concessions contracts indicated the increased level
of attention being afforded national park issues. The new popularity of the
parks posed serious problems for the NPS. Government facilities, like those
of the concessioners, were run-down, staffing levels low, funds exhausted.
Yet burgeoning numbers of visitors expected to be housed, fed, and entertained; they had been sold numerous images of the park over the years and
now wanted reality to reflect their personal image of Yellowstone. Both the
NPS administrators and concessioners struggled to meet ever-increasing
demands for services. Complaints poured into park headquarters across the
country and into Washington, D.C., insisting that visitor desires be
addressed. When the inevitable breakdown occurred early in the 1950s, well
documented in the popular press, public pressure necessitated drastic measures to remedy the critical situation.

Widespread national publicity regarding the state of the parks began in
1953 and escalated over the next two years. In October 1953 Bernard DeVoto,
an influential writer and member of the National Parks Advisory Board, published a disheartening description of conditions in Yellowstone. As "the oldest, most popular, and most important national park," it had "reached the
limit of performance and begun to slide downhill." He bemoaned the lack of
sufficient NPS personnel necessary to "protect tourists from the conse-
quences of their own carelessness" and the shortage of funds that allowed
water, sewage, and garbage collection services to become overloaded. DeVoto
suggested closing Yellowstone, Yosemite, the Grand Canyon, and other
prominent parks, since Congress was unable to fund them adequately, until

"letters from constituents unable to visit Old Faithful . . . would bring a nationally disgraceful situation to the really serious attention of the Congress which is responsible for it."

Other, similar diatribes followed, with various levels of accuracy. A 1954 article in *Motor News* magazine titled "Our Crumbling National Parks" detailed the rotting timbers supporting Yellowstone's famed Fishing Bridge and the hundreds of tourists forced to sleep in their cars because of insufficient accommodations. The same author, like DeVoto, blamed Congress for inadequate appropriations and sympathized with concessioners, who, according to his sources, found it difficult to operate under the oppressive NPS guidelines. "The government regulates wages, hours, percentage of return on capital, and offers only short-term leases to concessionaires," he quoted one operator. "No preference is given in contract renewal, and there's no assurance a group will be permitted to retain the concession long enough to recover its investment." This assertion, although patently false, effectively rallied support for congressional funding. Other articles, with titles such as "Is Yellowstone Really a Mess?" and "Crisis in Our Parks," further fueled the debate, which even reached schoolchildren when the scholastic magazine *Every Week* published a simplified summary of DeVoto's column. And a Livingston, Montana, newspaper published a nostalgic reminiscence of the "good old days" of the 1920s, reassuring readers that, despite the present deplorable conditions, "the Spirit of Yellowstone never dies."[6]

Perhaps the most illustrative example of how competing stories, all of which utilized national parks as symbols, had complicated the old consensus ideology of promotion and development to "improve" nature and render it accessible came from prominent author Wallace Stegner. In an article in *Sports Illustrated* in 1955, Stegner acknowledged the long-standing dilemma between preservation and use, first mandated in 1872, but ignored the changes that creative marketing had imposed upon collective ideas about such things since Yellowstone's creation. Stegner opined that the 1933 expansion of NPS management responsibilities had proved confusing, stating that "too many kinds of things are included in the 24 million acres which the Park Service must administer. No wonder Joe Smith is confused; no wonder he sometimes falls for the notion that the parks ought to be 'developed.'" He then asserted that a true national park like Yosemite or Glacier "is not a playground and not a resort," but that such places existed "to preserve scenery, beauty, geology, archaeology, wildlife, for permanent use in living natural museums." Later in the article he called on Congress to appropriate more money for "the backlog of construction that every year is more frantically needed" and then closed by referring to Yosemite, Yellowstone, and the other natural parks as "primeval," offering "values that are close to the values of religion."

Stegner was expressing many commonly held and sometimes contradictory ideas. The belief that Americans were, in the popular phrase of the day, "loving the national parks to death," infused most such critiques of government park policy. Such a belief was understandable: tourist numbers had risen dramatically by 1955. When compared with 1940, before the war, the increase was obvious and alarming. Great Smoky Mountains National Park, close to population centers and since its inception the most visited park in the system, hosted over 2.6 million people in 1955 as opposed to only 861,000 fifteen years earlier. Similar gains were posted throughout the system: at Rocky Mountain National Park, the increase was 140 percent, from 628,000 to over 1.5 million; at Yellowstone, up 167 percent, from 526,000 to 1.4 million; Yosemite, from 507,000 to 1.06 million, an increase of 109 percent; Glacier tourism rose an amazing 264 percent during the period; and Olympic National Park went from accommodating 92,000 visitors in 1940 to over 700,000 in 1955, an increase of 664 percent. For Stegner to insist that national parks were not playgrounds or resorts was wrong; decades of NPS and concessioner activities had turned parks like Yellowstone, Yosemite, Rocky Mountain, and the others into resorts and playgrounds because that was what visitors desired. Stegner argued that development was too extensive, but he also called for more construction. Development itself was not the issue being debated, but rather the kind of development. Swimming pools, movie theaters, golf courses, and other similar tourist draws were now being perceived by ever-increasing numbers of people as distracting from the true value of the parks, nature. Beliefs were changing. Such development was losing fashion, while other kinds — access roads, interpretive displays, museums featuring natural and historic exhibits — were acceptable forms of transforming the landscape because they focused attention on the right qualities of the parks. Talk of "overdevelopment" simply meant, in most cases, that development should be refocused to emphasize nature, not eliminated, and that such development would once again allow national parks to fulfill their symbolic national roles.[7]

Interior Secretary Chapman appointed Conrad Wirth as NPS director to repair the damage done to the parks and their images by continued neglect and negative publicity. Appointed in 1951, Wirth brought admirable credentials and a family history of park work to the post. His father, Theodore Wirth, a Swiss immigrant, arrived in the United States late in the 1880s with a degree in horticulture. He immediately found employment as a park planner for New York City, working on Central Park; he later was superintendent of parks in Hartford, Connecticut, where son Conrad was born. In 1906 Wirth moved his family to Minneapolis, where for the next thirty years he developed one of the most extensive and respected municipal park systems in the country. Conrad Wirth followed his father's career path, enrolling at Massachusetts Agricultural College (now the University of Massachusetts) and earning a bachelor of science degree in landscape gardening. In 1925 he and a partner founded the landscape architecture and town planning firm of Neale and Wirth in New Orleans, but it survived only two years. In 1928 Wirth — by virtue of his father's connections — moved to Washington to work for the National Capital Park and Planning Commission under Ulysses S. Grant III, where he caught the attention of Horace Albright. In 1931 NPS director Albright employed him as an assistant director in charge of the Branch of Land Planning. During the 1930s, Wirth served as Civilian Conservation Corps administrator, hiring many men for low-paying jobs, then promoting them until by the 1950s he had established a loyal base of support within the NPS and was the logical choice to head the agency in 1951.[8]

During the first three years of his tenure, Wirth reorganized the NPS, which centralized authority and improved his working relationship with concessioners, including those at Yellowstone. He partially streamlined the agency by moving regional concessions supervisors out of NPS regional offices (the regional chief for Yellowstone, Ben Dickson, had offices in Omaha) and concentrating them in Washington. He then appointed an on-site chief of concessions management for Yellowstone, who reported directly to the Washington office. Through this formula Wirth eliminated a level of bureaucracy. In August he visited Yellowstone and spent considerable time with Nichols and the other operators, to whom he became affectionately known as "Connie." While in the park, Wirth outlined a joint five-year construction program that the NPS and the concessioners would undertake together. He wanted the Lake area expanded first; Canyon area facilities moved to a new location called Canyon Village; and a new area developed at the West Thumb of Lake Yellowstone. By the time Wirth departed, he and Nichols appeared to have agreed on a five-year development plan designed once again to reshape the park, the product, to fit what the partners believed was popular customer demand.[9]

Shortly thereafter, the tone of their relationship changed. In November 1953 Nichols received a request from Yellowstone superintendent Edmund Rogers, asking that he provide a comprehensive program detailing company construction plans for the next five years. Nichols immediately began working on such a plan, mindful of Wirth's desire to begin at Lake and then complete Canyon Village and the West Thumb development. In November 1953 he traveled to Washington, D.C., to clarify the proposal further, discussing the layouts for each new area (Wirth, a landscape architect by training, always desired well-planned "villages" for Yellowstone guests). Less than a week after returning from his trip, however, Nichols received a somewhat baffling missive from the NPS director, who confirmed the general development program but now informed him that Canyon Village, not the Lake area, was the top priority. Nichols was dismayed; the Lake development he could finance out of earnings and retained capital, but if Wirth insisted on completing Canyon Village first, millions of dollars in outside financing would have to be raised. The confusion lingered for a full year, but from that day forward, Nichols distrusted Conrad Wirth.[10]

By 1954 the YP Company was approaching a crisis of unprecedented proportions. Nichols and his assistants, although well aware of the poor condition of park facilities, had spent little money on maintenance and repairs over the past decade. Nor had they added many new accommodations since World War II — only a smattering of cabins to house greater numbers of visitors. Most facilities dated from the 1930s or, in the case of the large hotels at Lake, Canyon, and Old Faithful, much earlier. One reason for this neglect was simply a loss of interest by management; Adelaide Child, the matriarch of the family, died in 1951, the last of the founding generation; Billie Nichols was himself approaching seventy-five years and, concerned about leaving his family financially sound, wanted desperately to reduce his dependence on as capricious an enterprise as Yellowstone concessions. In addition, his apparent heirs, John Nichols and Huntley Child Jr., lacked what he believed was the necessary experience to sustain long-term profitability. Nichols had concerned himself with these matters for years; he had investigated a public stock offering to reduce the family's holdings shortly before Harry Child died in 1931 but discovered little interest due to the inherently unstable nature of the business. In 1952, he and the other stockholders — still overwhelmingly family members — quietly offered the YP Company for sale through a New York investment banker, but for two years no prospective buyer emerged. In 1953 he spent less on improvements than the net profit for the year. In 1954 Nichols authorized thirty new housekeeping cabins for the Lake Lodge area, but even this project depended on the NPS completing the necessary road, water, sewer, and other utility infrastructure, all of which was the government's responsibility. In 1954 a decision was at hand: the YP Company contract, signed in 1936 for twenty years, would expire shortly. Wirth was pressing for construction commitments that could be met only by acquiring massive amounts of outside money. Nichols faced only two choices: find a buyer — a difficult task, with Congress threatening regularly to weaken franchises and the public outcry over poor facilities — or commit vast amounts of capital to upgrade and expand his operations.[11]

While pondering his decision, Nichols attempted to stem the tide of negative publicity. He ordered Huntley Child Jr. to draft a statement, for distribution to company employees throughout the park, which presented the company's observations on poor conditions. The completed "prospectus," as he called it, lacked any sense of apology; instead, it shifted the blame for run-down facilities and complications of doing business in such a remote locale with a limited season to the NPS. "Building in Yellowstone is far different from building in or near a city," he insisted. Before he could accommodate greater numbers of tourists, the NPS must "build roads, install water and sewer systems and prepare the ground for building. This requires appropriations from Congress . . . [that] have been hard to obtain since World War II." He noted that in addition to erecting visitor facilities, the company had to construct dormitories and employee dining halls. "All of this," he pointed out, "adds considerably to the expense of the development." Nichols also informed his employees of the financial difficulties involved in upgrading his operation, listing as obstacles "the hazardous nature of the investment, a limited franchise, buildings on ground to which title is in the government and not the operator, the possibilities of decreased travel, and a comparatively short season." Furthermore, "we find it impossible to secure long term loans from banks, trusts and insurance companies, or private capital. Hence, annual reinvestments in betterments must come out of annual earnings, which in the very nature of resort operations are problematical." Despite these difficulties, Nichols stated that the YP Company intended to "replace or rehabilitate every lodge and tourist cabin now operated," and to build additional accommodations as needed.[12]

In 1955 an unusual opportunity for Nichols to sell his company presented itself. The torrent of negative publicity about park conditions, and the failure of Congress to address the problem, led Wyoming governor Milward Simpson to announce brashly his intention of correcting the situation himself. Shortly after being elected in the fall of 1954, he prodded the Wyoming state legislature into passing a resolution stating that Yellowstone facilities were "so inadequate, old, and worn out" that their condition verged "on a national scandal." In February 1955 he obtained authority from lawmakers to appoint a state commission that would investigate the feasibility of Wyoming taking over park concessions. As chairman of this body, Simpson appointed Glenn E. Neilson, president of Husky Oil Company, who had long coveted the exclusive right to supply park service stations held by Conoco since 1917. As advisers the commission hired a Chicago appraisal firm, Duff, Anderson, and Clark, which later estimated that company assets totaled $4.9 million and annual net profits were $300,000 — both of which were, in reality, substantially higher. In the spring of 1955, commissioners met with Interior Secretary Douglas McKay, who had replaced Chapman two years earlier, and NPS director Conrad Wirth, neither of whom voiced any objections to a state takeover. Throughout the summer, Interior Department officials, state commissioners, and NPS administrators met regularly, and delegations of U.S. congressmen toured the park to investigate public complaints and apprise themselves of the Simpson plan.[13]

Nichols had no objection to selling his company to Wyoming. Others, however, protested furiously. National parks like Yellowstone were among the most valuable commodities in the nation, and those who controlled visitor services virtually owned them. Montana governor Hugo Aronson vowed to block the proposal, as did the Idaho legislature, convinced that Simpson wanted simply to use concession profits — especially the lucrative gasoline franchise — to supplement his state's treasury. The U.S. Chamber of Commerce also opposed the plan, calling it "socialistic," and many U.S. congressmen, including Keith

Thomson of Wyoming, expressed concern about the precedent such a sale would set. Several Wyoming businessmen also questioned the Simpson scheme, noting that the concessioners to be bought out had paid over $950,000 in Wyoming taxes during the previous four years — over $1 million if Hamilton Stores was included in the acquisition, which Simpson had not made clear — money the state earned without the headaches of operating the businesses.[14]

Simpson had one reply to his critics: "Come up with a better answer." Wirth already had. He called it Mission 66, a comprehensive program to improve visitor services in national parks and publicize NPS efforts to alleviate miserable tourist experiences. Wirth conceived the plan in 1955 as the first long-term project in agency history and scheduled it for completion in 1966, the fiftieth anniversary of the NPS. It entailed massive development of concessions facilities such as cabins, restaurants, lodges, and trailer courts in nearly every national park, in addition to extensive government improvements. In February 1955 Wirth appointed a committee staffed by NPS department heads to flesh out his idea. Over the next twelve months, committee members requested and received "wish lists" from every national park; Mission 66 would include improvements for all. By February 1956 Wirth possessed a thorough, well-researched plan that virtually the entire agency had participated in drafting.[15]

Mission 66 was without question the largest, best-organized, and most slickly packaged initiative ever undertaken by the NPS, as well as the most ambitious attempt to redesign national parks. It was also the most comprehensive such proposal, providing for new buildings in almost every unit of the national park system. The plan called for a ten-year appropriation in excess of $785 million, with more than $48 million of that total to be spent in 1956 alone. On January 27, 1956, Wirth presented the program to President Dwight D. Eisenhower during a cabinet meeting and received unconditional support. Two weeks later he launched his project amid much fanfare at a dinner in Washington, D.C., hosted jointly by the NPS and the American Automobile Association, a powerful interest group that had long badgered the agency to improve tourist accommodations. Soon thereafter, a barrage of articles in the popular press hailed Mission 66 as the salvation of the national parks. Wirth wrote some of these pieces himself and circulated memorandums encouraging NPS personnel at all levels to do the same. The package was most impressive from an administrative standpoint; Wirth involved practically all agency employees in the planning process, raising NPS morale appreciably during those first, heady months. He rallied his troops as never before by appealing to tradition, to the memory of Stephen Mather, to NPS mystique. Their enthusiasm carried over to the general public; Mission 66 appeared to be an overwhelming success almost before it began. Even politicians became caught up in the excitement; before seeing the details, President Eisenhower had requested that Congress appropriate sufficient funds to complete the ambitious program. Led by Wyoming senators Joseph O'Mahoney and Frank Barrett, the legislature quickly approved the necessary money.[16]

While diagramming his overall strategy, Wirth, with cooperation and input from park officials, developed a Mission 66 plan for Yellowstone. In the spring of 1955, he appointed a park working committee to recommend necessary improvements. The resulting document institutionalized the previously unofficial practice of regimenting and systematizing tourism begun by Harry Child. Many of the points were reminiscent of language in the 1883 YNPIC leases, which opponents referred to as "the park steal." Committee members included the superintendent, Edmund Rogers, chief ranger Otto Brown, park naturalist David Condon, landscape architect Frank Mattson, and Ben Dickson, NPS head of Yellowstone concessions management. They suggested that "the terrain and size of the park alone will permit, under control, the providing of accommodations within the park without detriment to the thermal and natural resources (features) for which the park was established." They insisted that the "area of the park and type of terrain" would allow almost unlimited development but, adopting Child's plan of systematized tours, urged that "the location and development should be controlled to definite sites and capacities to retain a pattern of day-use and traffic flow." In a twisted logic only NPS staffers seemed to understand, they further emphasized that "full development of existing sites is a definite aid in protecting the surrounding areas," meaning that by concentrating visitors in congested campgrounds, cabin developments, and lodges, the majority of the park would remain untouched. In this way, the NPS could fulfill its obligations, set forth in 1916, to "preserve and promote" the park. Child had tried to accomplish the same thing; his motive was profit; theirs remained unconvincing. The very parts that the committee intended to preseve — the so-called untouched parts — were those most visitors were increasingly interested in. Yet the development plans called for guests to be discouraged from visiting such places, to be funneled instead into developed areas. Such plans only exacerbated the eventual problem, as more and more people came to believe that nature existed only in places unaltered by human activity. This conceptual division between natural and unnatural later proved immensely problematic for those trying to package Yellowstone to fit popular perceptions.[17]

The committee members further advised that, in order to protect the park from tourists — to preserve nature — the NPS and concessioners should transform parts of Yellowstone into virtual metropolises. Not surprisingly, their recommendations included much of what Wirth had been urging Nichols to undertake for two years. They suggested the development of new "use areas" in addition to the expansion of those at Lake, Fishing Bridge, and Roosevelt Junction, near Tower Falls, which they called, aptly enough, "villages." The committee members advocated locating the new sites at Canyon (Canyon Village, which had been planned since before World War II) and the West Thumb area (to be called Grant Village). They also recommended that facilities at Old Faithful — including the splendid Old Faithful Inn — be moved to a new location in the Midway Geyser Basin, where greater expansion room existed. The new settlement would be called Firehole Village. Members also proposed a smaller development, including a marina for private power boats, at Bridge Bay on the northwest shore of Lake Yellowstone. At each site, concessioners would be required to supply adequate (as decided by the NPS) services. In addition, members advised that smaller settlements, consisting mainly of government-run campgrounds, museums, visitor centers, and other such miscellany, be located at strategic sites around the park. They also recommended that as the NPS prepared to construct each new development, it should open concession contracts to competitive bidding and extend preferential rights only to the limits of a specified location — a proposal similar to the Krug plan of 1949 and the Cordon amendment of 1953, both of which the concessioners had refused to accept. Through such a program, the NPS desired to increase overnight accommodations in the park from the present 8,500 to over 14,500, but first Nichols would have to agree to a massive construction program — unlikely if the competition clause remained intact.[18]

Before any such agreement could be finalized, Nichols still had to reach a decision about his company's future course. The YP Company franchise expired on December 31, 1955, and Nichols had not convinced himself of the wisdom of remaining involved in Yellowstone concessions. His concerns multiplied as he learned of the immense commitment that his company would be forced to make under Mission 66. Furthermore, he did not trust Wirth, who, he had learned from an informant in the park superintendent's office, had hired a spy to provide information about YP Company facilities and operations. In March 1955 Wirth goaded him toward a decision, informing him that the NPS was prepared to begin appraisal proceedings to determine the value of possessory interest, implying that the NPS might offer Wyoming a discount on purchasing his company. During the spring of 1955, therefore, Nichols sought the advice of his most trusted adviser, accountant and company auditor Hugh Galusha.[19]

Writing from his home in La Jolla, California, Nichols outlined for his friend and financial adviser those aspects of Wirth's Mission 66 proposal that troubled him. He recalled the confusion over the relative priority of the Lake and Canyon Village developments and reiterated his belief that, if Wirth remained adamant on constructing Canyon Village first, the YP Company would have to acquire outside financing. Nichols estimated that he would have to invest over $1 million, at Canyon, which would pose two serious difficulties. First, interest on outside money would outstrip any profit from the development — the Canyon area was losing popularity as an overnight location. Most tourists, being more mobile, spent less time in the park than in previous years, and developed areas like Canyon were becoming less attractive than places perceived as "natural." Visitors were as interested in avoiding congestion as they were in seeing features like the canyon. Second, the possibility of borrowing such an amount remained remote because, as Nichols noted, "there is no equity for a bank to foreclose on in case of bankruptcy." He also questioned the wisdom of NPS officials in selecting a site without "any background and no view of any kind," believing the location offered "no inducement for people to stay there, except to be there overnight in lieu of being some other place." Nichols asked Galusha directly if, based on the language in the current contract, the company could expect compensation for its investment if it abandoned the park now, although he desired no such withdrawal: "I would much prefer to have Wirth change his mind about spending all the money at the Canyon Village first instead of at Lake Lodge."[20]

The elderly Galusha responded with some fatherly advice that left no doubt about his position. Stating that he was "dismayed" by Nichols's thoughts of quitting Yellowstone, he insisted that the Canyon Village versus Lake debate was trivial. "I can't see where it makes any difference which one is completed first," he professed. Nichols should stand firm with the NPS, he advised, first negotiating a new contract, then ensuring that the NPS complete all its utility and site preparation work prior to any construction. Galusha mistakenly believed that the NPS could not possibly acquire adequate appropriations for at least two years. He then addressed the finance question, showing Nichols how, with such a two-year cushion, the company could fund Canyon Village and the rest of the new construction out of earnings. In closing, Galusha pointedly recalled how the company founder would have handled such a situation. "I can remember Mr. Child's advice on many occasions," he reminisced, "that the best thing to do was to go to bat with the powers that be, sit on their lap and cry on their shoulder. I once waited in the anteroom of the White House while he fixed up his end of it with the President. He was a firm believer in starting just as high in the echelon as he could."[21]

While pondering Galusha's advice, Nichols received another bit of counsel in the mail. Instead of invoking fond memories, however, the author of this dispatch, Hugh D. Galusha Jr., encouraged Nichols to modernize not only the company's physical assets but also its corporate philosophy. Galusha Jr. had just returned from a six-week journey around the country, acquainting himself with the latest business trends and meeting financial and corporate leaders across the nation. The information that he gathered, which he summarized in his letter to Nichols, led to perhaps the most significant decision in YP Company history. Galusha Jr. began by stressing the positive aspects of the company position: it held a monopoly in a market of historically demonstrated value; almost complete freedom from unions (as well as exceptions from government wage scales); a twenty-year franchise with a practical assurance of reasonable compensation in the event of loss; and a record of successful operation and experience. The problem, as he perceived it, was simply how to capitalize on those positive points. He advised Nichols to "throw the book away" and approach the business in fresh terms, specifically recommending that the company agree to NPS demands for a marina at Bridge Bay (noting the "phenomenal expansion of the boat business" around the country) and a trailer park at Fishing Bridge ("parks charge from $30.00 to $40.00 per month for a location"). He also suggested that Nichols abandon the longtime practice of building on-site, using regional architects and contractors, in favor of world-class talent and new, modern, prefabricated structures (such as those being used in the vast subdivisions springing up around the United States). Apparently, he believed that the product — Yellowstone — was so valuable that the packaging, formerly carefully designed to invoke certain beliefs about the park, was irrelevant. Galusha Jr. encouraged adopting equally inventive means of financing the plan, asserting that "in the field of finance, there are almost as many new techniques as there are in building." Banks no longer required mortgage security on large industrial loans, he assured Nichols; therefore, a favorable loan package "could be obtained for the Yellowstone Park Company." Finally, he addressed in a positive fashion the obvious desire of the NPS to include a construction commitment in any new contract negotiations: "If you approach these negotiations with a program of expansion in mind, you are going to catch the National Park Service off base. With such a program you might obtain provisions without previous precedent to provide favorable franchise tax treatment."[22]

Nichols accepted this advice almost immediately. On August 18, 1955, he authorized Galusha Jr. to negotiate in principle a loan of $2 million through the Security-First National Bank of Los Angeles. The next week he entered negotiations with the Los Angeles architectural firm of Welton Beckett and Associates and with McNeil Construction Company, also of California. By the end of August, he surprised Wirth with a monumental proposal for future development. He informed the NPS director that he was "anxious to proceed" with the installation of 250 cabins and a 250-room motel (the NPS preferred the term lodge, because it fit more comfortably into the rustic Yellowstone atmosphere) at Canyon Village and further committed the YP Company to construct a cafeteria, a lounge, public laundry and recreation facilities, dormitories, and a boiler plant. He promised a 150-room motel (lodge) at Lake; at the proposed West Thumb development, he promised another 250 cabins and a 250-room motel along with service facilities similar to those at Canyon Village. As his counselors had advised, Nichols made every point contingent upon the NPS completing its infrastructure work and the awarding of a new twenty-year contract by December 31, 1955.[23]

During the next three months, contract negotiations proceeded smoothly, and the abrupt reversal of policy had its intended effect. On September 1, 1955, Nichols and his management team met with Wirth at Mammoth Hot Springs and immediately received a substantial reduction in franchise taxes from the baffled NPS director. They also secured assurances that the proposal by Wyoming governor Milward Simpson would be rejected, since the NPS and the YP Company had worked out a mutually satisfactory arrangement. The two sides reached tentative agreements on Canyon Village, Bridge Bay, and the West Thumb development, christened Grant Village in honor of President Ulysses S. Grant, who had signed the legislation establishing Yellowstone in 1872. In October, after the YP Company officially committed to allocate $3.5 million for improvements by April 1, 1956, both parties signed a twenty-year franchise agreement. As required by the revised Cordon amendment of 1953, the NPS submitted the document to Congress for review — a step that all of those involved believed was only a formality.[24]

They were wrong. On December 16, 1956, Nichols learned that he faced a concerted effort by Wyoming legislators to increase the YP Company financial commitment. Governor Simpson, frustrated by being rebuffed in his attempt to buy the concessions, was obviously behind the move. Representative Keith Thomson, previously critical of the Simpson plan, now protested the YP Company contract renewal and forced the House Committee on Interior and Insular Affairs to schedule hearings on the matter for January 1956. At midnight, December 31, 1955, the YP Company contract of 1936 expired, and the future of the new agreement was still in doubt. Nichols and his advisers — attorney Taylor Weir and Galusha Jr. — traveled to Washington for the house committee hearing, at which Congressman Thomson voiced his objections. The hearing lasted only briefly before committee members approved the YP Company contract. The debate then moved to the Senate, where Frank Barrett and John C. O'Mahoney of Wyoming, previously friendly to the company, proposed an amendment that required it to commit an additional $10 million over the first ten years of the agreement. After several meetings, Weir and the legislators reached a compromise — both claimed victory, although no concrete assurances of additional spending were added to the contract.[25]

By March 1956 all obstacles to the launching of Mission 66 in Yellowstone had been removed. The NPS working committee in the park had submitted its recommendations to the national Mission 66 panel in Washington, D.C., and a tentative program of improvements emerged over the next few months. Nichols had decided to remain in business and had agreed to participate in the program, as had the other concessioners, Hamilton and Haynes. President Eisenhower had endorsed the project, and Congress had appropriated the money. On March 30 Nichols signed a loan agreement with Security-First National Bank of Los Angeles, establishing a $3 million unsecured revolving line of credit. His family, in the form of the H. W. Child Corporation, guaranteed the note. Detailed plans for each individual developed area remained flexible — negotiations regarding exact numbers of cabins, campsites, and other facilities continued throughout the next several years — but the basic framework for massive change was in place. The YP Company thus commenced yet another era of transforming the landscape of Yellowstone National Park.[26]

6

Mission 66

Mission 66 fit the mood of Americans in the 1950s. Many were almost compulsively acquisitive, expressing national pride through the accumulation of material possessions. As consumerism drove a booming economy, a burgeoning population expected its every desire to be met. Instead of the pre–World War II workweek of seven days, most Americans now spent only five days working and had weekends off. Over fifty million workers enjoyed paid vacations as well. Automobiles became sleeker and housing more affordable; washing machines, refrigerators, and vacuum cleaners were no longer luxuries but necessities. Television sets multiplied in subdivisions populated by young families determined to enjoy their newfound affluence. Motorboats or campers — tents no longer sufficed — parked beside garages signified status. This tendency toward gratification, toward fulfillment through materialism, extended to public as well as private possessions. The National Park Service, as keeper of the most visible symbols of American public property, was expected to accumulate as well, to amass enough material possessions to serve the desires of the traveling public. Director Wirth conceived Mission 66 in direct response to what he perceived as an overwhelming popular mandate for development, understanding all the while that a vocal minority with different ideas about how nature should be preserved and protected was gaining adherents and had the potential to alter collective beliefs about the parks.

Potential conflict notwithstanding, Wirth promoted Mission 66 as the solution to all national park problems. For those who desired increased access to scenery, Mission 66 provided almost 1,200 miles of new roads, mostly in areas previously inaccessible by automobile, as well as 30 miles of airport runways. Included in the road mileage was the Blue Ridge Parkway, a favorite project of Wirth's close friend Senator Harry F. Byrd of Virginia. An additional 1,502 parking lots were constructed, with a total capacity of nearly 156,000 vehicles, and 577 miles of new trails penetrated the back-country of the parks. Interpretive exhibits along roads and trails were expanded by 1,116, and 114 visitor centers, some housing souvenir shops, food service facilities, and auditoriums, were built. For campers, the NPS cleared 575 new campgrounds and expanded others for a total of 29,782 sites. At developed areas, outdoor amphitheaters with audiovisual equipment provided seating for more than 41,000 guests. The NPS also built fifty marinas, boat ramps, and docks for recreational use and added over 740 new picnic areas. Much of the construction was in response to complaints about the need for more and better accommodations, a problem that the NPS and concessioners together tried to solve. The park service added 535 fresh-water systems, 521 sewer systems, and 271 electric power generation or delivery systems for concessioner use. For their part, park concessioners spent over $33 million on facilities ranging from new cabins at Grand Teton, Grand Canyon, Shenandoah, Everglades, Yellowstone, and Lassen to elaborate "villages" in some of the larger parks.[1]

Although Mission 66 was a nationwide undertaking, Yellowstone served as the showpiece of the program. As a consequence, the NPS spent a tremendous amount of time planning new facilities for the nation's most famous and visible national park. Wirth's Mission 66 council in Washington, D.C., along with the NPS committee at Yellowstone, debated various proposals throughout 1955, while Yellowstone Park Company officials were negotiating a new contract. Any scheme to accommodate greater numbers of visitors would necessarily include improvements to both government and concessions facilities. In April the park committee submitted its recommendations, proposing a significant amount of expansion and new development. But the members of the national committee were not convinced that more was necessarily better. Upon receiving the proposal from Yellowstone, they raised such basic questions as whether visitor accommodations should be located within the park at all; they noted that "the service cannot control hotels in parks because they are concession owned and operated. Best to have hotels outside parks wherever possible." If the concessions had to remain within park boundaries, should such facilities be limited to one large developed area or several, as the Yellowstone committee proposed? The Washington, D.C., council members even challenged NPS tradition by suggesting that park headquarters and concessions facilities be moved from within the boundaries of the reservation (Mammoth Hot Springs had served in this capacity since the army days) to Gardiner, only five miles north but across park lines.[2]

Despite such questions, the responses were inevitable. Wirth would not allow any drastic departures from the long-standing NPS policy of development, promotion, and partnership, especially while negotiating with the chief park concessioner to build more and bigger facilities. Public opinion, as reflected in the national press, clearly favored such growth. NPS surveys and investigations indicated similar approval for the idea of facilities expansion. One "average interested and intelligent park visitor," a "young stenographer who liked to travel during vacations," was interviewed by the Mission 66 committee, and she wanted

> to go to the large parks; have private bath facilities in room or cabin; have clean linen; take a conducted tour; drive to parks in car; would not object to a reasonable fee for services within a park; would pay a guide fee; would want to see everything worth seeing; would visit museums to get history of park; would attend lectures at night on park subject, but one or two would be enough; would not expect man-made recreational facilities in the parks; would not expect to pay more than $3 a night in a 2-bed cabin or motel-type quarters; would bring walking shoes and hike; would want signes [*sic*] and markers telling where things of interest are located and what they are; would buy souvenirs; would buy lots of picture post cards; would want to sit at a table for meals; would not look for fancy accommodations, and would not want to dress for dinner; would want good, tasty, hot, inexpensive food; would prefer to stay overnight inside park — thought that would have a real although intangible value — would even pay more to stay inside the park; would be disappointed if there was not the opportunity to stay inside the park; would want to get to high places and look at the scenery, would not expect to find cocktail bars; would not expect or like to find a resort-type development in the parks; prefer motel-type accommodations because of convenience and luggage; would stop at park orientation center; would not want too much information thrust upon her — just a little, with the chance to ask for more if she wanted

it; would not object to staying overnight in park some distance from one of its principal features; above all, would want cleanliness and simple comforts in overnight accommodations and public rest room facilities.[3]

NPS tradition demanded that the agency and its concessioner partners provide adequate facilities to meet all these desires.

Eventually, the NPS staff in Washington approved the Yellowstone committee proposals wholesale. In April 1956, a year after planning had begun and shortly after agreeing with YP Company officials on a new twenty-year contract that included provisions for added construction, agency planners drafted a broad agenda of development for both the government and the concessioners. The program that emerged from the Washington, D.C., planning office included general recommendations for building new "use areas," consisting of government and concessioner services, at Canyon Village, Grant Village, and Bridge Bay; moving all facilities from Old Faithful to a larger area away from the geyser basin; expanding the small settlement at Fishing Bridge to include a trailer court; and increasing the capacity of existing services at the Lake Hotel and Lodge developments. In addition, the NPS proposed to double its existing campground capacity to fifteen hundred sites and to build over fifty day-use picnic areas near roads and "visitor concentration points." To further systematize tourism, roadside exhibits and parking areas would highlight nearby attractions for those guests unwilling to leave their vehicles. According to the Washington committee, "the majority of people will not camp or stay overnight at places in the parks where there is not a special attraction. The majority of people will go to slum campgrounds rather than to new, wholesome ones in good wilderness environment, if man-made attractions and entertainment are at or near the former." In addition, the committee cited research that indicated "women want good trails, trails that they can walk on in high heels. Many are not prepared to change into walking shoes for short walks to points of interest. Trails to points of interest should be hard surfaced for all-weather use and smooth enough for all kinds of shoes." The agency also planned museums and interpretive centers at Norris Junction and Madison Junction, areas with campgrounds but lacking concessions services.[4]

With these general suggestions in place, NPS officials immediately requested that Nichols supply them with a proposal for YP Company expansion. He had already done so once (in October 1955) during contract negotiations; now he simply restated his objectives broadly. He had already discussed most of the main points with Wirth before signing the new franchise agreement. Specifically, Nichols committed the YP Company to building facilities at Canyon Village and expanding services at Lake during 1956 and 1957. Then he hoped to add services at Fishing Bridge, Old Faithful, and Roosevelt Junction. Nichols also pledged to build a new cafeteria at Fishing Bridge and to overhaul his antiquated transportation fleet during 1958 and 1959. Later, over a three-year period beginning in 1960, he planned to add large-scale accommodations and services at Grant Village and Bridge Bay. Again, as Nichols had insisted before signing the new contract, his main goal was to construct facilities that would produce immediate income, allowing him to finance further development. Each phase of his program, however, depended on the government completing its part — roads, utilities, and other necessities — before he started.[5]

Even as the planning process continued through the spring of 1956, Mission 66 projects were well under way in Yellowstone. Yellowstone Park Company construction crews commenced refurbishing the Old Faithful Lodge, adding tile floors in the lobby and redecorating many cabins. Outside contractors began renovating the fifty-year-old Old Faithful Inn, installing steel beams in place of the original logs on the porte cochere and erecting an adjacent dormitory and office building. Other crews began removing cabins from the Canyon Lodge settlement, which was to be abandoned, and transferring them to Lake. At the same time, NPS contractors started installing 140 new picnic tables and fire pits at the Fishing Bridge campground, constructed boardwalks in all the main geyser basins, and resurfaced several miles of the main loop road and others near Lake. They also began building three amphitheaters — at Mammoth, Lake, and West Thumb — which the NPS euphemistically called "campfire circles," although twenty-foot-tall movie screens and rows of bench seats set into concrete created an atmosphere very different from that of the old Yellowstone camps.[6]

The focus of government work, however, was at the site of Canyon Village, which represented a new concept in national park development and was the cornerstone of Mission 66 nationwide. Superficially resembling the lodge-centered settlements that Child had utilized during the 1930s to concentrate paying guests in manageable locations, as designed it dwarfed any previous park community. The main portion of the proposed settlement surrounded a U-shaped parking lot and contained some familiar components. On the left side of the U would be a souvenir shop, general store, and ice cream counter to be built by Hamilton; a Haynes Picture Shop was to occupy an adjacent lot. Across the parking area, a lodge building 320 feet long would house a lounge, gift shop, and lunch counter with room for 65 diners. A cafeteria seating 250 and a coffee shop holding an additional 250 would occupy another end of the building. The lodge was also to contain a recreation hall encompassing 16,500 square feet, to be used for a variety of purposes and able to accommodate one thousand temporary seats. Behind the lodge, three roads led to 500 motel-type cabins — row upon row of connected units, not individual freestanding shelters — and three dormitories for concessions employees. At the base of the U-shaped parking lot, a 110,000-square-foot NPS visitor center — a composite headquarters and administration building that would also contain a museum, information desk, and auditorium — was designed to dominate the area. A miniature park relief map highlighted the information and orientation room and became an attraction as popular as any natural phenomenon. Nearby, the agency planned to revolutionize the concept of a campfire circle by constructing a thousand-seat amphitheater, complete with drive-in-movie-sized screen, where rangers could offer evening interpretive programs. Across the four-lane highway above the U-shaped lot was to be a service station, a NPS campground, as well as a government maintenance, utility, and housing area. South of the main settlement would be another maintenance garage, riding stables, and a sewage disposal plant. If built as planned and filled with visitors and employees, Canyon Village would be a small city of nearly five thousand people.[7]

Canyon Village was the single most important project of the entire ten-year scheme to rebuild and expand national park facilities; Wirth therefore promoted it heavily as the ideal solution to several perceived problems. It would replace existing developments that encroached upon the canyon, thus becoming a means of protecting fragile resources. It would provide accommodations for thousands of tourists, thereby relieving congestion, and would offer a wide range of clean lodgings and quality food services, both of which were currently in short supply. The NPS visitor center would enable staff members to, in NPS language, "interpret" for visitors exactly what they were experiencing. Interpretation — shaping public opinion through stories — was a vital part of the Mission 66 overall strategy to increase public support, and thus appropriations. Since Canyon Village was the first of the new, large "use areas," designed to the smallest detail, the NPS publicized it as an ideal model. Wirth wagered that such developments would solve the problem that every NPS director had faced since 1916— how to adhere to the "promote and preserve" clause in the enabling legislation — by dividing the parks into areas deserving of protection as "natural" and other zones of promotion and commerce. He also gambled that a success with Canyon Village would open the congressional coffers and allow him to proceed with the entire Mission 66 program nationwide.[8]

Nichols viewed the project less optimistically. Canyon Village represented the greatest risk ever taken by his company. Debt service on the loan could easily outstrip profits, even with the anticipated high rental prices for new accommodations. Nichols also questioned NPS assumptions equating increased park travel with a need for more lodgings; between 1954 and 1955, for example, tourism increased by approximately forty thousand people, but house counts at hotels, lodges, and cabins dropped by thirty thousand. Clearly, the nature of park tourism was again changing, this time toward camping or day use, making a heavy investment in Canyon Village extremely precarious. In addition to the possible financial jeopardy, the company rep-utation was on the line; the years between 1946 and 1955 had tarnished its prestigious character, and Nichols badly needed to repair the damage if he were to attract more capital — or even a potential buyer for the business. If the public lauded Canyon Village as a success, and utilized its expanded ser-vices, the YP Company would reap benefits both concrete and intangible; if tourists shunned the new facilities as too expensive, unattractive, or incon-venient, the company could face ruin.[9]

During the summer of 1956, Canyon Village dominated all other con-cerns. Wirth wanted it to be open for the 1957 season; consequently, the NPS and the YP Company both spent much of their available time and money to complete their respective portions. The architectural firm of Welton Beck-ett and Associates of Los Angeles designed a prefabricated, plywood, motel-type housing unit consisting of six to eight attached cabins. In May, McNeil Construction, also of Los Angeles, the company chosen to build concession facilities for the new area, set up a shop in Gardiner and began producing the first of five hundred structures. Other McNeil workers roughed in the three YP Company dormitories and the main lodge building, hoping to enclose them enough for interior finish work over the winter, and began installing the complex system of steam heat and hot-water piping. Meanwhile, the NPS, which had budgeted $1.5 million for utilities, $890,000 for roads, trails, parking lots, and paved walkways, and $1.2 million for general site preparation, engaged local contractors for its work. The agency hired a Casper, Wyoming, company to provide sewer and water systems, a Gardiner electrical contractor to design and build a power grid, and two Billings, Montana, firms to construct reservoirs, roads, and a trailer court for government employees. While the work commenced, Wirth informed Nichols that he would officially inaugurate Mission 66 at a Canyon Village groundbreaking ceremony on June 25, 1956.[10]

The NPS choreographed the event for maximum positive media exposure, with the notables atop the speaker's platform reflecting the traditional hierarchy of national parks management. Wesley A. D'Ewart, former U.S. representative from Montana and currently assistant secretary of the interior for national parks, a longtime political ally of the concessioners, represented the Interior Department. Wirth attended as the NPS delegate; Billie Nichols and his two top executives, John Q. Nichols and Huntley Child Jr., provided the YP Company with a significant presence; Charles Hamilton and Jack Haynes spoke enthusiastically about Mission 66 and the cooperative nature of the program. Park superintendent Edmund Rogers served appropriately as master of ceremonies, a role he had been playing for twenty years while concessioners and NPS officials in Washington dictated park policy. A month before, Wirth directed that publicity "should be slanted away from 'modernization' or such expressions as 'replacement of obsolete facilities.'" Speakers thus accentuated the nebulous conservation aspects of the development, stressing the removal of old facilities along the canyon rim; both were stated aims of Mission 66 but perhaps reminded visitors of the sad state of current operations. All of them urged attendees — and the press — to focus instead on the "positive approach to expansion problems" that the NPS and concessioners had chosen.[11]

The groundbreaking was the most formal event of a hectic 1956 park season. By the end of June, the NPS had spent over $1 million preparing the site and installing utilities at Canyon Village. The remodeling of Old Faithful Lodge and the Old Faithful Inn exacerbated the ongoing shortage of accommodations, as did the dismantling of Canyon Lodge. Portions of the

Canyon Hotel were shut down due to structural failure stemming from chronic instability along the foundation, adding to an already frenzied tourist scramble for suitable lodgings. The many contractors involved in work at Canyon Village and the other projects commuted from either Gardiner or West Yellowstone each day, contributing to a continuing traffic snarl caused by road improvement work and the constant moving of cabins between areas. Others commandeered space in the public automobile camps. Some, like the McNeil crews at Canyon, even bulldozed new camp space from pristine meadowlands when tourists filled all available space at existing facilities. Superintendent Rogers regularly complained to Nichols about the liberties that the McNeil workers had taken and futilely insisted that construction employees adhere to park regulations regarding sanitation, fire prevention, and equipment use. From early in the spring until after heavy snows limited much work, park officials, concessions managers, and construction company foremen argued almost weekly over some aspect of the ongoing projects, while together they turned Yellowstone into a vast construction site.[12]

Although the NPS heavily publicized its plans for improving visitor services, complaints continued with alarming frequency. Many criticized the condition of overnight accommodations, one tourist referring to the YP Company cabins at West Thumb (slated to be removed within five years when Grant Village was built) as "filthy shacks" that were a "disgrace to our national park system." Another protested the situation at Old Faithful, where "good accommodations were all closed or taken. . . . Old Faithful Hotel being closed, nothing left but cabins, equipped with running water, wood stove and slop jar." Some guests, including, oddly enough, a Canadian man, who insisted that his family's "whole holiday was ruined" by "false information and a miserable dirty shack," hoped to provoke changes by sending copies of their complaints to members of Congress. Other visitors, regardless of the national publicity surrounding Mission 66, still failed to understand that the federal government did not operate most services. One such misinformed guest insisted that "the trouble is that govt. is undertaking to operate these things itself, whereas it would be much better if contract was let to some operating company that would provide reasonable facilities. . . . private enterprise would get much better service." Visitors hounded company managers with complaints about "tasteless" food, "very indignant" staff, and a cafeteria with decor "like a penal institution," as well as almost every other aspect of concession operations. Even the still-incomplete Canyon Village drew the ire of one visitor, who wrote to protest "the 'chicken coop' style architecture" at the new site, which was "completely out of place" in a national park.[13]

By November, the tourists had departed — some happy with their visits, many displeased — and construction slowed due to harsh winter conditions. But in March 1957, crews returned for the season, again creating misery for vacationing tourists and headaches for park rangers. Because NPS director Wirth wanted Canyon Village open by July 1, the pace of work accelerated. McNeil Construction expanded its camp at Canyon — dubbed "McNeilville" by rangers — to house one hundred workers. Two other companies, Cop Construction and Studer Construction, moved into the area and built trailer courts and bunkhouses nearby for their workers. Cop crews started erecting the NPS visitor center, while Studer workers began grading the site for roads, parking lots, and drainage systems. Road work again created long delays for travelers, as hundreds of construction workers clogged travel routes with equipment and material. The YP Company became so involved in new construction that it delayed routine maintenance on cabins, cafeterias, and hotels, thereby inviting still more visitor complaints.[14]

Construction workers, unaccustomed to working in an environment as restrictive as Yellowstone, created daily problems for NPS rangers, especially those stationed at Canyon. In addition to committing frequent traffic violations, the workers regularly removed — or occasionally simply ran over — barricades across closed roads. Others drove through the park while drunk, a problem that reached epidemic proportions on Sundays, their day off. Frequent auto accidents involving workers occupied many hours of the rangers' time, as did searching for those who became lost after drinking and hiking. Some residents of "McNeilville," finding housekeeping cabins at Canyon more attractive than their spare bunkhouse quarters in the early spring chill, broke into several and destroyed beds, stoves, and sinks. After June 1957, when tourists again arrived for the season, complaints about the filthy condition of the construction camps — beer cans and other trash covering the ground at several — contributed to general visitor dissatisfaction. At times the construction workers posed direct dangers to travelers; in clear violation of park rules, they allowed their dogs to run loose in the camps, at least one of which displayed an appetite for tourist. Again, against all regulations, some workers carried firearms inside park boundaries, and one McNeil Construction laborer left a case of dynamite lying along a park trail.[15]

While Yellowstone received its Mission 66 facelift, the NPS was reorganizing as well. In June 1956 Wirth, not satisfied with the progress being made on his program, overhauled park administration. He replaced Edmund Rogers as Yellowstone superintendent with Lemuel A. "Lon" Garrison, former head of the Mission 66 planning committee in Washington, D.C. Nichols and the other concessioners received this news warily; they had become accustomed to Rogers, who stayed in the park only during the summer travel season and had proved to be particularly inept at restraining their collective enthusiasm for profits. They had little respect for his authority, regularly appealing his infrequent adverse operational decisions directly to Wirth. In addition, they had a close friend and informant within the park administration, Assistant to the Superintendent Joe Joffe, who often passed along confidential NPS memorandums regarding concessions policies; if Rogers left, Joffe might also.[16]

In November 1956 Garrison arrived in Yellowstone with a well-earned reputation for enforcing rules and accomplishing NPS goals. Shortly after assuming the superintendency, he walked from his house at Mammoth Hot Springs across the old army parade ground to the Mammoth Hotel for dinner. Once inside, he was presented with a "gold card" by the manager, who explained that the superintendent never paid for any concessioner services. Garrison inquired if this practice extended to all NPS staff at the park. Upon receiving the obvious answer, he replied that from now on it would not apply to anyone, including the superintendent. He demonstrated an intense interest in all aspects of YP Company operations, frequently inspecting laundries, kitchens, and warehouses. The results were sometimes absurd. During one of his kitchen examinations, he discovered that company beef was marked either "select" or "choice"; Garrison indignantly inquired how the company could list "prime rib" on its menus, since "it does seem that if you list 'Prime' beef you should serve it."[17]

Inside YP Company offices the situation bordered on chaos. The 1956 travel season proved dismal; existing accommodations filled to capacity only three times, and Canyon Village would add a projected 1,550 "pillows," increasing the odds that rooms would remain empty. The company had quickly spent its $3 million loan from Security-First National Bank of Los Angeles and by August 1956 had negotiated an emergency increase in its credit line to $5 million. To supplement that loan, the company desperately borrowed $150,000 from the H. W. Child Corporation and an additional $53,000 from the H. W. Child Trust — essentially, from the family. Soon thereafter, company management became more complex. At a stockholder's meeting on September 14, 1956, Billie Nichols resigned as president and became chairman of the board, a new position he created to distance himself from day-to-day operations. His son John Q. Nichols assumed the presidency, and Huntley Child Jr. remained as vice president. At the same time, the company expanded its board of directors for the first time to include non–family members. Hugh D. Galusha Jr., who had convinced Nichols to borrow money and build Canyon Village, and Alfred T. Hibbard, a Helena banker, became the first outside directors, both elected largely to stabilize the company's increasingly tenuous financial condition.[18]

Most of the financial troubles could be attributed to longtime company practices and shortsightedness by Billie Nichols. During the 1920s, Harry Child and his accountant Hugh Galusha Sr. had established a tradition, using accounting sleight of hand, of reducing net earnings and extracting maximum annual profits from the four separate Yellowstone Park Companies. When Nichols took over in 1931, he continued the practice, milking the companies for cash and reinvesting only minimal amounts. By the 1950s, years after the businesses had been merged into the YP Company, this constant draining of company funds caught up with him; in 1952, as usual, the YP Company paid its stockholders — nearly all of whom were family members — $200,000 in dividends out of net profits of $280,000. In 1953 Nichols declared another $200,000 in dividends from $275,000 in earnings, and shareholders continued to receive the same amount through 1956. By then the remaining annual profits fell short of funding needed improvements, so company managers had to subtract the balance of operating capital from equity — essentially lessening the net worth of the company. By the spring of 1957, with reserves all but depleted, the company was basically broke, and interest payments on the $5 million note further exhausted available funds. To exacerbate the situation, payments on the loan principal — $500,000 per year beginning in 1958 — promised to prevent any possible recovery. An accounting structure designed for maximum short-term profits combined with heavy interest payments were bleeding the YP Company dry, creating a difficult situation for new president John Q. Nichols.[19]

Only a dramatic upswing could salvage the business. By August 1957, company fortunes seemed to be improving, but further difficulties soon materialized. Park travel was at a record level, house counts were up, and YP Company profits followed suit. After nearly two tumultuous seasons of Mission 66 construction, NPS director Wirth scheduled a dedication ceremony at Canyon Village for July 1, 1957. But construction schedules had fallen far behind as winter temperatures of minus thirty-five degrees, heavy snows, and spring mud wreaked havoc on the inexperienced construction crews and indifferent supervisors. By the proposed opening date, only 117 of the projected 500 new cabins for Canyon Village were complete, and the lodge was still being furnished. Portions of the new development opened as scheduled, but Wirth, fuming, delayed the official ceremony until August 31. Then, on July 28, Billie Nichols suffered a heart attack at his Mammoth Hot Springs office; he died on August 6, leaving son John and nephew Huntley Child Jr. to manage the business.[20]

On August 31, 1957, Wirth returned to Yellowstone for the formal dedication ceremonies at Canyon Village. Unbeknownst to the many dignitaries gathered for the occasion, the new development would soon prove to be a financial and operational nightmare. McNeil construction crews did not complete the remaining cabins until October, after most tourists had departed. Those units that were serviceable rarely filled with guests even during the busiest months. The expensive steam-heating system never worked properly; in a single month, guests summoned maintenance crews 327 times with complaints about either too much or too little heat. Underground pipes were so poorly sealed that workers flushed rocks, rubbish, and welding beads out by the bucketful, and miniature "geysers" began appearing between cabins. Plumbers had also left gaps between fixtures and the floors, allowing ground squirrels unimpeded access to bathrooms, while frost heave occurring during the winter loosened waste pipes so that toilets flushed directly onto the ground. Equally disconcerting, the bare plywood walls between cabins were devoid of soundproofing materials; hence, complaints about noise plagued company maintenance personnel. Seas of mud surrounded the cabins, as neither the YP Company nor the NPS had landscaped as plans dictated. The new lodge, although relatively free from problems in workmanship, nevertheless stunned many guests with its decor. Instead of being greeted by the familiar, elegant, but rough-hewn visage of the old Canyon Hotel, visitors discovered a concrete-block-and-glass edifice boasting orange Formica tables. Upon seeing the new facilities, many preferred to stay in the more expensive hotel, whose occupancy rate rose for the first time in years — despite its shortcomings, it at least looked like a national park facility was supposed to look. The YP Company eventually had to close the old structure to encourage more people to stay in the new village, where rates were as much as double those in other areas of the park.[21]

Canyon Village, because of its financial importance, received the bulk of company problem-solving efforts. Yet other operational difficulties vexed company officials as well. Between 1957 and 1960, concessioner facilities and services continued to deteriorate, and Superintendent Garrison missed few opportunities to remind Nichols of company responsibilities. His personal inspections revealed poorly trained employees — some of whom could not even name the company by whom they were employed, much less direct guests to park attractions. He bemoaned an "indifferent operational attitude" among workers and requested that Nichols institute a broad-based training and motivational program. Recognizing the shortage of qualified food service help, Garrison allowed the company to close some dining areas during the 1958 season, thereby generating more tourist complaints. In 1959 Nichols responded by commissioning a survey of company management policies, but low wages, employee immaturity, and dismal living conditions — the dormitories were worse than the guest cabins — created high personnel turnover rates. The report concluded that by "clinging to tradition," the company had allowed its management and supervisory functions to become obsolete. Conditions worsened each year.[22]

As a result of operational troubles and financial peril, the company lagged behind in its construction schedule, and total accommodations actually decreased. In 1958 NPS officials began pressuring Nichols to finish current projects and begin others. Canyon Village still lacked almost 25 percent of its planned total of cabins; in June 1958, when Garrison inquired about their completion, Nichols informed him that the company could not afford to finish until the fall of 1961, especially since available cabins were rarely filled to capacity. Garrison erupted. "The government has invested over $200,000 in this special facility," he replied, and "we are not sympathetic with any move which leaves government investments of this type idle and unused." The NPS had reluctantly allowed Nichols to close the old Canyon Hotel before the 1959 season to stimulate business at the new development, so three hundred fewer rooms were available to tourists. Then, in August 1959, after an earthquake damaged the Old Faithful Inn and other company structures, terrified tourists fled the park for the year. Revenue slumped, but the NPS kept pressing. In October, Garrison asked Nichols to move several of the old cabins from the now-abandoned Canyon Lodge site to the village to fill the gap temporarily; the company, however, could not afford to undertake even this emergency measure. Increasingly, Mission 66 appeared to have crippled the YP Company, but the NPS demanded that Nichols submit plans for yet another "village" development, this one on the west shore of Yellowstone Lake, called Grant Village.[23]

Grant Village was, without a doubt, the single largest planned alteration of Yellowstone's landscape. NPS architects had chosen a site near the West Thumb, or bay, of the lake, just south of a small existing settlement with a few cabins and one of Hamilton's general stores. The terrain consisted of an elevated, wooded plateau about one-quarter mile from the shore, broken only by several small streams in deep, narrow gorges, with a sandbar jutting into the lake below. Preliminary surveys indicated that this "lovely site required extensive alteration to fit it for use," including cutting about eighty acres of timber, both on the plain itself and toward the lake, the latter for "vista clearing." The sandbar would also have to be dredged to accommodate the planned marina. By remaking this parcel of land that would otherwise be of little interest to tourists, the NPS hoped to construct what it considered a "typical and normal park atmosphere."[24]

To ensure that such an ambience emerged from the obscure site, the NPS, as it had at Canyon Village, proposed two distinct construction programs, one by the agency itself and one by the concessioners. The government contribution to a "typical and normal park atmosphere" would consist of, in addition to clearing the land of trees, building a 50-site picnic ground, a 400-site public campground, and a 150-site trailer park. So that visitors could better appreciate Yellowstone while at the lakeside site, the NPS would also construct a visitor center, complete with interpretive services and an auditorium to show films about the park; an outdoor amphitheater, or "campfire circle," in NPS dialect, designed to evoke some mythological connection with nature or the frontier; public boat docks and concrete launching ramps for recreationists; and a post office. To ensure the proper "atmosphere," the agency also planned considerable road construction, a water treatment plant and sewer system — which would return treated effluent into the lake — as well as ranger stations, employee apartments and dormitories, and numerous maintenance and utility buildings. All services would be powered by electricity brought in on high-tension wires across thirty miles of park.

The NPS proposed that concessioners build facilities similar to those at Canyon but much larger. According to NPS plans, the YP Company would contribute 900 cabins of three classes: 250 housekeeping structures, furnished with beds, tables, chairs, and heat, complete with kitchen, bathroom, and hot and cold water; 250 "class A" cabins, similar to the housekeeping structures but without a kitchen; and 400 economy-class units, sparsely furnished, without a bathroom, and having only cold running water. The agency also requested several levels of food services, including a relatively formal dining room, a cafeteria, a coffee shop, and a lunch counter. Planners wanted the company to provide a lodge building with barber and beauty shop services, meeting rooms to attract convention business, a bar, a gift shop, and ample lobby space; a marina to rent boats, sell supplies, and repair watercraft; public laundries and showers; as well as horses for hire, a service station, and an auto repair shop. The NPS suggested that Hamilton erect a general store to sell camp supplies, groceries, and curios, and that Haynes build another picture shop offering complete photographic services. The agency wanted all these services, plus the attendant employee dormitories and a medical clinic, so that visitors could more fully enjoy the Yellowstone experience, which by this time was beginning to mean many different things to many different people.[25]

Planning for the new area revealed conflicting philosophies among many groups. Between January 1958 and January 1960, NPS officials — including director Wirth — and YP Company executives met regularly to discuss plans for Grant Village, which was tentatively scheduled to open in 1961. But Mission 66 had fractured the traditional alliance between the agency and park operators; they no longer shared the same goals based on a common philosophy of marketing, development, and promotion. The NPS, responding to public criticism, desired to accommodate every tourist; the YP Company wanted to return to profitability before committing itself to further investment. The relationship thus became adversarial. While Wirth cajoled and threatened company officials, dissension among the NPS and its other customary partners erupted and compounded his problem. A number of conservation organizations strenuously opposed Mission 66, and Grant Village in particular, as did many citizens of the "gateway communities" of Gardiner, West Yellowstone, Cody, and other nearby towns.

Opposition to Mission 66 had existed since Wirth announced the program, both among concessioners wary of investing such sums and among the growing body of preservationists. Prior to 1955, however, the NPS had enjoyed widespread support for its policies. During the first decades of the twentieth century, the agency, together with tourism groups, concessioners, and conservation organizations, had discovered much common ground in developing national parks as places where nature could be designed, remade, and managed to fit popular ideas about what such landscapes should look like. Later, the same consensus ideas had made the parks more accessible in response to popular demands, and by the 1930s added recreation to the list of qualities national parks could provide. The NPS, along with such groups as the American Automobile Association, the National Parks Association (NPA), and the Sierra Club, in concert with concessioners and trade groups representing the petroleum, hotel, and publishing industries, formed a conservation "establishment," a coalition of public and private groups that worked together to set policy. Their goals included the preservation of certain areas and the development of tourist facilities at the most spectacular attractions — Old Faithful and the Grand Canyon, for example. Occasionally at odds over one issue or another, these organizations more often worked together, compromising regularly for the sake of greater numbers of visitors and broader political support for conservation.

By the end of World War II, this establishment had expanded and matured. Shortly before Wirth announced Mission 66, a battle over the construction of a dam in Dinosaur National Monument generated an enormous amount of publicity and marked the beginning of an important shift in attitude, the formation of a new mythology of preservation rather than development. This same shift altered the balance of power within the conservation establishment. For decades, concessioners, the tourism industry, and the NPS itself, which had a long tradition of development and whose bureaucratic survival depended on expanding accommodations and services, had dominated national park policy planning. Those who supported other plans, who insisted that the tradition of growth be modified to include new aesthetic values — the wilderness advocates — became much more influential after Dinosaur and brought a newfound effectiveness into the coming fight over Mission 66.[26]

The idea of wilderness had changed dramatically since Yellowstone was created in 1872, and by the 1950s it was rapidly becoming a divisive force within the conservation establishment and among the general public as well. Before the nineteenth century, wilderness was threatening, chaotic, something to be transformed into useful, organized nature. The impetus behind much of Yellowstone's design was a desire to shape those parts of the wilderness popular ideology deemed desirable into a pleasing nature scene. But during the 1930s new ideas emerged that challenged the concept of constructed nature as inherently dishonest; only landscapes unaltered by human activity — wilderness — were worthy of veneration as truly natural. Such ideas raised the bar impossibly high, and in reality no such places existed in the United States. Humans, whether Native Americans or later arrivals, had inevitably altered the landscape of the entire continent. Most Americans did not hold nature to such high standards; for them the term *wilderness* connoted places of nature, human intervention and alteration of landscapes notwithstanding. The founding of the Wilderness Society in 1935 demonstrated that the idea of untouched wilderness as a valuable commodity had gained some credence, and by the mid-1950s a significant movement arose to preserve those areas commonly perceived to meet the criteria of unaltered nature. Those who belonged to this movement emerged as important critics of Mission 66, whose opposition Wirth had tried to diffuse early on by insisting that his construction program actually guaranteed wilderness preservation by focusing development only in certain areas of the parks. Preservationists were not assuaged, however.

Among the most vocal of this new breed was Devereux Butcher, who had long been involved in national park issues. Early in the 1940s, as an editor at the American Forestry Association, he had attracted the attention of NPA president William P. Wharton. Subsequently, in May 1942, he became executive secretary of the association and forged a close relationship with Robert Sterling Yard, the organization's founder and guiding spirit. Butcher transformed the NPA by increasing membership dramatically and converting its

sporadic newsletter, the *National Parks Bulletin,* into a slick, quarterly publication titled *National Parks Magazine.* In 1947 he published *Exploring Our
National Parks and Monuments,* which soon became a standard text for visitors to the parks. He participated fully with other conservation leaders in
the fight to save Dinosaur National Monument, printing editorials and photographs to rally public support for preservation. But in May 1950, after citing health concerns, he resigned as executive secretary of the NPA, although
continuing his editorial duties.[27]

Most members of the national parks policy establishment greeted Mission 66 warmly, with the exception of Butcher. He had been skeptical of
Wirth's intentions since the 1940s, having been warned by his mentor,
Robert Sterling Yard, that the landscape architect possessed a vision of
national parks at odds with preservationist goals. He alone among the establishment leadership argued that Mission 66 shifted park policy toward
overdevelopment and away from what he considered "wilderness values."
Upon hearing of the program for the first time, Butcher stated that "it will
be but a matter of time before we have reduced the system to the level of
commercialized playgrounds." In 1957, frustrated at the lack of support from
others in the NPA, he resigned as editor of *National Parks Magazine* and
became a renegade, assailing Wirth and Mission 66 from outside the mainstream conservation circle.[28]

This extreme action cost Butcher credibility with some members of the
establishment. After 1957 many perceived him as a radical, unwilling to meet
the NPS halfway or to compromise on any issue. But some noted his resolve
and reexamined Mission 66, resulting in a flurry of opposition from conservationists. Such prominent individuals as Olaus Murie of the Wilderness
Society and David Brower of the Sierra Club, among many others, joined
Butcher's protest of NPS policy. Besides writing letters to Wirth imploring
him to reconsider his plans, they published sometimes scathing articles
about his program, both hastening and illuminating a shift of establishment
attitude toward preservation that the NPS and its concessioner partners had,
in their efforts to accommodate tourists, seemingly ignored. They repeatedly warned Wirth that Mission 66, with its emphasis on development, was
rapidly losing popularity not only within the establishment but also among
the general public. In an article in *National Parks Magazine,* Brower blasted
Wirth and Mission 66 as inappropriate, misguided, even dishonest. In a let-

ter to Wirth in 1957, Olaus Murie related random conversations with people "from all over the country" who were "extremely worried over the trend
in the NPS." Murie wrote that one acquaintance had remarked that "the
symbol of Mission 66 should be the bulldozer," and then asked the director
if the ideals of conservationists, who for so long had defended and protected
the national parks against incursion from mining, hydropower, and timber
interests, should not now have "something to do with what takes place inside
those boundaries which they defend?" For the first time, preservationists
were equating tourism with a loss in value, a dramatic departure from the
days when promoting tourism was perceived as an effective alternative to
more environmentally destructive commercial development. Murie, a resident of Moose, Wyoming, was especially critical of NPS actions in Grand
Teton National Park, where a road had recently been built along the east side
of the Snake River. He chided Wirth for placing an "urban veneer" upon a
landscape formerly known as "the foreground to grandeur" and concluded
that he, along with many others, believed that "we should not lose entirely
the remnants of the subtle but inspiring influences we suddenly plunged
into when we spread ourselves over a new continent."[29]

Murie was perhaps the most eloquent of Wirth's critics, but Butcher
remained the most vociferous. He criticized the NPS mercilessly for what he
perceived as the desecration of the parks and in the process helped popular-
ize an entirely new image of them as pristine wilderness areas whose inherent value was threatened by any alteration. An avowed enemy of Wirth,
whom he held personally accountable for all NPS problems, he rarely con-
veyed his sentiments directly, preferring to assail other conservationists and
politicians in an effort to rally support to his militant position. In 1959 he
began publishing a newsletter, the *National Wildlands News*, considered even
by other conservationists to be radical in its antidevelopment stance. He
spoke before such groups as the Federation of Western Outdoor Clubs and
the Garden Club of America, testified at Interior Department hearings on
park development, and published articles in magazines ranging from the
Atlantic Monthly to the *American Institute of Architects Journal*. Frank E.
Masland Jr., a trustee of the National Parks Association and member of the
National Parks Advisory Board, was one of his most frequent targets. Butcher
believed that Masland had "sold out" to Wirth, and he frequently wrote to
tell him so. He also allied himself with park gateway associations, formed by

businesspeople in towns near parks who objected to the expansion of concessions, and encouraged them to write letters to congressmen denouncing
Wirth, Mission 66, and "overdevelopment" in the national parks.[30]

In September 1959 merchants in West Yellowstone, Montana, established
one of the strongest such gateway alliances and, despite being courted as partners by park concessioners, immediately formed an odd, opportunistic coalition with preservationists like Butcher. The Yellowstone Park Gateways
Association, consisting of one hundred representatives from ten surrounding communities, opposed the expansion of YP Company facilities not
because such a program encroached upon some abstract, mythological wilderness values but because it intruded upon the members' profits. Concessioners regularly traveled to these local towns, attempting to convince citizens
that all area businesses, both inside the park and in the gateways, had common interests — hoping "to make Christians out of them," according to
Huntley Child Jr. — but to little avail. The situation became especially tense
when, in 1959, hoping to raise Canyon Village revenue, the company erected
large billboards along major highways in Montana, Wyoming, and Idaho,
advertising services within Yellowstone. Open conflict erupted early in 1960
when, after a precipitous drop in business, Nichols accused gateway businesses of steering tourists away from Yellowstone by denigrating the condition of park facilities; the locals insisted that poor services alone kept visitors
away from places like Canyon Village. The NPS quickly tried to mediate the
dispute, sending Garrison along on the annual concessioner goodwill tour
of surrounding towns — the "Yellowstone Evangelical Troupe" — but
Butcher, through frequent correspondence with the most strident members
of the Gateways Association, frustrated NPS attempts at reconciliation. Thus
Wirth, in addition to his continuing problems with the recalcitrant, financially stricken YP Company and the zealous wilderness advocates, who
wanted the park to be preserved unaltered, a goal long ago rendered impossible, faced opposition to Mission 66 from yet another corner.[31]

Butcher complicated Wirth's life immeasurably. Without question, he was
among a small, militant minority, a zealous fringe element among conservationists. In a letter to David Brower of the Sierra Club, Masland referred to
him as an "unconvertible maverick" and opined that "he isn't happy unless
he's tilting at a whole flock of windmills with a toothpick." A former NPS
official was also critical, assessing Butcher as "a flyweight" who was "inef-

fective in rallying support." But Butcher's presence on the fringe caused
other establishment conservationists to move in his direction — not as far,
perhaps, but closer toward park preservation and away from Wirth and Mission 66. In addition, he helped create the belief that wilderness should be
an attainable ideal for national parks, adding it to the long list of what the
parks should be.[32]

Wirth soon began to recognize the forces arrayed against him. His
response, however, tended more toward evasion and deception than moderation. In the press and in letters to concerned citizens, Wirth constantly
contradicted himself. Some such contradiction was understandable, because
he was still trying to sell the idea that parks like Yosemite, Yellowstone, and
the other large natural reservations could be both playground and wilderness area. He insisted that Mission 66 was not a construction program but a
conservation plan, designed to protect vast areas of Yellowstone by concentrating visitors in small developed areas. But those areas kept multiplying
and growing ever larger. While repeatedly stating that all new improvements
would occur within the existing framework of roads, which was patently
false, Wirth bulldozed sites for new "villages" and planned even more. He
urged Yellowstone superintendent Garrison to accelerate the building of new
structures, to spend money faster to ensure continued appropriations. And
while imploring NPS personnel to publicize Mission 66 and garner support
for its continued funding, Wirth cautioned park officials that "controversial
or confidential sections" of the program "should be removed" before being
distributed to interested parties.[33]

While Wirth battled to save Mission 66, YP Company executives had a
more pressing concern — rebuilding their financially stricken organization.
Between 1958 and 1960, Nichols, Child Jr., and Galusha Jr. all frantically, desperately attempted to forestall an imminent economic collapse. As early as
1958 they had hired IBM to install sophisticated accounting equipment to
provide detailed financial reports and other statistical data, hoping to identify troublesome areas of their operation. They had also commissioned
another large-scale company survey by Billings engineering firm Orr Pickering and Associates to provide an accurate evaluation of facilities and services. Galusha Jr. traveled to Minneapolis to explore a public stock offering
but discovered that years of draining company capital had rendered the
business unfit for such an undertaking. He next proceeded to New York

City, trying to entice a mortgage banker into loaning money and taking "possessory interest" as collateral; the banker had never heard of the term. Galusha Jr. next contacted insurance companies, including John Hancock and New York Life, hoping that they would invest, but again to no avail. He even explored a bond issue — and was rejected. By 1959, with the situation worsening, Nichols again borrowed money from the H. W. Child Trust and more from the H. W. Child Corporation, halting the flow of dividends to family members from those companies. The YP Company also expanded its board of directors, adding Robert J. Sevitz of Security-First National Bank of Los Angeles, who was worried about protecting his firm's $5 million interest, and E. Herrick Low of the First Western Trust Company of San Francisco, whom Adelaide Nichols Casserly had married two years earlier. Both advised against any further expansion; the company could not possibly commit to developing an area like Grant Village when revenues from Canyon were falling short of expenses. In 1960 the crisis worsened; Huntley Child Jr. resigned as vice president; of the family, only John Nichols and his mother, Ellen Dean Child Nichols, remained, he as president and she as chairman of the board, with outsiders filling the remaining positions. At the end of the year the directors hired another outsider, La Marr Bittinger, to direct operations, effective January 1, 1961. The family, although it still owned the YP Company, had effectively abandoned Yellowstone.[34]

Mission 66 was a catalyst for conflict. Despite the obvious problems at Canyon Village, the impossibility of constructing Grant Village, the continuing deterioration of facilities, and the constant visitor complaints — in short, the obvious failure of the program to reinvent the parks to fit contemporary ideals — Wirth insisted on pressing forward. He faced opposition from all sides: preservationists like Devereux Butcher, who was slowly convincing others to follow his lead; local business operators concerned about their economic situation, who did not believe that the federal government should subsidize their competition; and even the YP Company itself, which had been crippled by the program. After 1960, although Wirth and the YP Company officials all muddled onward, desperately clinging to outdated ideas and practices, neither Mission 66 nor Harry Child's family business had any hope of surviving much longer.

7

Collapse

During its first five years, Mission 66 solved few problems. In February 1961 the popular national magazine *Atlantic Monthly* published a group of articles under the heading "Our National Parks in Jeopardy" that revealed continuing concerns over policy and doubts about the program. One author, referring to the "devastating popularity" of the parks, suggested that Congress should appropriate more money for National Park Service programs, but that the agency should use the funds to add land to the system, not build more facilities, to alleviate congestion at existing locations. Another also advocated restraining development and pointedly criticized the NPS and Mission 66, calling the program "the prescription that may kill the patient." He insisted that the agency's desire to accommodate every tourist had "inevitably led to compromise in preservation of the natural landscape," and that a proper solution to the overcrowding problem should focus on "brains rather than bulldozers." But the most disparaging article was penned by Devereux Butcher, who exposed the inherent fallacy of Wirth's contention that Mission 66 was a conservation, not a construction, program. He openly challenged the NPS director to explain how the agency could promote Canyon Village as less intrusive on the natural scene in Yellowstone. He also derided the contradictory new NPS policy that closed portions of Yellowstone Lake to motorboats — a concession to the new, vocal preservationist lobby — while building marinas to accommodate five hundred such craft at Bridge Bay and Grant Village. At the end of Butcher's article, *Atlantic Monthly* editors encouraged readers to write their congressmen and the Interior Department to insist on a solution to overcrowding, poor facilities, and possible overdevelopment under Mission 66. The next month, Representative John

Dingell of Michigan inserted into the *Congressional Record* another of Butcher's articles denouncing overdevelopment in the parks. Public opinion seemed to be divided between accommodation and preservation.[1]

Such publicity heartened Butcher but, more important, heightened the pressure on Wirth. Many believed that newly appointed Secretary of the Interior Stewart Udall, who outwardly supported the NPS director, would balk at further construction in the parks. Early in 1961 he and Wirth had clashed over a proposed National Recreational Resources Commission report that recommended interagency cooperation between the NPS, the U.S. Forest Service, and other land management bureaus. Udall favored such a plan; Wirth, concerned about losing authority over parklands, opposed it strenuously. In April 1961 Udall hired Joe Carithers, who had been employed by Butcher's *National Wildlands News,* as a special assistant, lending credence to preservationist rumors of tension between the interior secretary and Wirth. By the end of the year even close friends of the director — and some within the NPS itself — questioned his policy of rapid growth. Butcher soon escalated his attacks, urging the Yellowstone Park Gateways Association to monitor closely new development in the park. He believed that Wirth was vulnerable: "Now is our chance," he wrote to a colleague, "let's build as big a fire under him as we can."[2]

But Wirth was not willing to abandon his policies. In March 1961, he defended his position to Udall, answering the criticism leveled at his agency by the *Atlantic Monthly* articles. He acknowledged the validity of several points, stating that he appreciated the opportunity for "reappraisal and self-examination," but contended that Butcher represented a "small but vocal minority which would insulate the parks from the people and preserve them from the obviously mounting pressures and demands" of American society. Critics who charged that the parks were being overdeveloped, he insisted, were mistaken; what they meant was that the areas were overcrowded, and only a concentrated effort to expand facilities would solve the problem. He justified Mission 66 development as being "in accordance with carefully prepared plans," as if no excess construction could possibly occur under such circumstances. Wirth considered his "villages" in the parks to be "zones of civilization in a wilderness setting," necessary to preserve the remaining lands from the ravages of overuse. He cited noted author Joseph Wood Krutch, who had penned a calm, rational defense of utilizing parks such as

Yellowstone as three different things: resorts, nature reserves, and wilderness areas. Resorts for "the majority whose tastes are not essentially different from those who frequent commercial resorts," nature reserves for "the larger minority which is interested in wild animals, in plant life and in natural scenery though unprepared for life in a real wilderness"; and wilderness for "the smallest minority — that which is physically and psychologically up to the strenuousness of really primitive living." Such ideas were very much in keeping with Wirth's plans to develop certain areas while leaving others "unspoiled" by human alteration. Typically, Wirth also quoted NPS founder Stephen Mather, reminding Udall that his policies were in line with agency tradition.[3]

Wirth's allies rallied around him; therefore, he continued promoting Mission 66 throughout 1961 and 1962 but refocused the program. Former NPS director Horace Albright assured Udall of the soundness of current policies and encouraged him to allow Wirth latitude in their implementation. Concessioners such as Don Hummel, who had begun his park career at Lassen Volcanic and later took over the Glacier National Park operations, and Paul Sceva of Rainier also encouraged the interior secretary to support Wirth. They believed that Mission 66 was being unfairly criticized by elitist preservationists who wished to eliminate tourism from the parks altogether. Executives from the Automobile Association of America and the U.S. Chamber of Commerce backed the director as well. Even officials within the office of the interior secretary urged Wirth to carry on his program. On March 20, 1961, the Interior Department issued a public statement on national parks policy. Despite the frequent divergence of opinion between the department and the NPS over concessions policy, dam building, and other issues, the statement mirrored Wirth's agenda. Udall had apparently decided to grant the NPS time to salvage Mission 66, to quiet the critics. Wirth seized upon the opportunity but disregarded the growing preservationist movement and instructed members of his planning division to accelerate their work and embark on new projects. Even within the NPS itself, many employees had become disillusioned with Mission 66 because the program seemed to emphasize construction rather than conservation. So, in April 1961, Wirth restructured the biennial NPS superintendents' meeting into a pep rally, calling it the "Mission 66 Frontiers Conference," in hopes of boosting morale. Critics of the first five-year phase had instilled caution; in his address at the conference, Wirth underscored his determination to redirect

Mission 66 toward augmenting staffing levels, increasing interpretive services, and professionalizing scientific research. Construction of facilities, he
insisted, would be subordinated to these new concerns. A consummate
politician, Wirth was still attempting to sell the idea that national parks
could be all things to all people. He scheduled the next conference for
Yosemite National Park in October 1963 and announced that guests would
include the entire NPS family — employees, concessioners, and Interior
Department officials — so that all could participate in planning the final
two years of Mission 66.[4]

Despite his apparent shift away from construction and the dismal, ongoing Canyon Village experience, Wirth remained convinced that Yellowstone
facilities had to be upgraded to meet tourist demands. But between 1960
and 1962, Yellowstone Park Company officials, rather than embarking on
new construction, instead desperately attempted to effect a financial turn-
around. And to a certain extent they succeeded. In 1960 the directors sold
the last of the company's $1 million in marketable securities to stave off
bankruptcy. They then hired Fargo businessman La Marr Bittinger as general manager, hoping that he could streamline procedures and reinvigorate
the lagging business. Upon assuming control, he was astounded at the lack
of oversight exercised by previous managers. He immediately slashed
expenses by eliminating company cars for managers, cut payroll costs by
reducing employee numbers, and trimmed food charges by negotiating contracts with discount suppliers. Bittinger also continued dismantling the
transportation division, a process that had been initiated in 1958 when John
Nichols had sold many obsolete buses and leased replacements from the Los
Angeles City School Bus System. In 1961, after the Union Pacific Railroad
announced the discontinuance of passenger service to West Yellowstone,
Bittinger proposed that other bus companies be allowed to operate in the
park as long as their passengers spent at least one night in a lodging facility
and purchased three meals. The YP Company would provide a guide for
each bus; such a plan reduced company investment in equipment. Bittinger
also reaffirmed a company contract signed in 1956 with Western Fleetlines,
an Avis car rental franchisee, that guaranteed the YP Company a 15 percent
commission on all automobiles rented in park gateway communities. In
1961, with costs thus diminished and revenue inching upward, the YP Company returned to profitability, netting $230,000 — not enough to appease

NPS officials pressing for improvements but better than the $540,000 loss of 1960.[5]

Company officials also struggled somewhat unavailingly to maintain a stable management structure. In 1961 the board of directors hired Les Scott, an executive with Grand Canyon concessioner Fred Harvey Company, to consult on future decisions. Soon thereafter Bittinger, although his program had stemmed the short-term outflow of cash, abruptly departed. Fred Burke, company controller and a vice president, quit in March 1961; Thomas Hallin, another vice president and chief of the engineering and construction division, resigned in December, as did President John Q. Nichols. In August 1962 the directors retained George Beall, an Arizona businessman, as executive vice president and general manager to halt the exodus and continue the recovery. In addition, the financially conservative California banker E. Herrick Low (Adelaide's husband) became chairman of the board and president of the firm. John Nichols and his mother, Ellen, the only other family members remaining as officers, served as vice president and treasurer — they controlled the majority of company stock but had little input on daily operations; both still believed that the only way to solve existing problems would be to sell the company.[6]

Late in 1961, Nichols and his mother had nearly succeeded in selling, but they were stymied by the NPS. In November, Galusha Jr. informed Wirth that he had located two possible buyers for the franchise, both of whom desired confirmation of NPS capital investment requirements. Wirth assured him that a $250,000 annual expenditure for upgrading and renovation, completion of the Bridge Bay Marina, basic food and camper services at Grant Village, a motel at Lake, and completion of Canyon Village would suffice. In addition, he seemed confident that any new operator could count on a new thirty-year contract, which would aid in securing investment capital. Galusha Jr. then relayed this information to his potential buyers — one a New York City investment group, the other Slater Food Service of Philadelphia. Negotiations proceeded smoothly until Galusha Jr. returned to Washington in March 1962 and learned that Wirth had reconsidered. The NPS would require any purchaser to spend at least $13 million over fifteen years. According to Wirth, a commitment of this size would be necessary because "it takes dollars to convince Congress that a thirty-year contract should be awarded," although he openly admitted that "the money probably would not be spent."

Galusha Jr., aware that such a demand effectively ended any possibility of a sale, angrily informed the YP Company board of directors that the NPS had sabotaged the deals.[7]

Thus, operations continued. Vice President George Beall, with regular advice from Low, utilized extraordinary means to maintain the recent upward trend. He, along with the other concessioners and the NPS, recruited members for a Yellowstone National Park Advisory Council, consisting of respected business representatives from Montana, Wyoming, and Idaho, as well as officers from Haynes, Incorporated, Hamilton Stores, Incorporated, the YP Company, and the NPS. He offered to sell the company's massive transportation garage in Gardiner to the NPS and hired an appraisal firm to arrive at a fair price. After closing company offices in La Jolla, California, and Bozeman, Montana, he reorganized housing for company managers by requiring that many relinquish their homes in Mammoth or Gardiner and move in together, or even into unused hotel space.[8]

At the same time, Beall tried conventional methods to develop a plan for future years and to stimulate company earnings. In 1962, shortly after being hired, he commissioned a comprehensive, in-house review of operations titled "A Blueprint for the Future" that addressed three specific problems: how to meet new visitor demands, how to comply with NPS construction requests, and how to fund these endeavors. The report concluded that tourists desired mainly motel-type accommodations, fast-food services such as cafeterias and coffee shops, and flexible transportation options. In addition, all services should be reconfigured to prolong park visits and thus increase revenue. The survey noted three primary construction projects; the largest of these, at the Lake area, included full-scale developments at Bridge Bay and Grant Village, a motel at the Lake Lodge site, and renovations to facilities at Fishing Bridge. The company estimated total cost for these projects at over $1.7 million. Two smaller construction ventures, one at Mammoth and the ongoing work at Canyon Village, added an estimated $400,000 to the total expense. The bulk of the report, however, focused on acquiring capital. Recommendations included refinancing the loan from Security-First National Bank of Los Angeles to increase cash flow, negotiating additional loans from outside sources, and selling all or part of the company's stock to investors. Since a sale remained unlikely because of the poor financial position and the unreliability of NPS officials, the report concluded that the best available option was to convince the NPS to guarantee long-term loans from institutional investors — a difficult and ultimately unsuccessful task.[9]

Not surprisingly, the federal government had become increasingly concerned about YP Company operations and had escalated park oversight functions. In 1961, Superintendent Garrison, who had always taken an intense interest in controlling concessioners, became disturbed after the company dismissed several longtime employees. Rumors of one man, a winter keeper at Mammoth, being summarily released "with less than one weeks notice after 38 years in the park and one year from his pension date," prompted an inquiry from the superintendent. In response, he learned that the YP Company had no pension plan; in fact, a trust fund, which had been set up in 1957 to provide retirement benefits, remained empty. In 1962, the Interior Department investigated complaints that the company was skirting minimum-wage requirements but was assured that such was not the case. Wirth personally inquired about questionable labor practices but received an answer so vague and intentionally indirect that he ordered an audit of company records. Then the U.S. House Appropriations Committee Division of Surveys and Investigations launched its own probe. The various investigators discovered that the company had underpaid government franchise fees, had allowed several contracts with suppliers to lapse, and had maintained incomplete and unacceptable accounting records. They also noted that management remained unsettled and requested that the company hire an experienced controller, since that position had been "filled by at least five different persons during fiscal year 1962."[10]

The audits and reviews failed to assure NPS officials that the YP Company could achieve stability; hence, their relationship with concessions managers became more adversarial. In February 1963, responding to yet another NPS request for information about accounting procedures, Beall informed associate park superintendent Luis Gastellum that "to understand professional problems of any nature requires a certain basic knowledge of the disciplines involved." His implication that park officials were incompetent to review company practices infuriated Garrison, who angrily responded directly to the company board of directors, questioning the ability of concessions managers and expressing displeasure over company operations. Although Beall, under pressure from the board, apologized for his remarks, his relationship with park officials deteriorated further. Garrison accepted the apology, asserted confidence in Beall, but nonetheless intensified his supervisory role. In June he expressed skepticism over YP Company advertising practices, telling Beall that "the problems of empty rooms and the need for more meal customers cannot be resolved in this manner." Rather, the company's "tradition of poor quality rooms and indifferent service all at high prices" was to blame and could only be reversed through improving performance. Since the company financial position required that "expenditures for advertising be most carefully screened for value," Garrison demanded that all such advertising material and programs be cleared through his office, thereby expanding NPS authority well beyond any previous level. He also convinced Wirth to finance yet another review of company operations, this one to be conducted by an independent hospitality services consultant.[11]

While the NPS was usurping company administrative authority, the deterioration of the relationship between the agency and the concessioner surfaced in discussion of other issues. The financial condition of the YP Company, combined with preservationist pressures on Wirth, necessitated slowing the pace of Mission 66 planning and construction. During 1961 the agency contracted site preparation work at Grant Village and built large campgrounds at Madison Junction and Lewis Lake, two sites with no other planned facilities. Workers also started dredging and building a breakwater at Bridge Bay, anticipating imminent YP Company construction. The company, however, continually frustrated agency plans, remaining financially unable to undertake any major projects and investing only $85,000 during the year on equipment and insignificant renovations. By 1962 Wirth reluctantly acceded to requests that Grant Village be built in stages, but he petulantly outlined a new, five-year program for YP Company capital investment and construction that totaled $2.78 million. He further informed managers that the NPS would require a $1 million annual commitment to retain their franchise after 1967. Since concession operations had remained slightly profitable, Garrison informed the YP Company that he wanted a minimum of one hundred cabins at Fishing Bridge and Old Faithful renovated by the end of 1962. He then recommended that the company erect the motel at Lake, complete Canyon Village cabin construction, and add accommodations at several other sites, but abandon the still-operational cabins at the site of the old Canyon Lodge. Again, the company failed to comply; it erected no cabins, instead spending over $500,000 on miscellaneous equipment and maintenance. Despite NPS entreaties, the owners staunchly resisted adding promised accommodations, since house counts continued to decline even though more tourists visited the park each year.[12]

This trend — that of more people in the park yet fewer guests utilizing concession facilities — further aggravated the increasingly tense relationship. Billie Nichols had noted such a pattern in 1955 when first faced with Mission 66 construction schedules but had failed to persuade Wirth that it portended catastrophe. NPS officials in Yellowstone had been conducting annual park censuses since the mid-1950s detailing populations on given days, and their information confirmed the divergence. For instance, greater numbers of tourists stayed overnight in the free NPS campgrounds than in the concessioner lodgings. But even this evidence failed to deter agency officials from insisting that the YP Company construct more facilities. In the six years of Mission 66 construction, the company, while adding a few additional "pillows," had not approached the original goal of increasing capacity from eighty-five hundred to over fourteen thousand. Meanwhile, tourists continued to complain about existing lodgings. Company executives would invest limited amounts of capital to upgrade these facilities but not to build new ones and have them sit idle. In August 1963, Beall informed Garrison that the company wished to retain the cabins at the site of the old Canyon Lodge — the same structures that the NPS had recommended be abandoned the previous year. He also stated that he had no intention of building any more cabins at Canyon Village, the first time that the YP Company openly declared its intention not to comply with Mission 66 construction plans.[13]

Based on available statistics, the company seemed to be pursuing the correct program. By concentrating on the renovation of existing facilities rather than the construction of new ones, officials hoped to stem the ever-rising tide of visitor complaints. Mission 66 had done little to alleviate tourist criticism — even the American Automobile Association advised its members that park accommodations were unacceptable. Many visitors wrote to Secretary of the Interior Udall; others sent their negative comments to their congressmen or directly to the YP Company. The specifics differed little from charges contained in similar missives over past years. One traveler complained about "disproportionate prices and antiquated methods of serving the public"; another described the lodgings and food services as "inexcusably poor." Canyon Village, only five years old, seemed "shameful" and the employees "slovenly dressed and not generally courteous." Others described themselves as "very much distressed" over conditions that were "filthy and greasy." An Arizona couple informed Udall that they were amazed that "the crowd made it this summer without an epidemic of some sort breaking out." One notable change in the complaints from previous years was public awareness of concessioners—perhaps an unintended side effect of Mission 66 publicity. Few visitors blamed the NPS for the conditions, instead placing responsibility squarely on the YP Company. "The concessioners have the public right by the tail," an Illinois man wrote, "and instead of making improvements are milking these obsolete 'accommodations' to the extreme limit."[14]

Conditions were equally miserable behind the scenes, where NPS inspectors supported tourist contentions of filth and apathy. During regular inspections in 1962 they discovered moldy fruit being served to breakfast guests at the Old Faithful cafeteria. The lodge kitchen at Canyon Village lacked hot water in employee rest rooms. Floors and equipment were uniformly squalid. Cooks and waitresses smoked over food preparation areas, wore uniforms for days without laundering them, and scorned hair nets. Meat-cutting tools displayed evidence of rancid flesh particles. Officials investigated regular reports of food poisoning among guests and employees alike. Not surprisingly, few facilities earned passing inspection grades.[15]

Such problems increased the tension between the NPS and the YP Company, especially when Garrison pressured managers to improve services and address complaints. In August 1962, he wrote to Ellen Nichols in La Jolla, hoping that she—as matriarch of the family—would motivate the board of directors to improve conditions. He told her that her company suffered from "chronic low employee morale" and was in a "generally unhealthy condition." Workers regularly quit in midseason or had their contracts terminated after displaying little interest in their jobs. As a consequence, the company had to close some rooms in the Old Faithful Inn because housekeepers were unavailable. Cabins at Canyon Village and Lake sat empty for the same reason. The Mammoth Grill and Canyon Village dining rooms closed frequently because workers abruptly departed. Garrison noted that "filthy cabins, unsanitary kitchens, and dirty restrooms" remained a source of "embarrassment and disgust" to visitors. He informed Mrs. Nichols that, in his opinion, the company had done little to alleviate this chronic situation and that he was "deeply concerned" that such conditions jeopardized the company's concession contract. Then, in October 1962, he notified general manager Beall that present company rates for accommodations and services "can no longer be justified and require downward revision," referring to the prices as "indefensible." He admitted that the NPS had been lax in supervising company operations, that it had accepted "in good faith that the company would initiate the needed improvements . . . [and thereby] justify the rates" — but would do so no longer.[16]

The company, while acknowledging problems but attempting only superficial means to correct them, increased Garrison's ire. After the 1962 season, upon learning that employee turnover for the year had exceeded 55 percent, managers tried to boost morale by honoring those workers who returned for two or more years of work with banquets, plaques, and lapel pins. They tried to organize an employee photographic contest. They even founded a "Miss Yellowstone Pageant" to promote company pride among seasonal employees. But they never raised wages, funded a profit-sharing or pension plan, or exhibited more than a cursory interest in employee housing conditions or food services. Consequently, visitor complaints continued unabated. In July 1963, Garrison insisted that "it is long past time to forget the balance sheet for a few minutes and start thinking of the customers served." He expressed doubts about the abilities of owners, managers, and employees to reverse the downward spiral and, responding to company complaints about excessive NPS regulation, opined that it was "doubtful if your operation could survive without the protecting umbrella of the franchise."[17]

By October 1963, when NPS officials and concessioners gathered at Yosemite National Park for the biennial superintendents' conference, the YP Company officers were in open rebellion. They reverted to past practices by investing nearly $500,000 of profits from 1963 in marketable securities instead of in new lodgings. They had spent approximately $300,000 on facilities, but none of that amount on NPS-mandated construction. All Mission 66 schedules had been abandoned. Wirth informed them that, unless they agreed to build planned facilities at Bridge Bay, the NPS would do so, and he would abrogate their franchise. On October 11 Beall protested officially, eliciting from Wirth a promise to reconsider and to meet with company officials at the Yosemite conference.[18]

Other matters, however, soon took precedence, as groups from all across the conservation spectrum began assailing Wirth. Butcher remained vocal in his opposition, but representatives from other quarters also pressured the NPS director to step down. The widely publicized problems with concessions at Yellowstone, especially the disastrous experiment of Canyon Village, had effectively discredited Mission 66 and cost Wirth the support of tourism advocates. In addition, Interior Secretary Udall had appointed respected scientist A. Starker Leopold to chair a National Academy of Sciences study of wildlife policy in the national parks. The Leopold report, issued in March 1963, soundly rebuked the NPS for its wildlife management policies of previous years and unleashed a new group of critics. Yet another report by the National Academy of Sciences Advisory Committee on Natural History Research in the National Parks, chaired by William J. Robbins, also criticized NPS policy decisions under Mission 66, insisting that such moves had "damaged naturalness."

The two reports demonstrated that a fundamental shift in popular perceptions of national parks was under way. The Leopold report, whose committee members had initially been charged with scientifically justifying elk reduction in Yellowstone, was in its final form much broader in scope and ultimately more influential. The report assumed that large natural parks like Yellowstone should, without question, be managed so as to "represent a vignette of primitive America," an idea certainly reflective of the growing influence of the wilderness lobby but not by any means a consensus among policy makers nor among the general population. Indeed, judging from the complaints and editorials, many people still desired the national parks to be resorts for recreation or, at the very most, nature reserves where they could appreciate scenery and wildlife and relive the stories about frontier pasts. For decades, such imagined places had been mirrored in reality as NPS officials and concessioners designed the parks to fit the collective imagination of the traveling public. Now, however, wilderness advocates and scientists in favor of ecological managment were insisting that such creations were unnatural, that only a landscape designed to provide "a reasonable illusion of primitive America" should be the objective managers aspired to design. The traditional custodians of the parks, the NPS administrators and the concessioners, had lost control of their product. Instead of being able to create a public image of what the parks should be and then design a scene to meet expectations, they now were faced with molding a landscape based on expectations that were impossible to fulfill. The Leopold report even acknowledged the futility of such endeavors, stating that management plans intended to "preserve, or where necessary to recreate, the ecological scene as viewed by the first European visitors" required "skills and knowledge not now in existence." In other words, the report created an unattainable goal but nonetheless chastised NPS officials for not reaching it.[19]

Then, on October 14, Assistant Secretary of the Interior John A. Carver blasted Wirth and his agency in a speech to the assemblage at Yosemite. He derided Wirth's admittedly feeble attempt to take credit for the recent wildlife policy study, remarking that "to credit the Park Service with the Leopold report is like crediting a collision at sea for a dramatic rescue effort." He scolded the director for opposing Udall's plan to coordinate national recreation resource agencies and, indirectly, for perpetuating an NPS administrative policy that rewarded and promoted incompetent officials. Carver then chided the agency for basing its entire philosophy on tradition rather than on sound — read scientific — management principles, boldly asserting that "when all else fails, the Park Service seems always able to fall back upon mysticism, its own private mystique." As evidence, he quoted from an agency manual, which stated that the "primary qualification" for most NPS jobs was that "employees be imbued with strong convictions as to the 'rightness' of National Park Service philosophy, policy, and purpose, and who have demonstrated enthusiasm and ability to promote effectively the achievement of National Park Service goals." Carver, frustrated after battling Wirth over policy issues for months, then exploded: "This has the mystic, quasi-religious sound of a manual for the Hitler Youth Movement. Such nonsense is simply intolerable. The National Park Service . . . isn't a religion, and it should not be thought of as such."[20]

The two scientific reports and Carver's diatribe all castigated Park Service officials for relying on mythology, for romanticizing their agency and their parks. According to these critics, not only was the NPS's traditional vision for national parks misguided, but its own heritage and stories, the agency's very identity, was nothing more than a romantic illusion ill suited to modern times. In reality, there were religious aspects, mythological significances, to the culture of the National Park Service that Carver, not being part of the agency, simply did not understand. From its earliest days under Mather and Albright, the NPS culture was defined by its people, who shared a strong sense of loyalty to the parks and to one another. The national parks were national icons, symbols that according to law were to be protected from exploitation and preserved for public enjoyment. As caretakers of these sacred places, NPS employees enjoyed a uniquely favorable public image and within a short time began to believe that they were indeed part of a special and elite group that understood better than any outsiders what was best for the parks. More than most such government agencies, the NPS personnel shared a collective belief system that placed the welfare of the parks above all other concerns. In trying to protect their charges from harm, NPS officials encouraged tourism and promoted concessions monopolies as a means of acquiring partners in the struggle against mining, timber, and water developers. Even as attitudes changed and tourism became one of the problems rather than a solution, the long-standing traditions of the NPS toward making the parks accessible would not allow the agency or its devoted employees, including Conrad Wirth, to consider any possible alternative. The mythology was simply too powerful.

The day after Carver's outburst, Wirth and assistant director Hillory A. Tolson, both of whom had been contemplating retirement, announced their resignations; Udall immediately appointed George B. Hartzog as NPS director effective January 10, 1964. Hartzog had been actively preparing for such an opportunity since early in 1962 after an altercation with Wirth that resulted in Hartzog's resignation. Udall, hoping to pressure Wirth into resigning, had rehired Hartzog as an associate NPS director in the spring of 1963. Hartzog had immediately begun developing a policy to replace Mission 66, which nearly everyone — even many within the service — by that time realized had failed miserably to satisfy its many critics, especially those advocating an ecological approach to park management. He unveiled the new NPS strategy statement, titled "The Road to the Future," to popular acclaim at the Yosemite conference the day that he was appointed director. While at Yosemite, Hartzog also met with YP Company directors and informed them that the NPS was canceling all Mission 66 schedules and that Udall had appointed yet another committee to develop, with concessioner input and mindful of recent criticism, a new master plan for Yellowstone.[21]

This committee replaced Wirth as arbiter of the Yellowstone concession controversy. Chairman A. Clark Stratton, the NPS associate director and

Hartzog's chief deputy, recruited several high-ranking agency officials, along with Yellowstone superintendent Garrison and prominent wilderness advocate Sigurd Olson, to serve on the review board. They immediately began working on a program to replace Mission 66 with smaller, less-intrusive park facilities. Within a month of the Yosemite meeting, they had suspended all federal expenditures for Yellowstone — the concessioner had fallen so far behind construction schedules that new roads led only to vacant sites, and government service buildings stood idle near proposed developments. Chairman Stratton reasserted the agency's plans to take over construction of all facilities at Bridge Bay, and YP Company directors accepted his decision but negotiated an operating lease. Soon thereafter, committee members received a company request for approval to build a swimming pool, shuffleboard courts, and a golf course inside the park. They scornfully rejected the application, believing that such development reflected the old, promote-at-all-costs tradition from which Hartzog was attempting to distance the agency. It seemed that the NPS had accepted a new vision for the park, one that was intended to create an image of restrained development and place a greater emphasis on nature, while the concessioners were still operating under the impression that Yellowstone could still be everything that visitors desired, that resort, nature preserve, and wilderness could all coexist, at least in the popular imagination, if marketed appropriately. The two longtime partners in promoting the park had grown apart ideologically.[22]

During 1964 the committee produced a tentative plan that departed dramatically from Mission 66 precepts. Members recommended that overnight accommodations be limited to four locations, advising that Grant Village be scaled back from nine hundred cabins to five hundred; the Lake Hotel be abandoned and replaced with cabins and motel rooms; the YP Company eliminate substandard units at Canyon and refrain from adding new facilities at that site; and Roosevelt Lodge be retained and upgraded. Concessioner accommodations at Fishing Bridge, West Thumb, Old Faithful, and Mammoth would be eliminated. The committee further recommended that at Bridge Bay, where the NPS had already spent months preparing for construction, services should be limited to a marina and boating services. It also scrapped Firehole Village, intended to replace Old Faithful under Mission 66 guidelines. Members counseled restraint in building new campgrounds, preferring that the U.S. Forest Service increase its capacity on surrounding lands. Unlike the Mission 66 program, this new plan did not assume a cor-relation between increased visitor counts and a need for more lodgings; rather, the committee believed that "congestion can be reduced through reduction in 'pillow' count and improved circulation." The NPS was still attempting to reconfigure Harry Child's old systematized tour while limit-ing concession services, to redesign the park yet again within the constraints of contemporary ideas about nature.[23]

During the remainder of 1964, NPS officials attempted to reconcile their new plans with those of the YP Company. In May, Director Hartzog removed Lon Garrison as Yellowstone superintendent and replaced him with John McLaughlin, issuing specific instructions to the new administrator to solve the concessions problem. In June, McLaughlin discovered that work on the Grant Village site had been halted for over a year. Now that the new plans specifically included this development, he requested that the YP Company provide a parkwide construction proposal, including building and financing plans for Grant Village, by August 10. The NPS demanded that the company participate in three stages of development by constructing 250 motel-type cabin rooms and a lodge building in 1965, as well as another 250 cabins in both 1966 and 1967. In July, Beall responded that the company was not in "any position to commit to a specific program" but outlined several tentative sug-gestions, many of which — such as retention of the Old Faithful, Mammoth, Fishing Bridge, and West Thumb facilities, as well as keeping the Lake Hotel operational — conflicted with NPS goals. He also informed McLaughlin that the company expected to be compensated for its possessory interest in any facilities that it eventually eliminated. He omitted, however, any reference to Grant Village, asking instead for a deadline extension until September 10 to develop a proposal. In September, he requested another thirty-day grace period; McLaughlin granted it. On October 30, Beall finally answered the NPS request for a Grant Village plan. He asserted that, if the company was to undertake even limited development at the site, the NPS would first have to approve a new thirty-year contract. Then he reiterated his belief that the government should reimburse the company for abandoned facilities. With-out these two conditions, Grant Village remained economically unfeasible. NPS director Hartzog summarily refused to consider paying the company for decrepit facilities and pressed for a more specific plan, but Beall delayed responding until the spring of 1965.[24]

Both the NPS and the YP Company pursued other options while nego-tiating over Grant Village. McLaughlin began compiling evidence to sup-port a government cancellation of the YP Company contract if a solution could not be reached. Meanwhile, the company was courting another poten-tial buyer, the Greyhound Corporation, and was reluctant to commit itself to any development program during ongoing negotiations. By April 1965, how-ever, NPS demands for future investment had deterred Greyhound from buying the concession operations. Soon Beall resigned as company general manager, and the NPS, still without any firm commitment for facilities at Grant Village, increased the pressure on company directors yet again.[25]

The concessioner's relationship with the NPS had completely disintegrated. In April, YP Company chairman E. Herrick Low, citing Beall's resignation as a contributing factor, requested yet another extension before submitting Grant Village plans. Hartzog, after ten months of trying to get a commitment from the company, flatly denied his application. Low then explained that company attorney Newell Gough Jr. and Hugh Galusha Jr. — neither of whom had any expertise in construction planning, a signal to Hartzog that the company was attempting to avoid Grant Village altogether — had been working on a pro-posal, but Galusha Jr.'s recent election as president of the Federal Reserve Board of Minneapolis had delayed its completion. Low suggested a personal meeting; Hartzog agreed. The two sides met in June 1965, whereupon the NPS demanded an immediate commitment of $6 million for Grant Village, aban-doning its previous position of a three-stage development. Gough Jr. coun-tered with an offer to spend $2.5 million if the company received a new thirty-year contract. Hartzog declined; therefore, Gough, Jr. notified him that, "most reluctantly, and without waiving any of its rights, the Yellowstone Park Company must inform you that it is unable to comply with the Park Service construction program at Grant Village."[26]

The company's legal right to refuse compliance was unclear; therefore, Hartzog attempted a reconciliation. In the contract that Billie Nichols had signed in 1957, the company had included a clause stating that any NPS demands for concession developments must be "economically feasible" and include a "reasonable assurance of profit." In July, aware that these condi-tions limited his options, Hartzog met with Art Bazata, the new executive vice president and general manager of the YP Company, and again requested firm company plans for the proposed $2.5 million commitment. Hartzog also expressed concern that the owners were once again taking profits at the expense of development funds; after a six-year moratorium the board of directors had authorized dividend payments in February 1964. He requested that the family members who controlled the company either sell portions of the H. W. Child Trust and H. W. Child Corporation to raise equity capital for improvements or actively pursue a sale of the YP Company itself. The family, however, had no intention of investing more capital in park operations, but it agreed to act more forcefully to attract a potential buyer.[27]

Despite Hartzog's conciliatory tone, the situation continued to deteriorate. Later in July, he met with the YP Company board of directors and detailed the NPS position on several issues. He asserted that prices for existing services were "unconscionable" and provided excess profits, which the company ownership insisted on applying to dividends rather than to needed improvements and new construction. He restated the fact that the government had spent over $3.5 million preparing sites at Grant Village, Canyon Village, and Lake in expectation that the concessioner would construct new facilities. And he demanded that the owners commit more risk capital — their own money — to complete planned work before taking dividends. If they refused, Hartzog was preparing to invite other concessioners to enter Yellowstone, build the new facilities, and compete directly with the YP Company. General manager Bazata, however, noted that the NPS plans for Grant Village were too extensive and questioned again the economic feasibility of any concessioner profiting from such a development; Hartzog replied that "the comment is moot and we cannot leave $3,442,000 in the ground unused." The NPS had already gone too far under Mission 66 to scale back, and the YP Company remained unwilling to construct accommodations without an assurance of profit — an impasse. Hartzog pleaded with the owners to find a buyer, to reconsider their asking price of $5 million, which had deterred several recent parties. He stated that a solution to the problem was vital; that, in his opinion, if the Yellowstone concessioner collapsed, "the entire concession system will fail." Additionally, he noted that "several congressional committees are concerned about the situation in Yellowstone," and that this interest further limited his range of negotiating options. The YP Company board remained unswayed. The members agreed to become more aggressive in searching for a buyer but refused to accede to NPS demands that they invest more capital or suspend dividend payments. In

August, the company submitted a final proposal for park development, which the NPS deemed "unacceptable." In September, Hartzog informed the board of directors that company facilities and services were "unsatisfactory" and that he intended to "find other means of meeting objectives considered to be necessary." Then, on October 8, 1965, he notified them that the NPS was "hereby giving notice of its intention to terminate" the YP Company contract. For the first time in its history, the agency was going to fire a national parks concessioner.[28]

The struggle between the NPS and the YP Company, which had allowed conditions in Yellowstone to become progressively worse and the image of the park to suffer, was nearly over. Ellen Dean Child Nichols and her son John — who, together with other family members still controlled 86 percent of company stock — immediately decided to appeal, but without much enthusiasm since neither believed the company could be saved. Their lackluster defense included claims that the company had been destroyed by a "vacillating government policy," an understandable accusation considering the apparent difference in vision between NPS directors Wirth and Hartzog and the mixed messages that emanated from the agency since 1963. Park Service officials had decided that science dictated a management philosophy tending toward moderation in development, but they were still pushing the YP Company to invest more money and develop new areas of Yellowstone. No wonder the concessioners were confused. Company officials also cited "the financial incubus of an ill-conceived and poorly executed major construction program" for which they were only partly to blame. In addition, they pointed out difficulties adjusting to "an entirely new set of operating conditions and requirements originating in the demands of the American traveling public."

In other words, company officials no longer knew how to shape the park to fit the demands of tourists, administrators, scientists, and preservationists, despite years spent trying to determine what those demands might be. A 1958 survey commissioned by the company, for example, asserted that park visitors expressed a much greater desire for luxury accommodations rather than for economy cabins. But the less expensive cabins filled to capacity, while hotel rooms remained vacant night after night, a contradiction noted in the survey as "tending to compromise the operational value" of the study. The survey did report "a rather clear indication that Yellowstone is serving several different populations of visitors having different character-istics and wants." This, essentially, was the basis for the company's problem: how to satisfy all the various visitor desires, which after all the company itself had played a significant part in creating in the first place. But the demands, previously harmonious, now seemed contradictory, and company officials were baffled. Some critics wanted newer and more facilities, a Yellowstone that lived up to its reputation as an entertainment attraction. Others wanted wilderness, no hotels, gift shops, or man-made distractions from the natu-ral features on display. The YP Company no longer knew which park it should sell, or if the park was indeed its product. During a meeting with NPS officials in 1960, company managers endorsed the idea of a "separation of appearances" between the government agency and their commercial operations. "It is better to have the Park Service sell birds and bees," one company official said, "and let the concessioners sell their services."[29]

Hartzog responded to the company statement with a well-documented assertion that the family had neglected its responsibilities to provide satis-factory accommodations and services. Both sides hoped to avoid years of litigation, but any possibility of a compromise solution had long since dis-appeared. Within six months Galusha Jr. resolved the dilemma by locating a buyer for the company, the Goldfield Corporation of New York, which had recently purchased concession operations in Everglades National Park. Con-sequently, in March 1966, Secretary of the Interior Udall postponed a sched-uled appeals hearing, and the family proceeded with final negotiations to leave the park.[30]

The NPS, elated at the prospects of attracting a cooperative concessioner, helped consummate the deal in extraordinary ways. Agency officials imme-diately agreed to a request for a new thirty-year contract by Goldfield chair-man Richard C. Pistell. They also overlooked his history of securities violations and stock exchange suspensions, apparently believing that oust-ing the recalcitrant Child-Nichols family was worth a substantial risk. They agreed to Pistell's proposal that Yellowstone be operated year-round, increas-ing both government expense and concessioner profit. Most remarkably, they sanctioned his scheme to eliminate Hamilton Stores from the long-standing and profitable Yellowstone Park Service Stations joint venture. The NPS also allowed Pistell to cancel Hamilton leases for hotel and lodge gift shops and take over those operations. In effect, the agency was forcing out a loyal concessioner with a long history of excellent service in favor of a rich newcomer.[31]

Thus ended the seventy-five-year history of Harry Child's family business. On August 8, 1966, NPS director Hartzog granted a new thirty-year contract to the Yellowstone Park Company. The family owners immediately sold all their stock in the company to the Goldfield Corporation, whose chairman, Pistell, promised to spend $20 million over twenty years on new lodgings and related services. No member of the Child or Nichols family attended the ceremony at Mammoth Hot Springs; perhaps the irony did not escape them. Ten years earlier, Conrad Wirth had promised to join the family in the park, on almost that very same day, and celebrate the NPS and concessioner partnership that had completed Mission 66 and had once again remade Yellowstone. But after those ten years, neither felt much like celebrating.[32]

CONCLUSION

Since the 1870s, when men like Matthew McGuirk, James McCartney, and Henry Horr first began erecting bathhouses and hotels around Mammoth Hot Springs, both the physical Yellowstone and its image in the collective imagination underwent tremendous change. From one of the most isolated areas of the American West, the park became a Mecca for tourists, intensively managed, promoted, and packaged to attract as many visitors as possible. Early stagecoach paths evolved into paved highways, isolated tent camps into grand hotels, and small groups of wandering curiosity seekers into masses of hurried visitors. The two entities most responsible for this transformation were the United States National Park Service and concessioners like the Yellowstone Park Company. Working together as promoters, they helped determine what visitors expected by constructing certain beliefs about the park. They then transformed the landscape to fit popular expectations, and as ideas about the proper role of national parks in America shifted, they adapted the park to fit. And because Yellowstone was the first and most famous national park, and national parks were such important parts of the American mythology, it became the benchmark against which all other ideas about nature, scenery, history, and recreation were measured. Through shrewd marketing by the NPS and concessioners, people became convinced that Yellowstone defined such ideas. It was the most natural place, the most scenic, the most representative of the past, the most enjoyable. Above all, Yellowstone was adaptable, in the words of the original legislation truly a "national pleasuring ground," open to entry and adventure, able to fulfill everyone's expectations of what a national park should be.

Harry Child and the other significant Yellowstone concessioners helped to shape the park in the popular imagination specifically to generate profits. For nearly a century they, along with Interior Department, army, and NPS administrators, constantly tinkered with a scene believed imperfect, a reality that needed modification to fit preconceived notions. To them the park was always a product and, as such, was always presented to potential customers in the best possible light. When visitor desires changed, the proprietors of Yellowstone responded by telling yet another story, weaving another image into the tapestry of Yellowstone mythology and, if necessary, reconfiguring their merchandise to appeal to greater numbers of people. Despite popular perceptions that the park was protected from commercial exploitation, the NPS and its conces-sioner partners virtually owned Yellowstone, selling it piecemeal to receptive customers as if it were an inexhaustible, self-replenishing commodity.

For years the partners conducted a flourishing trade in Yellowstone and else-where in the national parks, a robust business of selling nature, recreation, and frontier history to Americans. Stephen Mather and Horace Albright established a tradition of promotion and expansion within the NPS and encouraged con-cessioners to develop the national parks to suit popular demands. They shared a common vision. While the concessioners needed tourists to generate profits, the NPS needed them to ensure congressional appropriations and, in turn, bureaucratic survival. During the 1930s and 1940s, when the Interior Depart-ment, in a New Deal–inspired reform effort, attempted to rein in concessioner influence, the NPS supported its commercial partners. Even in the face of sci-entific challenges to management policies from within the agency itself, chal-lenges that presaged a later administrative coup, and a director, Newton P. Drury, who seemed less inclined than either his predecessors or his successors to adhere blindly to tradition, the old beliefs about promotion and development, about making the parks all things to all people, for the time being won out.

From the time of its founding the NPS was both part of and dependent upon a conservation establishment. Members included other government agencies like the United States Forest Service, concessioners like the Yellowstone Park Company, conservation groups like the Sierra Club, as well as boosters like the railroads and the American Automobile Association. This powerful establish-ment reacted forcefully and usually successfully to external threats from dam builders, timber harvesters, or mining companies, that threatened to alter irre-trievably areas more valuable for their scenery or history. To generate public support the establishment members called upon the mythology, the old story. They insisted that certain places be protected for the enjoyment of all Ameri-cans, not given over to destructive commercial development. Many of the estab-lishment members themselves, of course, had financial interests in promoting tourism, but all shared a belief that unique natural areas like national parks were indeed worthy of defense against the most transformative types of development. To that end they constructed popular images of parks and monuments as places of nature, recreation, history, and tradition and encouraged tourism develop-ment to prevent what they considered to be the possible physical destruction of the places themselves. The establishment lost at Hetch Hetchy, but for decades it successfully defended parks like Yellowstone against reservoir builders and Olympic against timber barons. The crowning achievment of this effort came in 1956, when the establishment halted construction of the Echo Park Dam in Dinosaur National Monument.

By that time, however, some members of the conservation establishment had begun to recognize that tourism itself could jeopardize the very qualities it had been encouraged and promoted to protect. The newfound status enjoyed after the Echo Park controversy by organizations such as the Sierra Club, the National Parks Association, and the Wilderness Society generated widespread popular support for their ideas about preservation and emboldened leaders of this nascent environmental movement — David Brower, Howard Zahniser, and even Devereux Butcher — to call for more government protection of wilderness. When NPS director Conrad Wirth announced Mission 66 in 1955, the establishment he counted on for support was on the verge of fragmenting, the old consensus mythology about right and wrong, about extractive industry being bad but tourism development being good, unraveling into two distinct and mutually exclusive stories.

Between the Echo Park fight in 1956 and the issuance of the Leopold and Robbins reports in 1963, the NPS suffered an identity crisis. The seeds had been planted in 1933, when the agency expanded its administrative responsibilities to include national monuments and historic sites. That same year, the issuance of George Wright's *Fauna No. 1*, the controversial report on natural resource policy, further muddled the previous beliefs of the Mather-Albright era about promotion and development of visitor services being paramount. By the time Interior Department officials used the National Academy of Sciences Report and the Leopold report to force Conrad Wirth out as NPS director, management philosophy had become divided and reflected the dissonance felt by the public at large. For the first time, really, people both within the NPS and on the outside were questioning what exactly Yellowstone was supposed to be, and for the first time coming up with contradictory answers.

Yellowstone had always been a malleable commodity, shaped and marketed in various ways. As long as the different beliefs about what the park was could be reflected in reality — that is, as long as the NPS and concessioners could make the park look like people expected it to look — visitors departed happy, their needs met. The challenge was making sure that the different images could co-exist, that the stories did not conflict. And for many decades, the stories fit together nicely. In the early days visitors wanted to see curiosities like geysers or impressive features like waterfalls and canyons; roads were built to accommodate them. Later, tourists began arriving from greater distances wishing to see not only specific features but also a more abstract commodity, nature. Administrators and concessioners, of course, understood that what these people really wanted was an idealized version of nature, a place where the frontier lived on. So they created one. They eliminated wolves to increase populations of elk, bred bison to repopulate the meadows, told stories about mysterious Indian tribes — while expelling living, breathing Indians, who were not part of the ideal — and built hotels of rough-sawn logs designed to fit into romanticized landscapes. Guests demanded more, wanted to be entertained; swimming pools, ballroom dances, and bear-feeding shows filled such needs in Yellowstone. As stories about the park entered the collective consciousness, hotels like those at Mammoth, Canyon, and Old Faithful themselves became part of what attracted visitors; the park had become a tradition, a place to experience nature as earlier generations had, from the seats of stagecoaches and windows of elegant hotels. And the stagecoaches and hotels themselves were now part of the experience, the YP Company itself an integral part of what visitors expected. Even when automobile tourism threatened to destroy the well-organized, systematic packaging of Yellowstone, Harry Child and his NPS partners invented new methods of marketing their product, dreamed up new ways of making stories come true. Lodges and camps supplemented hotels and provided the opportunity for visitors looking for the Old West to "rough it" as they wished. Gift shops offered as many items emblazoned with elk, moose, bison, and bear images as they did those depicting geysers, canyons, and waterfalls. Nightly campfires summoned forth national memories of the western past, and even the songs sung by guests (from a songbook published by the YP Company and distributed each evening) were intended to evoke images of the frontier. Later visitors arrived with other stories, telling them that Yellowstone was a place of outdoor recreation. The NPS and concessioners provided boating facilities, stocked lakes and rivers with fish for anglers, and constructed trails for hiking and horseback riding in addition to the campgrounds and picnic areas. And all these different groups, with all their different ideas about what the park was, were satisfied, because they all found their stories to be true.

And then Yellowstone failed to live up to expectations.

During the post–World War II 1940s and throughout the next decade, visitation to Yellowstone and other national parks exploded. Americans traveled in previously unimagined numbers, armed with substantial leisure time, material prosperity, a heightened sense of national pride, and images of national parks as traditional vacation destinations. Yellowstone, as the flagship park, attracted an immense amount of tourist attention. Visiting Yellowstone was almost a sacred pilgrimage. Fathers and mothers brought children as they themselves had been brought, to see the elk, bison, and bears, to sing around the campfires, fish in the streams, marvel at the lobby of the Old Faithful Inn, and buy souvenir postcards. They came to take pictures of the mountains, the canyon, and the falls, to be awed by hot springs and geysers or to hike in the forests. They came to ride horses, cook over open fires, and relive the mythological frontier experiences that made America special. They came, as the saying goes, to "get away from it all." And they came in greater numbers than ever before, numbers greater than could be accommodated.

Conrad Wirth proposed the traditonal solution: Mission 66 would redesign the park yet again to fit demands for services. But he and his concessioner partners had a more complicated mission this time, for ideas about what Yellowstone was supposed to be had diverged. Many visitors still expected the park to be what it had been for so long, the epitome of nature, history, tradition, and recreation. But the growing preservationist lobby insisted that tourism development be restrained. Wirth found himself caught between a tradition of shaping the park to fit visitor demands with concessioners as "partners" and a reality of growing environmentalism and pressure from scientists to manage the park as a "primeval" place. It was an impossible situation, one that never had a chance of success. Yellowstone enjoyed unprecedented popularity with the mobile, affluent American public; tourists were coming to the park in ever-increasing numbers. Following the pattern set by Mather and Albright, however, Wirth insisted on accommodating them. But he soon discovered the traditional solution to be no longer viable. With Mission 66, he and the NPS followed an established policy that had worked in the 1920s, when national parks were perceived as playgrounds, when tourism was by any definition good. The same policy would not work in the 1950s, with a financially weakened concessioner partner and a new public interest in preserving America's remaining natural areas from encroachment. Wirth, in an attempt to apply the customary NPS solution to a new problem, discovered himself and his most favored project, Mission 66, in an untenable situation, caught between a tradition that he could not abandon and a modern environmental ethic that he did not understand.

Mission 66 itself did not destroy the YP Company. The owners, themselves bound by tradition and their own personal story of how the family business should operate, did that themselves. Like Wirth, they failed to recognize changing environmental attitudes and refused to alter longtime practices that dictated profits be foremost. Harry Child had achieved a balance, managing to earn healthy profits and alter the park to suit both his needs and those of his guests. He operated in a time of consensus, when everyone knew almost instinctively what Yellowstone was supposed to be. His hotels, stagecoaches, camps, and buses all fit into the constructed image visitors brought with them to the park. His family business became part of a national experience.

But after World War II his successors could not duplicate this feat. Perhaps circumstances prevented them from doing so — the explosion of tourism and Mission 66 placed unprecedented demands on the company at a time when Billie Nichols was desperately attempting to recover lost wartime profits. But something else changed after Harry Child died. Neither Nichols nor any of the other company leaders through ensuing decades demonstrated the intense personal feelings that Child had for Yellowstone. In that respect this story is not unique: family businesses often follow such patterns of success during the reign of the founder, then stagnation under second-generation owners who enjoyed their prosperity, and finally ruin when grandchildren exhibited little interest in perpetuating the legacy. There was more to this story, however. The YP Company officials took their product for granted; they forgot what the park meant to people. Instead of constructing facilities to meet expectations about nature and tradition, they built modern structures that seemed incongruous in such a setting. They offered diesel-powered buses like those found on city streets rather than the stagecoaches or the popular open-top vehicles of earlier days. They built concrete-block laundry facilities and colorful, modern service stations, because people were demanding such things. Instead of the rough-hewn logs of the old hotels, they offered shoddily constructed motel rooms and chrome-and-glass coffee shop decor. They forgot where they were operating, that people wanted their services cloaked in a facade of tradition, of naturalness. They failed to realize that, more than ever, visitors wanted to be greeted by these familiar, traditional facilities, and that the increasing visibility of preservationism and calls for ecological protection shaped new perceptions about how Yellowstone should look. They stopped selling the park, their most valuable asset, and began selling motel rooms and cafeteria meals, and they lost the ability to make themselves part of the Yellowstone experience.

In some ways Conrad Wirth pulled the company along this path to destruction. Changing American attitudes elevated ecological science and wilderness preservation to places of importance. These same attitudes within the NPS challenged the tradition of promotion and accommodation. An ideological divide, the collapse of the old story about what national parks should be, ousted Conrad Wirth in 1963. Two years later, the same force finished off the pitiful remnant of Harry Child's family business.

Ironically, little changed within the NPS. The debate over proper policy, about how the national parks should look and what people expect, continues to this day. The divisions within that agency that became apparent with publication of the Leopold and Robbins reports of 1963—documents that constituted, in the words of the service's own most respected historian, an "ecological countermanifesto"—grew wider during Hartzog's administration between 1964 and 1973. If anything, the debate has become more strident as the NPS has become more politicized and the parks continue to gain popularity. Issues such as overflights of the Grand Canyon, overcrowding on the Colorado River, mass transit systems to lessen the environmental "footprint" of tourism all are current and controversial. Despite the calls for scientific management, for ecological concerns to take priority over visitor desires, the political reality requires a delicate balancing act and results in policies that continue to vacillate from promotion to preservation.

Although the Child and Nichols families withdrew from Yellowstone after selling the YP Company in 1966, the concessions controversy endured for several more years. Charles Hamilton's heirs, Ellie and Trevor Povah, withstood the challenge from Goldfield Corporation and remained active in park operations. In 1968 they purchased the Haynes Picture Shops from Jack Ellis Haynes's widow, Isabel, thereby solidifying their position. Richard Pistell, chairman of the Goldfield Corporation, transferred the YP Company stock to a subsidiary, General Baking Company, later in 1966. General Baking then became General Host, a speculative conglomerate whose subsidiaries included Cudahy Meats, Allied Leather, the Solar Salt Company of Salt Lake City, Royal Baking Company, Eddy

Bakeries, and national park concessions in Everglades and Yellowstone. Pistell, despite promising to invest millions in Yellowstone facilities, spent almost nothing to improve park services. Ten years after he bought the YP Company, the NPS initiated proceedings to cancel his franchise. In 1979, the U.S. Congress approved a buyout of over $19 million, providing Pistell with a profit of nearly $14 million in addition to ten years of earnings. The NPS then contracted with TW Recreational Services, a subsidiary of yet another conglomerate, Trans World Corporation, whose holdings included Trans World Airlines, Hilton International Hotels, and Century 21 Real Estate. After a two-year trial period, the NPS and TW Recreational Services negotiated a new thirty-year contract in 1982. In 1996, after improving facilities and services dramatically, TW sold its interest to Amfac Parks and Resorts.

Similar scenarios played out in other parks, as family-owned concessions companies withdrew in favor of conglomerates. In Glacier, the Great Northern Railroad maintained a financial interest in the hotels until 1961, when Don Hummel, concessioner at Lassen Volcanic National Park, took them over. Hummel sold out in 1981 to the Dial Corporation, and later the Viad Corporation purchased most concessions in the park. The NPS bought Mount Rainier concessions in 1952, after years of conflict between officials and Rainier Park Company management, especially the militant Paul Sceva. In the 1970s the NPS contracted with Guest Services to operate the park facilities. Union Pacific operations at Bryce Canyon, Zion, and the North Rim of the Grand Canyon were donated in 1972 to the NPS, which contracted with TW Recreational Services to manage them. The Yosemite Park and Curry Company remained family owned until 1969, when Shasta Telecasting Corporation purchased the assets. In 1973 MCA bought the business, and in 1993, Delaware North Companies took over. The Fred Harvey Company operated El Tovar and other Atchison, Topeka, and Santa Fe concessions at the Grand Canyon's South Rim until 1954, when Fred Harvey's sons purchased the facilities outright. In 1968 the Fred Harvey Company was sold to TW Recreational Services and, along with the Yellowstone, Bryce, Zion, and North Rim businesses, became part of the Amfac Parks and Resorts operation in the mid-1990s.

Yellowstone itself, of course, survived the tumult of the 1960s and continues to present some of the most frustrating management problems for NPS administrators. Hartzog's agreement to open the park for year-round use, at the demand of the new concessioner Richard Pistell, has caused much of the controversy. By 1990 more than sixty-five thousand snowmobiles used park roads in winter, stressing elk and bison and emitting noxious clouds of exhaust. Politicians from Montana, Wyoming, and Idaho lobby for more winter facilities, even while environmental groups insist the park be closed to such traffic in winter. In 2000 new rules limiting winter use were implemented, but they will likely be challenged in Congress as well as in the courts. The same kind of divisivness appeared in 1988, when fires swept across large portions of the lodgepole pine forests that were themselves creations of policy decisions undertaken to present the park as visitors demanded. When the NPS announced its new policy of letting the forests burn, the public outcry was unprecedented, with many insisting that the park was being destroyed. Ecological integrity was noble, the public shouted, but not at the expense of our vision of what Yellowstone should be.[1]

Interest in national parks and concessions remains high. Congress holds hearings regularly to review new contracts and explore options for streamlining operations and providing travelers with optimum services. Newspapers, both national and regional, frequently feature stories about Yellowstone and the other "crown jewels" of the national park system that focus on traffic problems, overcrowded facilities, and environmentally damaging management policies. The Public Broadcasting System and National Public Radio stations air documentaries and discussions of how best to solve the continuing problems of managing the parks. Early in the 1990s, the NPS, facing budget shortfalls, transferred the administration of most campgrounds in Yellowstone to the concessioner; visitors can now reserve a small tract of "wilderness" at any one of nine national parks through Ticketmaster, the national electronic reservations company. Much has changed over the past fifty years, but much more remains the same.

For over one hundred years, the story of the Old West was the story of America. One generation read it in books like Owen Wister's *The Virginian,* the next watched it play out on movie screens with Roy Rogers, the Lone Ranger, and John Wayne. Of course, this mythological place was not the real West. But it hardly matters, because the stories remained so powerful. Even today, reenactors hold weekend rendezvous dressed in the skins that they imagine the mountain men wore. Others stride across western prairies alongside reproduction Conestogas wagons and eat beans for weeks on end to demonstrate their national heritage, their belief in the mythology. A quick search of the local public library reveals 247 titles by Louis L'Amour. Children play computer games in which winning means arriving at a virtual Oregon without succumbing to digital representations of cholera, dysentery, or snakebite. When they tire of fording imaginary streams and hunting pixilated bison, they can move to the television and watch reruns of *Little House on the Prairie, Bonanza,* or *Grizzly Adams.* The more enamored conquer their own backyard frontiers with cap guns and bandannas from Wal-Mart. The sense of adventure lives on. Middle-class families spend hundreds of dollars to pan for gold in icy dude ranch streams; others invest hundreds of thousands to breed and ride cutting horses. We wear cowboy hats and boots because it says something about who we are, or at least who we think we are. We dress our Olympic athletes in the same garb, showing the world that Americans still possess those traits that allowed us to conquer the frontier. We keep telling the story because it tells us the things we want to hear. And we still make pilgrimages, in greater numbers than ever, to national parks like Yellowstone, and revere them as symbols of our American past.

INTRODUCTION

1. William Kittredge, *Owning It All* (St. Paul, Minn.: Graywolf Press, 1987), p. 62. This collection of essays masterfully explains the power of the western myth. William Cronon, "A Place for Stories: Nature, History, and Narrative," *Journal of American History* 78 (March 1992): 1374.

2. Coy F. Cross II, *Go West, Young Man! Horace Greeley's Vision for America* (Albuquerque: University of New Mexico Press, 1995), summarizes nicely the boosterism of Greeley.

3. Donald Worster, "Two Faces West: The Development Myth in Canada and the United States," in *Terra Pacifica: People and Place in the Northwest States and Western Canada*, ed. Paul W. Hirt (Pullman: Washington State University Press, 1998), pp. 71–91, offers a fascinating analysis of the ideological and mythological forces that drove western economic development.

4. Kittredge, *Owning It All*, p. 157. Frederick Jackson Turner, "The Significance of the Frontier in American History," in *The Frontier in American History* (New York: Henry Holt, 1986), is of course the most famous articulation of why the frontier and its stories meant so much to so many.

5. Wonderful examples of how powerful national parks became as symbols can be found in John Muir, *Our National Parks* (Boston: Houghton Mifflin, 1916); and Freeman Tilden, *The National Parks: What They Mean to You and Me* (New York: Knopf, 1951).

6. For the texts of these acts, see Lary M. Dilsaver, ed., *America's National Park System: The Critical Documents* (Lanham, Md.: Rowman and Littlefield, 1994).

7. The school of "New Western History" abounds with examples of assaults on traditional western mythology. The work most often cited as typical remains Patricia Nelson Limerick, *The Legacy of Conquest: The Unbroken Past of the American West* (New York: Norton, 1987). Richard White, *"It's Your Misfortune and None of My Own": A New History of the American West* (Norman: University of Oklahoma Press, 1991), offers the most complete integration of new stories with old. Alfred Runte, in *National Parks: The American Experience* (Lincoln: University of Nebraska Press, 1979), first and most forcefully articulated the worthless lands thesis.

8. William E. Grant, "The Inalienable Land: American Wilderness as Sacred Symbol," *Journal of American Culture* 17 (spring 1994): 84; David Chidester and Edward T. Linenthal, eds., *American Sacred Space* (Bloomington: Indiana University Press, 1995), p. 28; Neil Smith, *Uneven Development: Nature, Capital and the Production of Space* (New York: Basil Blackwell, 1984), p. 57. The most influential work on the role of nature in America is Roderick Nash's classic *Wilderness and the American Mind* (New Haven, Conn.: Yale University Press, 1967); all successive references are to the third edition, published in 1982. Hal Rothman, *Devil's Bargains: Tourism in the Twentieth-Century American West* (Lawrence: University Press of Kansas, 1998), is a broad-ranging analysis of the importance of national mythologies to tourism. Discussions about the importance of nature and national parks to American mythology can also be

found in Catherine Albanese, *Nature Religion in America: From the Algonkian Indians to the New Age* (Chicago: University of Chicago Press, 1990); Simon Schama, in *Landscape and Memory* (New York: Knopf, 1995), p. 7, refers to wilderness as "the holy park of the West." National parks as repositories of history are analyzed by David Lowenthal, *Possessed by the Past: The Heritage Crusade and the Spoils of History* (New York: Free Press, 1996); and Michael Kammen, *Mystic Chords of Memory: The Transformation of Tradition in American Culture* (New York: Knopf, 1991).

1. BEGINNINGS

1. Richard A. Bartlett, *Nature's Yellowstone* (Tucson: University of Arizona Press, 1993), pp. 3–22; Merrill J. Mattes, "Yellowstone Cavalcade," MS, box B-3, Merrill J. Mattes Collection, American Heritage Center (hereafter cited as AHC), Laramie, Wyoming, pp. 1–25. Bartlett describes the geology in great detail, while Mattes provides a chronicle of those few who ventured into the region during the first half of the nineteenth century.

2. Bartlett, *Nature's Yellowstone*, pp. 3–24. A valuable early topographical description can be found in Henry Gannett, *Report on the Geographical Field Work in the Yellowstone National Park Extracted from the Twelfth Annual Report of the Survey for the Year 1878* (Washington, D.C.: United States Department of the Interior, U.S. Geological and Geographic Survey, 1883), pp. 466–484.

3. Bartlett, *Nature's Yellowstone*, pp. 81–92; Robert H. Keller and Michael F. Turek, *American Indians and National Parks* (Tucson: University of Arizona Press, 1998), p. 22. The best treatment of native people in Yellowstone, as well as the most recent incarnation of the Sheepeater myth, is in Mark David Spence, *Dispossessing the Wilderness: Indian Removal and the Making of the National Parks* (New York: Oxford University Press, 1999), pp. 41–49. Wayne Replogle, *Yellowstone's Bannock Indian Trails* (Yellowstone National Park, Wyo.: Yellowstone Library and Museum Association, 1956), is a synthesis of many early studies.

4. Bartlett, *Nature's Yellowstone*, pp. 81–85; Spence, *Dispossessing the Wilderness*, pp. 43–44; Ake Hultkrantz, "The Indians in Yellowstone Park," *Annals of Wyoming* 29 (October 1957): 125–149; Susan S. Hughes, "The Sheepeater Myth of Northwestern Wyoming," *Plains Anthropologist* 45 (February 2000): 63–83, presents a compelling argument that Sheepeaters did not reside in Yellowstone in the manner ascribed to them by the mythology of the park.

5. Robert M. Utley, *A Life Wild and Perilous: Mountain Men and the Paths to the Pacific* (New York: Henry Holt, 1997), p. 15. Burton Harris, *John Colter: His Years in the Rockies* (New York: Scribner's, 1952), pp. 107–112, provides a credible account of Colter's visit to the region.

6. Utley, *A Life Wild and Perilous*, p. 93; Gerald C. Bagley, "Daniel T. Potts," in *The Mountain Men and the Fur Trade of the Far West*, ed. LeRoy R. Hafen (Glendale, Calif.: Arthur H. Clark, 1972), 3:259.

7. Bartlett, *Nature's Yellowstone*, pp. 93–111; Osborne Russell, *The Journal of a Trapper*, ed. Aubrey L. Haines (Lincoln: University of Nebraska Press, 1964), pp. 25–29; J. Cecil Alter, *James Bridger: Trapper, Frontiersman, Scout and Guide* (Columbus, Ohio: Long's College Book Co., 1951), pp. 380–391. See also Frances Fuller Victor, *The River of the*

West: The Adventures of Joe Meek (Missoula: Mountain Press, 1983); and Stanley Vestal, *Joe Meek: The Merry Mountain Man* (Lincoln: University of Nebraska Press, 1952), for accounts of other travels. Bernard DeVoto, *Across the Wide Missouri* (New York: Houghton Mifflin, 1947), remains a valuable account of how the Yellowstone region fit in the West of the trappers.

8. Bartlett, *Nature's Yellowstone*, pp. 117–119; Utley, *A Life Wild and Perilous*, pp. 279–281. Kenneth H. Baldwin, *Enchanted Enclosure: The Army Engineers and Yellowstone National Park: A Documentary History* (Washington, D.C.: Historical Division, Office of the Chief of Engineers, U.S. Army, 1976), pp. 5–14, offers a concise overview of the expedition of 1859. For the Montana gold rush, see Michael P. Malone and Richard B. Roeder, *Montana: A History of Two Centuries* (Seattle: University of Washington Press, 1976), pp. 50–69. The story of catching a fish and cooking it at the same time was one of the most frequently repeated and least-believed tales of early years and is recounted by most travelers throughout the nineteenth century. See Sir Rose Lambart Price, *A Summer on the Rockies* (London: S. Low, Marston and Co., 1898), p. 166.

9. Charles W. Cook, David E. Folsom, and William Peterson, *The Valley of the Upper Yellowstone: An Exploration of the Headwaters of the Yellowstone River in the Year 1869*, ed. Aubrey L. Haines (Norman: University of Oklahoma Press, 1965), provides the most comprehensive account of this journey.

10. The famous Washburn-Langford-Doane expedition was the catalyst for the creation of Yellowstone National Park but certainly not the genesis of the national park idea. The campfire story was first published in Nathaniel Pitt Langford, *The Discovery of Yellowstone Park* (Saint Paul, Minn.: Haynes Foundation, 1905; reprint, Lincoln: University of Nebraska Press, 1972); other accounts can be found in Hiram Martin Chittenden, *The Yellowstone National Park*, ed. Richard A. Bartlett (Norman: University of Oklahoma Press, 1964), pp. 67–85. Several other works contain further discussion. See Aubrey L. Haines, *The Yellowstone Story: A History of Our First National Park* (Yellowstone National Park, Wyo.: Yellowstone Library and Museum Association in cooperation with Colorado Associated University Press, 1977), 1:105–140; and Bartlett, *Nature's Yellowstone*, pp. 164–183.

11. The most recent and thoughtful analysis of the campfire story as useful mythology can be found in Paul Schullery, *Searching for Yellowstone: Ecology and Wonder in the Last Wilderness* (Boston: Houghton Mifflin, 1997), pp. 51–64. For accounts of Catlin's contribution to the idea, see Roderick Nash, "The American Invention of National Parks," *American Quarterly* 22 (fall 1970): 728–730.

12. Haines, *Yellowstone Story*, 1:134–141; Bartlett, *Nature's Yellowstone*, pp. 166–167; Chittenden, *Yellowstone National Park*, pp. 80–82.

13. Mattes, "Yellowstone Cavalcade," pp. 32–33; Bartlett, *Nature's Yellowstone*, pp. 188–193; Chittenden, *Yellowstone National Park*, pp. 74–76; Haines, *Yellowstone Story*, 1:140–155. James G. Cassidy, *Ferdinand V. Hayden: Entrepreneur of Science* (Lincoln: University of Nebraska Press, 2000), is a thorough study of Hayden, his experiences in Yellowstone, and his contributions to the founding of the park.

14. Bartlett, *Nature's Yellowstone*, pp. 198–210; Haines, *Yellowstone Story*, 1:156–173; Cassidy, *Ferdinand V. Hayden*, pp. 230–232.

15. Haines, *Yellowstone Story*, 1:179; Runte, *National Parks*, pp. 5–9; John Ise, *Our National*

Park Policy: A Critical History (Baltimore: Johns Hopkins Press, 1961), pp. 20–21; "An Act to Set Apart a Certain Tract of Land Lying Near the Headwaters of the Yellowstone River as a Public Park," in *America's National Park System: The Critical Documents*, ed. Lary M. Dilsaver (Lanham, Md.: Rowman and Littlefield, 1994), pp. 28–29.

16. Haines, *Yellowstone Story*, 1:196–198; Richard A. Bartlett, *Yellowstone: A Wilderness Besieged* (Tucson: University of Arizona Press, 1985), pp. 116–119; David A. Clary, *"The Place Where Hell Bubbled Up": A History of the First National Park* (Washington, D.C.: U.S. Department of the Interior, National Park Service, Office of Publications, 1972), pp. 50–51; Cassidy, *Ferdinand V. Hayden*, pp. 172–173; Edwin J. Stanley, *Rambles in Wonderland; or, Up the Yellowstone, and Among the Geysers and Other Curiosities of the National Park* (New York: D. Appleton and Company, 1878), pp. 54–57.

17. Haines, *Yellowstone Story*, 1:196; Mattes, "Yellowstone Cavalcade," p. 36; Dunraven, Windham Thomas Wyndham-Quin, 4th Earl, *The Great Divide* (London: Chatto and Windus, 1876), pp. 194–225; W. E. Strong, *A Trip to the Yellowstone National Park in July, August, and September, 1875*, ed. Richard A. Bartlett. (Norman: University of Oklahoma Press, 1968), pp. 38–40; Harry J. Norton, *Wonder-Land Illustrated; or, Horseback Rides Through the Yellowstone National Park* (Virginia City, Mont.: Harry J. Norton, 1873). Norton's guidebook, consisting of a series of published letters to the *Virginia City Montanan*, offered valuable descriptions but in an unorganized format.

18. Haines, *Yellowstone Story*, 1:216–239; Bartlett, *A Wilderness Besieged*, pp. 21–28; Mark H. Brown, *The Flight of the Nez Perce* (New York: Putnam's, 1967), pp. 313–334.

19. Spence, *Dispossessing the Wilderness*, pp. 58–60; Hughes, "The Sheepeater Myth," pp. 74, 76.

20. Mattes, "Yellowstone Cavalcade," p. 45; Haines, *Yellowstone Story*, 1:252–254; Bartlett, *A Wilderness Besieged*, pp. 116–120; "Geo. W. Marshal[l] Housing and Transportation," file "G. W. Marshall and G. G. Henderson," box C-17, Yellowstone National Park Research Library (hereafter cited as YNP), Mammoth Hot Springs, Wyoming.

21. Bartlett, *A Wilderness Besieged*, p. 33; Haines, *Yellowstone Story*, 2:263.

22. Carlos Schwantes, *In Mountain Shadows: A History of Idaho* (Lincoln: University of Nebraska Press, 1991), p. 171; J. William T. Youngs, *The Fair and the Falls: Spokane's Expo '74, Transforming an American Environment* (Cheney: Eastern Washington University Press, 1996), pp. 58, 59; J. W. Buel, ed., *Louisiana and the Fair: An Exposition of the World, Its People, and Their Achievements* (St. Louis: World's Progress Publishing Co., 1905), 7:2745–2757; Neil Harris, ed., *The Land of Contrasts, 1880–1901* (New York: George Braziller, 1970), p. 297; Jonathan Raban, *Bad Land: An American Romance* (New York: Random House, 1996), offers an enlightening account of how actively and sometimes irresponsibly railroads promoted the Old West; Michael P. Malone, *James J. Hill: Empire Builder of the Northwest* (Norman: University of Oklahoma Press, 1996), profiles one of the most successful boosters.

23. Marta Weigle and Barbara A. Babcock, eds., *The Great Southwest of the Fred Harvey Company and the Santa Fe Railway* (Phoenix, Ariz.: The Heard Museum, 1996); Malone, *James J. Hill*, pp. 249–250; Alfred Runte, *Trains of Discovery: Western Railroads and the National Parks*, rev. ed. (Niwot, Colo.: Roberts Rinehart, 1990), pp. 22–30; Kirby Lambert, "The Lure of the Parks," *Montana The Magazine of Western History* 46 (spring 1996): 42–55.

24. Malone and Roeder, *Montana,* pp. 130–133; Bartlett, *A Wilderness Besieged,* pp. 120–121; Haines, *Yellowstone Story,* 2:31–32.
25. Bartlett, *A Wilderness Besieged,* pp. 122–129; Haines, *Yellowstone Story,* 2:32–33.
26. M. L. Joslyn to Patrick Conger, August 10, 1882, file "C. T. Hobart, Yell. Park Improv. Co.," box C-17, YNP; Conger to Henry Teller, September 20, 1882, ibid.; lease between Department of the Interior and C. T. Hobart and H. M. Douglas, September 1, 1882, ibid.; assignment of lease from C. Hobart, R. Hatch, and H. Douglas to YNPIC, December 4, 1883, ibid.
27. Bartlett, *A Wilderness Besieged,* pp. 129–131; Haines, *Yellowstone Story,* 1:272–273.
28. Baldwin, *Enchanted Enclosure,* pp. 85–93; Bartlett, *A Wilderness Besieged,* p. 44; Haines, *Yellowstone Story,* 1:277.
29. C. T. Hobart to F. J. Haynes, May 5, 1883, file "F. J. Haynes," box C-17, YNP; Mattes, "Yellowstone Cavalcade," pp. 48–49; Bartlett, *A Wilderness Besieged,* pp. 45–53; Haines, *Yellowstone Story,* 1:279–289.
30. *New York Times,* January 29, 1885, p. 3; Louis C. Cramton, *Early History of Yellowstone National Park and Its Relation to National Park Policies* (Washington, D.C.: U.S. Government Printing Office, 1932), n.p.; Bartlett, *A Wilderness Besieged,* pp. 137–144; Haines, *Yellowstone Story,* 1:268–270; Ise, *Our National Park Policy,* p. 36.
31. Haines, *Yellowstone Story,* 1:268–269; Ise, *Our National Park Policy,* pp. 37–38; Bartlett, *A Wilderness Besieged,* pp. 138–144; Chittenden, *Yellowstone National Park,* pp. 190–191; Cramton, *Early History of Yellowstone,* n.p.
32. *Livingston Enterprise,* March 4, 1893, p. 1; Haines, *Yellowstone Story,* 2:46-53; Bartlett, *A Wilderness Besieged,* pp. 146–152; L. Q. C. Lamar to Charles Gibson, March 20, 1886, including lease, file "Yellowstone Park Assoc.," box C-16, YNP.
33. Wayne Replogle, "History of Yellowstone National Park Concessions," MS, vertical file, YNP; Yancey lease, April 1, 1884, file "J. Yancey," box C-16, ibid.; contract between Department of the Interior and Eleanor N. McGowan, May 1, 1884, file "E. Wilson/W. Nichols, E. N. McGowan," ibid.; Joslyn to Conger, January 21, 1884, file "G. W. Marshall and G. G. Henderson," box C-17, ibid.; "Geo. W. Marshal[l], Housing and Transportation," ibid.; lease, Helen L. Henderson and Walter J. Henderson, March 3, 1885, file "H. L. and W. J. Henderson," ibid.; Joslyn to Haynes, October 7, 1884, file "F. J. Haynes," ibid.; "Haynes," chronology, ibid.; assignment of lease, James A. Clark to T. Stewart White, Thomas Friant, and Francis Letellier, February 17, 1885, file "Yellowstone Park Assoc.," box C-16, ibid.
34. *Livingston Enterprise,* June 12, 1885, p. 5; Lamar to Gibson, March 20, 1886, YNP; Replogle, "History of Yellowstone National Park Concessions," pp. 2–3; Bartlett, *A Wilderness Besieged,* pp. 152–157.
35. Henry Jacob Winser, *Yellowstone National Park: A Manual for Tourists* (New York: Putnam's, 1883), p. 90; Replogle, "History of Yellowstone National Park Concessions"; YNP; Haines, *Yellowstone Story,* 2:478.
36. Winser, *Yellowstone National Park,* p. 84; F. Jay Haynes, *Catalogue of Views Mammoth, Imperial, Stereoscopic* (Fargo, Dakota Territory: F. Jay Haynes, 1887).
37. Bartlett, *A Wilderness Besieged,* pp. 155–157; Haines, *Yellowstone Story,* 2:42–48.
38. Bartlett, *A Wilderness Besieged,* pp. 157–158; Haines, *Yellowstone Story,* 2:46.
39. Bartlett, *A Wilderness Besieged,* p. 159; Haines, *Yellowstone Story,* 2:46.

2. HARRY'S GRAND TOUR

1. See Raymond W. Rast, "Vistas, Visions, and Visitors: Creating the Myth of Yellowstone National Park, 1872–1915," *Journal of the West* 37 (April 1998): 80–89; and Chris J. Magoc, *Yellowstone: The Creation and Selling of an American Landscape, 1870–1903* (Albuquerque: University of New Mexico Press, 1999), for analyses of early efforts to shape opinion about the park. For a discussion of constructed landscapes, see William Cronon, ed., *Uncommon Ground: Rethinking the Human Place in Nature* (New York: Norton, 1995), particularly the essays by Ann Whiston Spirn, "Constructing Nature: The Legacy of Frederick Law Olmsted," and William Cronon, "The Trouble with Wilderness: or, Getting Back to the Wrong Nature."

2. "Miscellaneous files of Harry W. Child," microfilm, reel no. 1, Yellowstone Park Company Records, Burlingame Special Collections, Montana State University–Bozeman Libraries, Bozeman, Montana (hereafter cited as MSU-Bozeman); Carl J. White, "Financial Frustration in Territorial Montana," *Montana The Magazine of Western History* 17 (spring 1967): 44–45; B. C. Forbes, *Men Who Are Making the West* (New York: B. C. Forbes, 1923), pp. 322–343; Michael P. Malone, "The Gallatin Canyon and the Tides of History," *Montana The Magazine of Western History* 23 (summer 1973): 7; *The Anceneys of the Flying D Ranch* (Bozeman, Mont.: Gallatin County Historical Society, 1986).

3. Forbes, *Men Who Are Making the West,* pp. 335–338; White, "Financial Frustration," pp. 44–45.

4. Replogle, "History of Yellowstone National Park Concessions," YNP; "Wiley," file "W. W. Wylie, O. Anderson," box C-17, YNP; "Haynes," file "F. J. Haynes," ibid.; Haines, *Yellowstone Story,* 2:126.

5. Robert Shankland, *Steve Mather of the National Parks,* 3d ed. (New York: Knopf, 1970), p. 130; *Livingston Enterprise,* June 10, 1893, p. 5; June 17, 1893, p. 1; June 1, 1895, p. 1; May 15, 1897, p. 5; June 26, 1897, p. 5; November 27, 1897, p. 5; "Monida-Yellowstone," file "YPC," box C-4, YNP.

6. *Livingston Enterprise,* November 24, 1894, p. 1; October 12, 1895, p. 1; September 5, 1896, p. 5; July 3, 1897, p. 5.

7. *Livingston Enterprise,* December 5, 1896, p. 1; April 23, 1898, p. 4; transfer of lease, YPA to Yellowstone Park Hotel Company, December 9, 1909, file "Yellowstone Park Assoc.," box C-16, YNP. Petition, "YPA v. Northern Pacific RR Co. and Thomas F. Oakes, Henry C. Rouse, and Henry C. Payne, receivers," United States Circuit Court for the Eastern District of Wisconsin, ibid. Bartlett, in *A Wilderness Besieged,* pp. 173–177, provides a detailed discussion of the complex series of stock transfers that concluded with Child controlling the businesses.

8. Runte, *Trains of Discovery,* pp. 2, 24–25; Ise, *Our National Park Policy,* pp. 120–122; Arthur D. Martinson, *Wilderness Above the Sound: The Story of Mount Rainier National Park* (Niwot, Colo.: Roberts Rinehart, 1986), pp. 42–45.

9. Martinson, *Above the Sound,* pp. 42–45; Runte, *Trains of Discovery,* p. 52; Christine Barnes, *Great Lodges of the West* (Bend, Ore.: W. W. West, 1997), pp. 26, 33–35.

10. Department of the Interior, Yellowstone National Park, Office of the Superintendent, "Memo of Park Travel Season of 1913, 1914, 1915, 1916," file "Yellowstone National Park–Miscellaneous," box 3, Howard H. Hays Collection, AHC; *Livingston Enterprise,*

July 3, 1897, p. 5. A large contingent of Christian Endeavor tourists entered the park in 1897, forcing Child to more than double the number of coaches in his fleet. He began searching for larger coaches and by 1907 had commissioned the massive Abbot-Downing vehicles. See *The Land of Geysers: Yellowstone National Park* (St. Paul, Minn.: Northern Pacific Railway, 1910), p. 7. Bicyclists invaded the park in comparatively large numbers during the period between 1890 and 1910, causing administrators to post special rules to avoid conflict between wheelmen and horses. See *Livingston Enterprise,* May 16, 1896, p. 5; September 9, 1896, p. 1. For an exhaustive collection of park travel accounts and anecdotes, see Haines, *Yellowstone Story,* 2:100–160.

11. *Land of Geysers,* pp. 1–2; Winser, *Yellowstone National Park,* p. 90; Robert D. Kenney, *From Geyserdom to Show-Me Land* (Clyde Park, Mont.: Robert D. Kenney, 1926), pp. 9–10. Most arrivals at Livingston were couponers who had purchased package tickets, compelling them to travel on Yellowstone Park Transportation Company stages and stay in the hotel company lodgings. Others who debarked in Livingston with only rail passage were fair game for agents of the many independent camp and stagecoach companies.

12. *Land of Geysers,* pp. 5–7; Haines, *Yellowstone Story,* 2:102–106.

13. Haines, *Yellowstone Story,* 2:107–112; *Livingston Enterprise,* November 27, 1897, p. 1; September 23, 1899, p. 5.

14. Price, *A Summer on the Rockies,* p. 185; *Land of Geysers,* p. 10; Bartlett, *A Wilderness Besieged,* pp. 64–65; Haines, *Yellowstone Story,* 2:116–117.

15. Alfred Runte, *Yosemite: The Embattled Wilderness* (Lincoln: University of Nebraska Press, 1990), pp. 96, 144; Richard West Sellars, *Preserving Nature in the National Parks: A History* (New Haven, Conn.: Yale University Press, 1997), pp. 79–80.

16. *Land of Geysers,* pp. 10–11; David Leavengood, "A Sense of Shelter: Robert C. Reamer in Yellowstone National Park," *Pacific Historical Review* 54 (1985): 502–504; Mrs. Edward H. Johnson, "Diary of a Trip Through Yellowstone Park, 1905," vertical file, Burlingame Special Collections, MSU-Bozeman; Thomas Ryan to acting Superintendent, Yellowstone National Park, June 12, 1899, file "H. E. Klamer and C. A. Hamilton," box C-16, YNP; "Chronology of Concessions Contracts — Yellowstone National Park," MS, ibid.

17. Forbes, *Men Who Are Making the West,* p. 333. See Leavengood, "A Sense of Shelter," pp. 495–513, for an excellent overview of Reamer's architectural style. By the turn of the century, Child had adopted La Jolla as his winter headquarters, and his family purchased several homes there over the next two decades.

18. Leavengood, "A Sense of Shelter," p. 497; Bartlett, *A Wilderness Besieged,* pp. 180–186.

19. Haines, *Yellowstone Story,* 2:18–19, 49–51; *Livingston Enterprise,* June 13, 1896, p. 5; July 18, 1896, p. 5; October 30, 1897, p. 5; Edward H. Moorman, "Journal of Years of Work Spent in Yellowstone National Park, 1899–1948," MS, vertical file, accession no. 92-6, pp. 4, 6, YNP.

20. Harry Child to Howard Elliott, June 23, 1910, file "YP Boat Company, 1914–1930," box YPC-24, YNP; Eli Waters to Britton and Gray, June 21, 1910, ibid.; Britton and Gray to Hofer, June 22, 1910, ibid.; Thomas Cooper to Child, June 8, 1911, ibid.; Child to Elliott, June 4, 1911, ibid.; Warren Delano to Child, June 27, 1911, ibid.; Delano to De Witt Van Buskirk, May 18, 1911, ibid.; Delano to Elliott, May 18, 1911, ibid.; Elliott to

Child, May 26, 1911, ibid.; Delano to Child, May 31, 1911, ibid.; "Boat Co.," financial organization as of May, 1911, ibid.; contract between U.S. Department of the Interior and Thomas Elwood Hofer, November 12, 1907, file "T. E. Hofer," box C-16, YNP; articles of incorporation, Yellowstone Park Boat Company, May 1911, file "Yellowstone Park Boat Company," box C-1, YNP.

21. *Land of Geysers*, p. 10; Barbara H. Dittl and Joanne Mallmann, "Plain to Fancy: The Lake Hotel, 1889–1929," *Montana The Magazine of Western History* 34 (spring 1984): 32–45.

22. Menus from Lake Hotel, file "historical 1," box YPC-3, YNP; *Livingston Enterprise*, April 13, 1895, p. 5; May 30, 1896, p. 5; May 15, 1897, p. 5. Henry E. Klamer, who later operated a general store at Old Faithful, contracted to furnish the hotels with fresh beef and mutton. Howard Eaton, later a famous dude rancher who would have a major Yellowstone hiking trail named after him, first started in the park by supplying the milch cows from his ranch in Medora, North Dakota. See *Livingston Enterprise*, May 29, 1897, p. 5.

23. "Yellowstone National Park," promotional brochure published by the Burlington-Northern Pacific System, 1927, located at the Center for American History, University of Texas, Austin, Texas; Leavengood, "A Sense of Shelter," pp. 504–506; J. H. Raftery, *A Miracle in Hotel Building: The Dramatic Story of the Building of the New Canyon Hotel in Yellowstone Park* (Yellowstone National Park: Wyo.: Yellowstone Park Company, n.d.), pp. 9–13.

24. Leavengood, "A Sense of Shelter," p. 504; Raftery, *Miracle in Hotel Building*, pp. 3–5. A photograph of Reamer and the workers playing baseball in the snow is in a scrapbook at the Yellowstone National Park photo archive.

25. Bartlett, *A Wilderness Besieged*, pp. 153–155, 175; "Monida-Yellowstone," file "YPC," box C-4, YNP; J. E. Haynes, "Permanent Record," ibid.; "Haynes," file "F. J. Haynes," box C-17, YNP.; *Livingston Enterprise*, October 13, 1894, p. 6; November 27, 1897, p. 1; June 25, 1898, pp. 1, 8; September 3, 1898, p. 8. The record of the Haynes business ventures and contributions to Yellowstone is well documented. Jack Ellis Haynes was an amateur historian who carried on the family business, one aspect of which was publishing an annual park guidebook. Before his death in 1962, he was collaborating on a project with park historian Aubrey L. Haines that eventually became *The Yellowstone Story*. Many of the documents cited are handwritten notes that he compiled in the course of that research. The Haynes papers are held at Montana State University–Bozeman. Hamilton's story, much more intricately interwoven with that of the Child-Nichols family business, is less available. See Acting Superintendent to Secretary of Interior, June 16, 1915, file "H. E. Klamer and C. A. Hamilton," box C-16, YNP; "Chronology of Concessions Contracts," ibid.

26. Bartlett, *A Wilderness Besieged*, pp. 187–188; *Livingston Enterprise*, November 11, 1897, p. 1; June 25, 1898, p. 8; "Wiley," p. 1, YNP; Moorman, "Journal of Years in Yellowstone," pp. 1–9, ibid.

27. Ise, *Our National Park Policy*, pp. 39–40; Moorman, "Journal of Years in Yellowstone," p. 8, YNP; "Wiley," p. 2, ibid.; F. J. Haynes to James R. Hickey, September 2, 1917, box 16, folder 13, collection 1500, F. J. Haynes Papers, MSU-Bozeman; Dan Miles to Jack Ellis Haynes, May 9, 1951, box 39, folder 25, collection 1504, Jack Ellis Haynes Papers,

ibid.; *Livingston Enterprise*, September 4, 5, 1919. Miles, a nephew of the famous Indian fighter General Nelson A. Miles, was easily as polished a promoter as was Child. Some years earlier, he had purchased a "petrified man," believed to be the remains of General Thomas Francis Meagher, another notable soldier, discovered buried in a bank along the Missouri River. He exhibited the specimen around the country, garnering widespread attention and not inconsiderable profits. See *Livingston Enterprise*, January 13, 1900, p. 1. Child and Charles Anceney would eventually purchase Wylie's Gallatin Valley holdings as well and add them to their own Flying D Ranch.

28. Moorman, "Journal of Years in Yellowstone," p. 8, YNP; "Wiley," p. 2, ibid.; "Statement of Net Earnings, Wylie Camping Company, Dividends," box 16, folder 12, collection 1500, MSU-Bozeman; Department of the Interior, "Memo of Park Travel Season of 1913, 1914, 1915, 1916," AHC; "Earnings of Wylie Permanent Camping Company 1906–1916," ibid.; Maury Klein, *Union Pacific: The Rebirth, 1894–1969* (New York: Doubleday, 1990), p. 327.

29. Moorman, "Journal of Years in Yellowstone," YNP, provides some information on guest activities, especially during the early years of the camps. See also *Songs of the Yellowstone Park Camps* (Yellowstone National Park, Wyo.: Yellowstone Park Lodge and Camps Co., n.d.), file "miscellaneous," box 41, Arthur E. Demaray Collection, AHC; Haines, *Yellowstone Story*, 2:02, 137. Haines defines "rotten-logging" as "love in the moonlight," as discreet a description as any.

30. Runte, *Yosemite*, pp. 96, 102–103; Martinson, *Wilderness Above the Sound*, pp. 42–45; Barnes, *Great Lodges of the West*, p. 94; Shankland, *Steve Mather of the National Parks*, pp. 131–139.

31. "Wiley," p. 2, YNP; Richard A. Ballinger to Child, July 10, 1909, box 16, folder 11, collection 1500, MSU-Bozeman; contract between F. J. Haynes and Harry Child, September 22, 1909, ibid.

32. "Miscellaneous Files of Harry W. Child," p. 173, MSU-Bozeman; Leavengood, "A Sense of Shelter," p. 497; Forbes, *Men Who Are Making the West*, p. 328.

33. Rufus Steele, "Summer Savages," *The Outlook*, May 12, 1926, pp. 56–58; Haines, *Yellowstone Story*, 2:101–102.

34. John T. McCutcheon, *Drawn from Memory* (New York: Bobbs-Merrill, 1950), p. 76; Haines, *Yellowstone Story*, 2:113.

35. *Livingston Enterprise*, July 11, 1896, p. 5; August 7, 1897, p. 4; September 2, 1899, p. 1.

36. Press release, August 24, 1908, file "Historical 1, AP Reports, Resolutions," box YPC-3, YNP; S. B. M. Young to Major Allen, August 24, 1908, ibid.; *Livingston Enterprise*, September 4, 1897, p. 5; Haines, *Yellowstone Story*, 2:149–153.

37. William M. Nichols to Child, August 25, 1908, file "Historical 1," box YPC-3, YNP; George Whittaker to Nichols, August 25, 1908, ibid.; Child to Miss Frenzel, August 30, 1908, ibid.; Frenzel to Child, August 30, 1908, ibid.; Sergeant Weiss to Child, n.d., ibid.

38. Bartlett, *A Wilderness Besieged*, p. 175; contract, Anna K. Pryor and Elizabeth Trischman, April 10, 1916, file "Pryor and Pryor, Holm Trans. Co.," box C-16, YNP; "Permanent Record of J. E. Haynes," file "YPC," box C-4, YNP; *Livingston Enterprise*, August 7, 1897, p. 1; August 13, 1898, p. 1; June 10, 1899, p. 1; February 10, 1900, p. 5; Paul Schullery, "A Partnership in Conservation: Roosevelt & Yellowstone," *Montana The*

Magazine of Western History 28 (summer 1978): 2–15. Contingents of army troops and concessions executives escorted many of the dignitaries around the park, but all employees participated in the creation of a family atmosphere among Yellowstone personnel. On July 4, 1896, for example, Independence Day festivities at Mammoth included a baseball game between company workers and the soldiers stationed at Fort Yellowstone. See *Livingston Enterprise*, June 27, 1896, p. 1.

3. TRANSITIONS

1. "Holm," file "W. W. Wylie, O. Anderson," box C-17, YNP; "Hefferlin Camps," ibid.; "Monida-Yellowstone," file "YPC," box C-4, YNP; "Travel Memorandum, Yellowstone National Park for June, July, and August 1916 and 1917," file "historical 2," box YPC-3, YNP; "Chronology of Concessions Contracts, Yellowstone National Park," file "H. E. Klamer and C. A. Hamilton," box C-16, YNP; assignment of lease, George R. Pryor to Elizabeth Trischman, October 19, 1912, file "Pryor and Pryor, Holm Trans. Co.," ibid.; Acting Superintendent, Yellowstone National Park, to Secretary of the Interior, October 21, 1914, ibid.; blueprint of Canyon area, file "George Whittaker," ibid.

2. Congress authorized the secretary of the interior in the Sundry Civil Act of 1883 to call upon the military for assistance in managing the park. See Haines, *Yellowstone Story*, 1:325.

3. The ratio of rail to automobile travel was perhaps the most significant factor in forcing concessioners to change their well-constructed park routines. The effects of autos on the park were both immediate and permanent. In 1916, Yellowstone rail passengers totaled 15,762, while those visiting in private cars numbered 13,599. Ten years later, 40,960 arrived by train and 141,644 by auto; by 1936 the ratio was over twenty to one in favor of automobiles: 409,471 to 19,472. See box YPC-12, YNP, for statistics.

4. Richard A. Bartlett, "Those Infernal Machines in Yellowstone," *Montana The Magazine of Western History* 20 (July 1970): 16–26; Shankland, *Steve Mather of the National Parks*, p. 151; Ruth Kirk, *Sunrise to Paradise: The Story of Mount Rainier National Park* (Seattle: University of Washington Press, 1999), p. 75; "Travel Memorandum, 1916 and 1917," YNP; Child to James Hannaford, September 10, 1915, file "Railroads 1918–1938," box YPC-14, ibid.

5. Bartlett, "Those Infernal Machines in Yellowstone," pp. 16–26; Bartlett, *A Wilderness Besieged*, pp. 82–87; "Minutes of Concessioner Meeting," November 18, 1916, folder 20, box 22, collection 1500, MSU-Bozeman; "Travel Memorandum, 1916 and 1917," YNP. The Cody–Sylvan Pass Motor Company was owned by Child, Haynes, and the operators of the Shaw and Powell Camps Company; Child held approximately 35 percent, and Haynes 40 percent.

6. Nash, *Wilderness and the American Mind*, pp. 161–181; Stephen Fox, *John Muir and His Legacy: The American Conservation Movement* (Boston: Little, Brown, 1981), pp. 139–147; Elmo R. Richardson, "The Struggle for the Valley: California's Hetch-Hetchy Controversy, 1905–1913," *California Historical Quarterly* 38 (1959): 249–258; Ise, *Our National Park Policy*, pp. 85–96.

7. Public Law 235, *Statutes at Large*, (1915–1917), vol. 39, pt. 1, p. 535; William C. Everhart, *The National Park Service* (Boulder, Colo.: Westview Press, 1983), p. 16; Donald C. Swain, *Federal Conservation Policy, 1921–1933* (Berkeley: University of California Press, 1963), pp. 126–127; Shankland, *Steve Mather of the National Parks*, p. 14.

8. Franklin K. Lane to Stephen T. Mather, May 13, 1918, file "Mather-Albright 1915– 27," box 22, Conrad L. Wirth collection, AHC; Hubert Work to Mather, March 11, 1925, ibid.; *New York Times,* December 6, 1920, p. 18; "National Park Monopolies," *New York Times,* January 30, 1921, sec. 6, p. 5; "National Park Franchises," *New York Times,* February 13, 1921, sec. 6, p. 6. Mather's views were expressed in letters that he and assistant Horace Albright drafted for Interior secretaries Lane, Hubert Work, and John B. Payne.

9. Moorman, "Journal of Years in Yellowstone," pp. 14–15, YNP; Shankland, *Steve Mather of the National Parks,* pp. 120–128. Horace M. Albright and Robert Cahn, *The Birth of the National Park Service: The Founding Years, 1913–33* (Salt Lake City: Howe Brothers, 1985), discuss the relationship between Mather and Albright. For a comprehensive biography of Albright, see Donald C. Swain, *Wilderness Defender: Horace M. Albright and Conservation* (Chicago: University of Chicago Press, 1970).

10. "Minutes of Concessioner Meeting," November 18, 1916, MSU-Bozeman; F. J. Haynes to James R. Hickey, July 18, 1917, folder 13, box 16, MSU-Bozeman.

11. "Minutes of Stockholders' Meeting, Yellowstone Park Camping Company," May 11, 1918, file "YP Lodges and Camps," box YPC 14, YNP; "Minutes of Concessioner Meeting," November 18, 1916, MSU-Bozeman; F. J. Haynes to Hickey, July 18, 1917, ibid.

12. Kirk, *Sunrise to Paradise,* p. 79; Martinson, *Wilderness Above the Sound,* pp. 50–51; Barnes, *Great Lodges of the West,* pp. 69–77.

13. Oswald Garrison Villard, "A Park, a Man, and the Rest of Us," *Survey,* February 1, 1926, pp. 542–544; Shankland, *Steve Mather of the National Parks,* p. 36; Forbes, *Men Who Are Making the West,* pp. 333–334; John C. Miles, *Guardians of the Parks: A History of the National Parks and Conservation Association* (Washington, D.C.: Taylor and Francis, in cooperation with the National Parks and Conservation Association, 1995), pp. 15–20. Robert Underwood Johnson, *Remembered Yesterdays* (Boston: Little, Brown, 1923), pp. 192–195, details the role of *Century* magazine as a forum for national park promotion. See also Arthur John, *The Best Years of the Century: Richard Watson Gilder, Scribner's Monthly, and* Century Magazine, *1870–1909* (Chicago: University of Illinois Press, 1981).

14. Gerard J. Pesman and Helen I. Pesman, "Yellowstone's Transition from Stagecoaches to 'Yellow Buses,' " MS, p. 14, YNP; Richard P. Carlsberg, "The Lander-Yellowstone Transportation Co.," *Wind River Mountaineer* (Fremont County, Wyoming), April 1993, p. 13. Child's extension of his transportation business beyond park boundaries stimulated regional commerce in many ways, as park tourism was far and away the main source of income for northwestern Wyoming. Such establishments as the Brooks Lake Hotel, built specifically to serve Yellowstone travelers between Lander and Moran, rivaled the great park hotels and have remained popular.

15. W. H. Murray, *Geyserland: Yellowstone National Park* (Omaha, Nebr.: Union Pacific System, 1925), p. 33; Gerard J. Pesman, "Geysers and Gears," MS, pp. 19–21, YNP; Replogle, "History of Yellowstone National Park Concessions," p. 3, YNP. The obsolescence of the Fountain Hotel, which was closed in 1917, signified like no other single event the end of the stagecoach era. When NPS director Mather visited Yellowstone in 1925, shortly after a well-publicized excursion to Glacier National Park, where he dynamited a troublesome sawmill, Child, never one for sentiment, suggested that "if he has any sticks of dynamite left, he may slip them under the Fountain

Hotel." Child to Howard Hays, September 5, 1925, file "1925–26 correspondence," box 3, Howard H. Hays collection, AHC.

16. Murray, *Geyserland,* pp. 34–35; "Yellowstone National Park," promotional brochure issued by the Burlington Route and Northern Pacific Railroads, [1927], Center for American History, University of Texas, Austin, Texas, pp. 39–47.

17. Pesman, "Geysers and Gears," pp. 7–8, YNP; Bartlett, *A Wilderness Besieged,* pp. 93–94.

18. Pesman, "Geysers and Gears," pp. 6, 10, 16, YNP; Bartlett, *A Wilderness Besieged,* pp. 93–94.

19. Pesman, "Geysers and Gears, pp. 16, 18, 19, YNP; Bartlett, *A Wilderness Besieged,* p. 93.

20. Gerrit Fort to Hays, January 2, 1919, file "1916–19 correspondence," box 3, Howard H. Hays collection, AHC; Pesman and Pesman, "Yellowstone's Transition from Stagecoaches to Yellow Buses," p. 14, YNP; "Yellowstone Park Camping Co.," MS, file "Yellowstone Park Company," box C-4, YNP; U.S. Department of the Interior, Yellowstone National Park, Office of the Superintendent, *Annual Report of the Superintendent, Yellowstone National Park, for the Year 1917* (Washington, D.C.: U.S. Department of the Interior, National Park Service, 1917).

21. The classic work on tourism in the West, including changes created by the automobile, remains Earl Pomeroy, *In Search of the Golden West: The Tourist in Western America* (New York: Knopf, 1957). Rothman, *Devil's Bargains,* updates and expands the scholarship on tourism and landscape. Both the railroads and Child (and his successor, Billie Nichols) would spend the better part of the next twenty years trying to limit the impact of private autos on their businesses.

22. The stockholders of the new company included A. W. Miles, John D. Powell, Dan Miles, Eunice C. Shaw, Jessie E. Shaw, L. C. Shaw, W. C. Shaw, Alice Hight, and Viola Powell. See the two escrow receipts dated May 5, 1919, file "Yellowstone National Park Miscellaneous," box 3, Howard H. Hays Collection, AHC; also, escrow receipt, May 6, 1919, ibid.; Horace M. Albright, "Yellowstone's Camps," *New York Times,* February 20, 1921, sec. 7, p. 7; Moorman, "Journal of Years in Yellowstone," YNP. The stock transaction that was to have occurred became the basis for a later lawsuit between Haynes and Child. The stock had split in 1912, which meant that Haynes, although still owning one-third of the company, now held 666⅔ shares of stock. Mather's deal specified that Child was to purchase Haynes's interest, but he only had to deliver into escrow 333⅓ shares. Hence, Child divided the remaining 333⅓ between Miles and Nichols. Later, when Mather discovered this loophole in the agreement, Child surrendered the stock. See F. J. Haynes to Hickey, July 18, 1917, folder 13, box 16, collection 1500, MSU-Bozeman; Hickey to Haynes, August 20, 1917, ibid.; Hickey to Haynes, September 15, 1917, ibid.

23. Howard H. Hays, "Occupation: Howard H. Hays' Chronology to the Present," file "Yellowstone National Park — Miscellaneous," box 3, Howard H. Hays Collection, AHC; *Salt Lake Evening Telegram,* October 30, 1914.

24. Bartlett, *A Wilderness Besieged,* p. 174; Shankland, *Steve Mather of the National Parks,* p. 125; Hays to Walter White, March 27, 1919, file "1916–1919 correspondence," box 3, Howard H. Hays Collection, AHC; Hays to Fort, December 28, 1918, ibid.

25. James H. Pickering, foreword to *The Rocky Mountain Wonderland,* by Enos A. Mills (Lincoln: University of Nebraska Press, 1991), p. xxx; Hays to Fort, December 28, 1918, file "1916–1919 correspondence," box 3, Howard H. Hays Collection, AHC; Fort to Hays, January 2, 1919, ibid.; Horace M. Albright to Hays, January 2, 1919, ibid.; Emery

to Hays, [December 1918?], ibid. White was well equipped to finance such a transaction; his war-tax bill for 1918 totaled over $4 million. He also likely bankrolled Emery in his Rocky Mountain Transportation enterprise.

26. Hays to Emery, January 4, 1919, file "1916–1919 correspondence," box 3, Howard H. Hays Collection, AHC; Hays to Fort, January 4, 1919, ibid.; Hays to Mather and Albright, January 4, 1919, ibid.

27. Hays to Mather and Albright, December 28, 1918, file "1916–1919 correspondence," box 3, Howard H. Hays Collection, AHC; Hays to Albright, January 20, 1919, ibid.; Hays to Fort, January 22, 1919, ibid.; Child to Hays, January 27, 1919, ibid.; White to Hays, January 28, 1919, ibid.; A. W. Miles to Hays, January 31, 1919, ibid.

28. Hays to White, January 29, March 27, 1919, file "1916–1919 correspondence," box 3, Howard H. Hays Collection, AHC; Hays to Emery, January 30, 1919, ibid.; Hays to Fort, February 3, April 10, 1919, ibid.; Child to Hays, February 14, 1919, ibid.; escrow receipt, May 6, 1919, ibid.; escrow receipt, May 5, 1919, ibid.

29. Moorman, "Journal of Years in Yellowstone," pp. 17–19, YNP; "Comparative Travel Statistics for Yellowstone Park During 1919 and 1920 to September 18th," file "travel 1918–1920," box YPC 12, YNP; Haines, Yellowstone Story, 2:361.

30. White to Hays, October 2, 1922, file "1920–1924 correspondence," box 3, Howard H. Hays Collection, AHC; White to Hays, October 7, 1922, March 17, 1924, ibid.; Hays to Emery, April 2, 1923, ibid.

31. Bartlett, A Wilderness Besieged, p. 174; White to Hays, March 17, 24, April 2, 28, 1924, file "1920–1924 correspondence," box 3, Howard H. Hays Collection, AHC; Hays to Child, March 23, 1924, ibid.; Child to Hays, March 24, 1924, ibid.; Emery to Hays, March 29, 1924, ibid.

32. Press release, [1924], file "YP Lodges and Camps," box YPC 14, YNP; Vernon Goodwin to Hays, February 28, 1924, file "1920–1924 correspondence," box 3, Howard H. Hays Collection, AHC; Hays to Child, March 25, 1924, ibid.; E. H. Moorman to Emery, April 24, 1924, ibid.; Emery to Moorman, April 25, 1924, ibid.; Taylor B. Weir to Vard Smith, April 28, 1924, ibid.; White to Hays, April 13, 1925, ibid.; "Minutes of Directors' Meeting of Yellowstone Park Camps Company," May 8, 1924, ibid.

33. Hays, "Occupation," AHC; Emery to Hays, March 29, April 25, 1924, file "1920–1924 correspondence," box 3, Howard H. Hays Collection, AHC; Hays to White and Emery, May 9, 1925, file "1925–1926 correspondence," box 3, AHC; Child to Hays, July 6, 1925, ibid. Hays, White, and Emery profited handsomely in the transaction and remained active in national park operations elsewhere. That same year Hays became president of the Sequoia and Kings Canyon National Parks Companies; in 1926 he added the Glacier National Park Transport Company to his portfolio. He retained these businesses for almost thirty years. White and Emery, close friends as well as business associates, likely benefited financially from his acquisitions.

34. Lane to Mather, May 13, 1918, AHC; Work to Mather, March 11, 1925, ibid.; "For National Park Needs," New York Times, December 6, 1920, p. 18; "National Park Monopolies," New York Times, January 30, 1921, sec. 6, p. 5; "National Park Franchises," New York Times, February 13, 1921, sec. 6, p. 6.

35. Barnes, Great Lodges of the West, pp. 91–94; Runte, Yosemite, p. 145; Don Hummel, Stealing the National Parks (Bellevue, Wash.: Free Enterprise Press, 1987), pp. 64, 88–89.

36. Barnes, *Great Lodges of the West,* pp. 23–31, 79–87; Shankland, *Steve Mather of the National Parks,* pp. 138–140. Rothman, *Devil's Bargains,* pp. 50–80, provides the best discussion of concessions and tourism at the Grand Canyon.

37. Bartlett, *A Wilderness Besieged,* pp. 327–341; Sellars, *Preserving Nature in the National Parks,* pp. 47–82.

38. Bartlett, *A Wilderness Besieged,* pp. 194–202. The loose standards of concessioner control are discussed in Shankland, *Steve Mather of the National Parks,* pp. 114–127.

39. Annual Report, 1925, Yellowstone Park Transportation Company, file "YP Transportation company," box C-4, YNP; Annual Report, 1928, ibid.; Annual Report, 1929, ibid.; Annual Report, Yellowstone Park Hotel Company, 1925, file "YPHC," box C-1, YNP; Annual Report, 1928, ibid.; Annual Report, 1929, ibid.; Annual Report, 1925, Yellowstone Park Lodge and Camps Company, ibid.; Annual Report, 1928, ibid.; Annual Report, 1929, ibid.; Annual Report, Yellowstone Park Boat Company, 1928, ibid.; Annual Report, 1923, file "YP Boat Company, 1914–1930," box YPC-24, YNP; "History of the Yellowstone Park Company," auditor's report, MS, n.d., box YPC-149, YNP.

40. "Interior Department Schedule, 1929," box C-8, YNP; Annual Reports, 1925–1929, Yellowstone Park Hotel Company, ibid.; Annual Reports, 1925–1929, Yellowstone Park Lodge and Camps Company, ibid.; Annual Reports, 1925–1929, Yellowstone Park Transportation Company, ibid.; Annual Reports, 1923–1928, Yellowstone Park Boat Company, ibid.

41. Correspondence file, Inter-Mountain Secret Service Detective Bureau, Inc., file "Business Correspondence 1930," box YPC-34, YNP; Nichols to B. H. Taylor, March 8, 1931, file "Railroads 40 #1," box YPC-12, YNP; Max Goodsill to Nichols, March 5, 1931, file "Railroads 40 #2," ibid.; W. S. Basinger to Nichols, September 24, 1931, file "Hertz Drive ur Self System," box YPC-16, YNP.

42. John Hertz to Mather, May 10, 1926, file "Hertz Drive ur self system," box YPC-16, YNP; "Brief of the Yellowstone Park Transportation Company and Yellowstone Park Hotel Company Opposing Application in the Matter of the Application of Hertz Driveurself System for License in Yellowstone National Park," ibid.; "Brief of the Rainier National Park Company in Opposition," ibid.; "Brief of the Glacier Park Transportation Company in Opposition," ibid.; transcript of Department of Interior hearing, Washington, D.C., November 13–15, 1926, pp. 40–41, 50–51, ibid.; Mather to Nichols, June 7, 1927, ibid.; Bartlett, *A Wilderness Besieged,* p. 175.

43. Bartlett, *A Wilderness Besieged,* p. 195; Haines, *Yellowstone Story,* 2:460; Albright and Cahn, *Birth of the National Park Service,* pp. 123–125, 227. Albright insists that he was rigorous in his oversight of park concession matters and not at all friendly with Child, but correspondence among participants in the camping company episode suggests otherwise. See Hays to Fort, January 22, 1919, file "1916–1919 correspondence," box 3, Howard H. Hays collection, AHC; Albright to Hays, February 2, 9, 1919, ibid.; Child to Hays, February 14, 1919, ibid.; Child to Hays, July 6, 1925, file "1925–26 correspondence," ibid.

44. Forbes, *Men Who Are Making the West,* pp. 330–332.

45. *New York Times,* November 20, 1931, p. 20; Guy D. Edwards to Albright, January 19, 1932, file "YPHC Annual Report," box C-1, YNP; Forbes, *Men Who Are Making the West,* pp. 328–329.

4. DEFENDING THE EMPIRE

1. The legacy of Mather and Albright was especially influential in future dealings between the NPS and concessioners. They had established a tradition of promotion and development that required a partnership with park operators, and tradition was the most important force in guiding NPS policy in later years. Directors Arno B. Cammerer, Arthur Demaray, and Conrad Wirth, career NPS men, carried on this practice of close cooperation; Newton P. Drury, the one outsider to hold the directorship, broke from tradition and consequently earned the enmity of concessioners and fellow NPS administrators alike.

2. Taylor Weir to A. M. Gotttschald, December 6, 1938, file "Railroads 1938," box YPC-14, YNP; E. H. Moorman to Hugh D. Galusha, March 17, 1932, file "YP Lodges and Camps," ibid.; Guy D. Edwards to Albright, January 19, 1932, file "YPHC Annual Report," box C-1, YNP; W. M. Nichols to Galusha, March 25, 1940, file "Auditor 1937–42," box YPC-78, YNP; Galusha to Nichols, March 21, 1940, ibid.; Roger Toll to Arno B. Cammerer, October 21, 1935, file "YP Lodges and Camps 1932–37," box YPC-14, YNP.

3. W. M. Nichols to R. H. Kelley, December 20, 1930, file "YP Lodge and Camps," box YPC-14, YNP; Nichols to Douglas MacArthur, April 17, June 10, 1951, file "M," box YPC-151, YNP.; press release, October 16, 1926, file "Park travel 1926," box YPC-11, YNP.; Bartlett, *A Wilderness Besieged*, p. 175.

4. Nichols to Galusha, December 16, 1936, January 11, 1937, file "Auditor 1937–42," box YPC-78, YNP; Nichols to Goodwin, January 11, 1937, ibid.; Galusha to Nichols, December 16, 1936, ibid.; Nichols to Galusha, August 20, 28, 1941, file "Wood, Struthers and Co.," box YPC-47, YNP; M. B. Milligan to Weir, Clift & Bennett, November 26, 1941, file "Historical," box YPC-2, YNP. Albright championed the concessioner cause both during his tenure as NPS director and after resigning to become head of United States Potash Company in 1933. He regularly advised Nichols, Haynes, and Hamilton on contract matters and visited Yellowstone each year through the 1970s. For insight into the relationship between Albright and the concessioners, see Albright to J. E. Haynes, March 15, 1933, folder 6, box 2, collection 1504, MSU-Bozeman; collection of letters in folder 10, box 2, ibid.

5. Haynes to Albright, October 29, 1920, file "Operators," box C-1, YNP; Albright to Haynes, November 4, 1920, ibid.; Nichols to Paul R. Greever, June 16, 1936, file "Gasoline Tax 1937–42," box YPC-17, YNP.

6. W. M. Nichols to Huntley Child Jr., February 16, 1938, file "Historical," box YPC-2, YNP; F. E. Kammermeyer to Nichols, May 10, 1933, file "Supt. of Trans. 1929–1932," box YPC-15, YNP; Nichols to Kammermeyer, December 17, 1935, ibid.; J. R. Van Slycke to H. B. Brown, March 21, 1940, file "American Automobile Association," box YPC-31, YNP; Nichols to Brown, January 15, 1945, file "Art Shops, 1940–45, box YPC-6, YNP.

7. Press release, October 1929, file "Park Travel 1929," box YPC-12, YNP; press release, October 1931, file "Park Travel 1931," ibid.; press release, October 1932, file "Park Travel 1932," ibid.; E. E. Nelson to Nichols, July 18, 1934, file "Railroads 1933–1934," box YPC-12, YNP; Goodsill to Nichols, January 21, 1932, file "Railroads 40 (3)," box YPC-13, YNP.

8. House counts for Canyon, Mammoth, Lake, and Old Faithful hotels for years 1929–1933, file "Park travel 1933," box YPC-12, YNP; Nichols to Goodsill, March 20, 1931, file "Railroads 40 (1)," ibid.; E. E. Nelson to Nichols, December 19, 1932, file "Railroads 40 (3)," box YPC-13, YNP.

9. Ise, *Our National Park Policy,* p. 356; Goodsill to Nichols, January 21, 1932, YNP; A. Cotsworth Jr., "Memorandum of Yellowstone Park Matters for Season of 1938," file "Railroads 1938," box YPC-14, YNP; itinerary for Tour No. 16, file "Railroads 40 (3)," box YPC-13, YNP; Nelson to Nichols, July 18, 1934, file "Railroads 1933–34," box YPC-12, YNP; Goodsill to Nichols, February 18, March 5, 1931, file "Railroads 40 (2)," ibid.; R. W. Clark to Nichols, April 7, 1936, file "Railroads 1936," ibid.; Nelson to Nichols, April 6, 1936, ibid.; press release, October 1933, file "Park travel 1933," ibid.; Nichols to Goodsill, April 6, 1933, file "Railroads 40 (4)," ibid. Ironically, the Yellowstone Park Company, which had developed the regimented tours and had made it possible to see the park in a short time, was now attempting to lure tourists for stays of longer duration.

10. Hillary A. Tolson, *Historic Listing of National Park Service Officials* (Washington, D.C.: U.S. Department of the Interior, National Park Service, 1964), p. 9; "History of the Yellowstone Park Company," box YPC-149, YNP; Weir to Gottschald, December 6, 1938, ibid.; Nichols to Huntley Child Jr., February 16, 1938, ibid.; "Yellowstone Park Company Income and Expense Report for Year Ended September 30, 1936," file "YPC Annual Report 1936–48," box C-2, YNP.

11. Annual Reports, Yellowstone Park Lodge and Camps Company, for years 1932–1935, file "YPLCC Annual Report," box C-1, YNP; Moorman, "Journal of Years in Yellowstone," pp. 17–19, ibid.; Haines, *Yellowstone Story,* 2:361.

12. The best way to track the growth of individual developed areas in the park is through the excellent location maps published in the *Haynes' Guides* of the 1920s and 1930s.

13. "Yellowstone National Park," promotional brochure issued by the Burlington Route and Northern Pacific Railroads, [1927], Center for American History, University of Texas, Austin, Texas, pp. 20–21; Yellowstone Park Lodge and Camps Company pamphlet, file "YP Lodges and Camps," box YPC-14, YNP; "Number of Cabins at Lodges and Tourist Cabins, October 15, 1936," file "YP Lodge and Camps 1932–1937," ibid.; "1936 Lodges and Tourist Cabins Records," file "Park travel 1936," box YPC-12, YNP; Jack Ellis Haynes, *Haynes' New Guide to Yellowstone National Park* (Yellowstone National Park, Wyo.: Haynes, Inc., 1936). The Haynes location maps provide detailed schematics of each area.

14. "Yellowstone National Park," Burlington Route and Northern Pacific brochure, p. 21; Pesman, "Geysers and Gears," pp. 10–11, YNP; Goodwin to Goodsill, August 30, 1935, file "Railroads 1935," box YPC-12, YNP.

15. House counts for Canyon, Lake, Mammoth, and Old Faithful hotels, YNP; Cotsworth Jr., "Memorandum of Yellowstone Park Matters," ibid.; Roger Toll to Goodwin, September 4, 1935, file "YP Lodges and Camps 1932–1937," box YPC-14, YNP; "Memorandum of Conclusions Reached on Yellowstone Park Matters, November 4, 1938," file "Railroads 1938," ibid.; press release, October 1934, file "Park Travel 1934," box YPC-12, YNP; press release, October 1935, file "Park travel 1935," ibid.; press release, October 1936, file "Park travel 1936," ibid.; press release, October, 1937, file "Park travel 1937," ibid.

16. Notice of sale, April 25, 1938, file "Supt. of Trans. 1929–1932," box YPC-15, YNP; Suzanne

Miotti to Nichols, December 28, 1942, file "buses 1935–1944," box YPC-17, YNP; inventory of sale items, June 29, 1939, ibid.; Nichols to E. C. Crimmins, April 25, 1938, ibid.; purchase order, F. E. Kammermeyer to White Motor Company, April 1, 8, 1925, ibid.; option agreement between YPC and Gregory Linder, March 9, 1940, ibid.

17. Jack Croney to W. M. Nichols, May 23, 1931, March 30, 1934, file "Yellowstone Park Boat Company 1930–34," box YPC-25, YNP; Joe Joffe to Arno Cammerer, March 26, 1934, ibid.; W. M. Nichols to Croney, February 22, 1934, ibid.

18. *Park Structures and Facilities* (Washington, D.C.: U.S. Department of the Interior, National Park Service, Branch of Planning, 1935), p. 3. NPS policy under Mather is well summarized in Richard West Sellars, "Manipulating Nature's Paradise: National Park Management Under Stephen T. Mather, 1916–1929," *Montana The Magazine of Western History* 43 (spring 1993): 2–13, and in Sellars's *Preserving Nature in the National Parks*, pp. 47–90. Albright's record as director is less easily unearthed: his own account, in Albright and Cahn, *Birth of the National Park Service*, is often contradicted by primary documents. Without question, however, he attempted to follow the policies and practices Mather had instituted. Examples of NPS success in promoting the parks can be found in widely diverse publications. See "Glimpses of Summer Playgrounds," *Literary Digest*, June 7, 1930, especially Albright's sidebar; "Western National Parks Invite America Out of Doors," *National Geographic Magazine*, July 1934, pp. 65–80; Henry Wellington Wack, "Travel Through Our National Parks and Scenic West," *Arts and Decoration*, June 1930, pp. 68–69, 105.

19. Press release no. 1936-32, file "Publicity," box K-22, YNP; press release no. 1936-33, ibid.

20. Address by Harold L. Ickes, secretary of the interior, at 1934 Superintendents' Conference, Washington, D.C., November 20, 1934, file "Historical," box YPC-2, YNP.

21. Sellars, *Preserving Nature in the National Parks*, pp. 91–101; Runte, *National Parks*, pp. 138–139.

22. Ickes address, YNP; Dilsaver, *America's National Park System*, pp. 135–136; Ronald A. Foresta, *America's National Parks and Their Keepers* (Washington, D.C.: Resources for the Future, 1984), pp. 45–46; Martinson, *Wilderness Above the Sound*, pp. 54–57; Albright and Cahn, *Birth of the National Park Service*, p. 254.

23. A. C. McIntosh, "Who Owns Yellowstone Park?" *American Mercury*, April 1936, pp. 493–496.

24. A. A. Tison to John Eric Bibby, June 28, 1940, file "1940 B Miscellaneous," box YPC-38, YNP; D. B. Martin to Tison, June 25, 1940, ibid.; Galusha to Bibby, January 12, 1940, ibid.; Helen Connors to Bibby, October 9, 1939, ibid.; Connors to Bureau of Licenses, State of California, September 29, 1939, ibid.; William J. Burns National Adjustment Service, Inc., to YPC, August 24, 1940, ibid.

25. Nichols to Galusha, August 29, 1942, file "1942 Wm. Nichols," box YPC-50, YNP; Goodwin to Galusha, February 22, November 22, 1942, file "Vernon Goodwin," box YPC-49, YNP; "Summary of Equipment on Hand and Sold," file "Buses 1935–44," box YPC-18, YNP.

26. Ise, *Our National Park Policy*, pp. 451–452.

27. "Accommodations and Services, Yellowstone National Park, Season of 1943," press release, August 30, 1943, file "Accommodations in Park, 1943–45," box YPC-5, YNP; press release, May 25, 1943, ibid.; "Schedule, Concession Facilities Available, Summer Season 1943," ibid.; Newton P. Drury, "Statement Concerning Facilities Available to

the Public in National Park Areas During the 1943 Season," ibid.; Nichols to Fred A. Noble, May 9, 1944, file "Office of Defense Transportation, 1941–46," box YPC-19, YNP.

28. W. M. Nichols to C. P. Dickson, May 4, 1944, file "Business Correspondence 1944," box YPC-34, YNP; W. M. Nichols to Charles A. Hamilton, January 23, 1945, file "Art Shops 1940–45," box YPC-6, YNP; W. M. Nichols to Robert S. Caird, November 16, 1942, file "Railroads 1942–43," box YPC-31, YNP; Hamilton to Galusha, December 6, 1942, file "1942 C. A. Hamilton," box YPC-49, YNP; Galusha to J. Q. Nichols, October 2, 1942, file "1942 J. Q. Nichols," box YPC-50, YNP; Joe Bill to Jack Ellis Haynes, various dates, folder 14, box 4, collection 1504, MSU-Bozeman.

29. Galusha to W. M. Nichols, March 8, 1944, file "Liquor in Park 1934–1946," box YPC-5, YNP; "Accommodations and Services, Yellowstone National Park, Season of 1944," file "Business Correspondence 1944," box YPC-34, YNP; W. M. Nichols to Galusha, December 27, 1944, file "J. Q. Nichols 1941–1946," box YPC-3, YNP; Galusha to W. M. Nichols, January 17, 1944, file "Auditor 1943–46," box YPC-78, YNP.

30. Galusha to W. M. Nichols, September 26, 1942, file "1942 J. Q. Nichols," box YPC-50, YNP; Galusha to Adelaide Casserly, September 26, 1942, ibid.; Galusha to Dean Nichols, September 26, 1942, ibid.; Galusha to John Q. Nichols, September 26, 1942, ibid.; allowance receipts, Marie Child, Huntley Child Jr., and Marion Child Sanger, file "1942 H. W. Child Trust," box YPC-48, YNP; Galusha to Adelaide D. Child, March 4, 1942, file "1942 Miscellaneous," ibid.; Dean Nichols to Galusha, November 13, 1941, file "1941 N Miscellaneous," box YPC-46, YNP; W. M. Nichols to Karl Kenyon, August 16, 1951, file "K," box YPC-150, YNP; Adelaide Casserly to W. M. Nichols, May 20, 1951, file "A," box YPC-151, YNP; Dean Nichols to W. M. Nichols, n.d., file "D," ibid.; Dean Nichols to W. M. Nichols, July 2, 1951, ibid.; Joan Casserly to W. M. Nichols, file "J," ibid.; W. M. Nichols to John Q. Nichols Jr., ibid. Box YPC-43 contains a file labeled "H. W. Child Trust Vouchers 1941," which provides numerous examples of allowance amounts and disbursements.

31. "Accommodations and Services, Yellowstone National Park, Season of 1945," file "Accommodations in Park 1943–45," box YPC-5, YNP; W. M. Nichols to Goodwin, June 26, August 24, 1945, file "Historical," box YPC-2, YNP; W. M. Nichols to Goodwin, J. Q. Nichols, and Huntley Child Jr., July 13, 1945, ibid.; press release, August 25, 1945, file "Business Correspondence 1945," box YPC-34, YNP; Edmund B. Rogers to Operators, Yellowstone National Park, ibid.; W. M. Nichols to Drury, August 31, 1945, ibid.; transcript of radio announcement, August 30, 31, ibid.

32. Press release, August 25, 1945, file "Business Correspondence 1945," box YPC-34, YNP; "Yellowstone Park — Travel Statistics," file "H," box YPC-151, YNP; press release, October 31, 1945, file "YNP Diamond Jubilee Material," box 3, Merrill J. Mattes collection, AHC. Rail travel to Yellowstone was by this time relatively insignificant except to Nichols and the lines themselves.

33. Hummel, *Stealing the National Parks,* pp. 25–29; Ronald A. Foresta, *America's National Parks and Their Keepers* (Washington, D.C.: Resources for the Future, 1984), p. 50; Stanford E. Demars, *The Tourist in Yosemite, 1855–1985* (Salt Lake City: University of Utah Press, 1991), pp. 22–24; Taylor B. Weir, "Statement," *Concessions in National Parks: Hearings Before A Subcommittee on Public Lands of the Committee on Public Lands, House of Representatives, Eighty-first Congress, First Session, Making Study of Problems in Connection with the Public Lands of the United States Pursuant to H. Res. 66, Held*

at Santa Fe, N. Mex., November 12, 1949 (Washington, D.C.: U.S. Government Printing Office, 1950), pp. 87–104.

34. Hummel, *Stealing the National Parks*, pp. 133–135; Byron Harvey Jr. to Members, Western Conference National Park Concessioners, May 2, 1947, file "Concession Contracts," box YPC-75, YNP; Daggett Harvey to Members, Western Conference National Park Concessioners, August 9, 1949, ibid.; Miller Matthews to Hugh D. Galusha Jr., January 29, 1955, folder 46, box 6, collection 1504, MSU-Bozeman; Howard H. Hays, "Occupation Chronology," file "Yellowstone National Park — Miscellaneous," box 3, Howard H. Hays collection, AHC.

35. Sellars, "Manipulating Nature's Paradise," pp. 4–6; Shankland, *Steve Mather of the National Parks*, pp. 207–208; Runte, *Yosemite*, pp. 152–153; Haines, *Yellowstone Story*, 2:459–460. Huntley Child Jr. to W. M. Nichols, February 11, 1953, file "WMN 1946–1947," box YPC-2, YNP; Nichols to Child Jr., March 17, November 2, 1953, ibid.; Wesley A. D'Ewart to Nichols, March 2, 1953, ibid. Despite disagreeing over closing facilities during the war, Nichols enjoyed a good relationship with NPS director Drury.

36. Hummel, *Stealing the National Parks*, pp. 130–140; Ise, *Our National Park Policy*, pp. 459–464; NPS press release, August 12, 1948, file "National Parks General Problems, 1948–1972," box 3, Devereux Butcher collection, AHC; J. E. Haynes to Daggett Harvey and W. M. Nichols, July 24, 1949, file "Business Correspondence 1948–49," box YPC-34, YNP; Weir, "Statement," pp. 51–53.

37. Hummel, *Stealing the National Parks*, pp. 130–140; Weir, "Statement," pp. 87–104; Goodsill to J. E. Haynes, October 4, 1949, folder 18, box 9, collection 1504, MSU-Bozeman; Haynes to Hays, July 30, 1949, folder 4, box 37, ibid.; Haynes to W. M. Nichols, April 16, 1948, folder 22, box 40, ibid.; Weir to W. M. Nichols, February 26, 1950, file "Concession Contracts," box YPC-75, YNP. Byron Harvey Jr. to Members, WCNPC, May 2, 1947, ibid. Throughout the unpleasant negotiations, concessioners continued to cultivate personal relationships with Interior Department officials. Jack E. Haynes, always a conciliatory presence, was perhaps the most active. He and Davidson belonged to the same college fraternity and addressed each other as "brother" in their correspondence. Haynes even entertained Krug on a visit to Yellowstone, but his loyalty to the concessioner cause was apparent in private correspondence with other members of the WCNPC. See Julius Krug to Haynes, August 15, 1947, folder 15, box 38, collection 1504, MSU-Bozeman; Haynes to C. Girard Davidson, January 1, 1950, folder 23, box 6, ibid.; Haynes to Hays, July 30, 1949, folder 4, box 37, ibid.

38. Ise, *Our National Park Policy*, pp. 462–463; Davidson to Oscar Chapman December 18, 1950, file "H," box YPC-151, YNP; Haynes to George Baggley, March 1, 1952, folder 26, box 2, collection 1504, MSU-Bozeman; Haynes to J. Q. Nichols, March 4, 1952, folder 20, box 40, ibid.; Weir, "Statement," pp. 88–92.

39. Herman Hoss, "Possessory Interest," MS, file "Yellowstone Park Company Background Information," box YPC-97, YNP.

40. Fred T. Burke, "Springtime in Yellowstone," *Yellowstone Gateway Post* (West Yellowstone, Montana), December 1993, pp. 13–16; W. M. Nichols to Weir, April 13, 1944, file "Liquor in Park 1934–1946," box YPC-5, YNP; W. M. Nichols to Rogers, March 29, 1944, ibid.; W. M. Nichols to Galusha, March 17, 1944, ibid.; B. O. Hallin, "List of Construction," September 2, 1952, file "historical 1," box YPC-3, YNP; "Statement of

Income and Expense," file "Annual Reports YPC 1949–1959," box C-3, YNP; Haines, *Yellowstone Story*, 2:372.

41. W. M. Nichols to Albright, September 15, 1951, file "A," box YPC-151, YNP; Olaus J. Murie to Frederick Law Olmsted, January 16, 1950, file "Correspondence 1950–1966," box 3, Adolph Murie collection, AHC; Foresta, *America's National Parks and Their Keepers*, p. 50; Haines, *Yellowstone Story*, 2:368–372.

5. THE COMING CRISIS

1. John Q. Nichols to Lelland M. Cowan, September 12, 1952, file "Hollenstein Case," box YPC-54, YNP; H. Sengstacken to J. Q. Nichols, March 14, 1951, file "Business correspondence 1951," box YPC-34, YNP; Fred T. Burke to Trevor Povah, February 17, 1953, file "YPSS and Trev Povah, 1953," box YPC-63, YNP; Charles Gallagher to Povah, January 28, 1953, ibid.; Povah to Burke, February 24, 1953, ibid.; Burke to W. M. Nichols, January 27, 1953, ibid.; Povah to Willis Johnson, January 30, 1953, ibid.; W. M. Nichols to Burke, February 2, 1953, ibid.

2. Hollis Farwell to Galusha, March 26, 1940, file "Hugh D. Galusha — Personal, 1940," box YPC-38, YNP; Hamilton to Mattson Navigation Company, March 21, 1940, ibid.; Hamilton to Galusha, November 20, 1942, file "C. A. Hamilton," box YPC-49, YNP; "Affidavit of May E. Hamilton,"ibid.; "Affidavit of Charles A. Hamilton," ibid.; Hamilton to W. M. Nichols, April 8, 1943, file "Accommodations in Park 1943–45," box YPC-5, YNP; Galusha to W. M. Nichols, March 8, 1944, file "Liquor in Park 1934-46," ibid.; Galusha to W. M. Nichols, January 15, 1946, file "Auditor 1943-46," box YPC-78, YNP; W. M. Nichols to Galusha, April 5, 1945, ibid.; Huntley Child Jr. to W. M. Nichols, February 11, 1953, file "W. M. Nichols 1946–57," box YPC-2, YNP; W. M. Nichols to Child Jr., February 16, 1953, ibid.; Edmund T. Fritz to Conrad L. Wirth, August 5, 1955, file "Yellowstone Park Service Stations," box YPC-19, YNP; Wirth to Solicitor, National Park Service, August 23, 1955, ibid.; Fritz to Wirth, August 26, 1955, ibid.; "Memorandum," W. M. Nichols to Child Jr., Galusha, and Weir, February 26, 1952, file "Business Correspondence 1952," box YPC-34, YNP; W. M. Nichols to Child Jr., February 27, 1952, ibid.; Hamilton to W. M. Nichols, February 20, 1952, ibid.; Galusha to W. M. Nichols, March 3, 1952, ibid.

3. For discussions of the NPS-concessioner relationship, see Sellars, "Manipulating Nature's Paradise," pp. 2–6; Peter J. Blodgett, "Striking a Balance: Managing Concessions in the National Parks, 1916–33," *Forest and Conservation History* 34 (April 1990): 60–68; Richard A. Bartlett, "The Concessionaires of Yellowstone National Park: Genesis of a Policy, 1882–1892," *Pacific Northwest Quarterly* 74 (January 1983): 2–10.

4. Tolson, *Historic Listing of National Park Service Officials*, pp. 1–3; Everhart, *National Park Service*, p. 26; Foresta, *America's National Parks and Their Keepers*, pp. 43–51.

5. Wesley A. D'Ewart to W. M. Nichols, March 2, 1953, file "Concession Contracts," box YPC-75, YNP; Lester C. Hunt to Child Jr., June 25, 1953, ibid.; Estes Kefauver to Child Jr., June 25, 1953, ibid.; John Sparkman to Child Jr., June 25, 1953, ibid.; Barrett to Child Jr., June 25, 1953, ibid.; Spessard Holland to Child Jr., June 26, 1953, ibid.; Hilmer Oehlmann to Ben Jensen, June 26, 1953, ibid.; George Smathers to Child Jr., June 27, 1953, ibid.; Barrett to Child Jr., June 27, 1953, ibid.; Child Jr. to Francis Case, June 30, 1953, ibid.; Child Jr. to John C. Stennis, July 7, 1953, ibid.; Child Jr. to Kefauver, July 7, 1953, ibid.; Child Jr. to Sparkman, July 7, 1953, ibid.; Child Jr. to Holland, July 7, 1953,

ibid.; Smathers to Child Jr., July 7, 1953, ibid.; Child Jr. to Case, July 7, 1953, ibid.; Stennis to Child Jr., July 8, 1953, ibid.; Child Jr. to Hunt, July 8, 1953, ibid.; Child Jr. to Barrett, July 8, 1953, ibid.; J. Q. Nichols to Galusha, April 29, 1954, file "Business Correspondence 1954, box YPC-34, YNP; Suzanne Miotti to J. Q. Nichols, April 2, 1958, file "Report of Concessions Advisory Group to Sec. Krug–1948," box YPC-78, YNP; "Supplement to Special List No. 7," file "VIPs," box YPC-63, YNP.

6. Bernard DeVoto, "Let's Close the National Parks," *Harper's Magazine*, October 1953, pp. 49–53; Len Barnes, "Our Crumbling National Parks," *Motor News*, August 1954, pp. 10–11, 31, 33; "Is Yellowstone Really a Mess?" *Business Week*, October 1, 1955, pp. 62–65; Anthony Netboy, "Crisis in Our Parks," *American Forests*, 61 May 1955, pp. 24–27, 46–47; "Should Our National Parks Be Closed?" *Every Week* 20 (May 17, 1954), 250–252; Hazel Holly, "National Parks Need $$ and Sense," *Woman's Home Companion*, May 1955, pp. 13, 15, 30, 60; "Parks Advisory Board," *Salt Lake Tribune*, August 4, 1955, p. 5; A. R. Patton, "Remember the Good Old Days in Yellowstone in the 1920s?" *Park County News* (Livingston, Montana), September 15, 1955, p. 3.

7. Wallace Stegner, "We Are Destroying Our National Parks," *Sports Illustrated*, June 13, 1955, pp. 28–29, 44–46; "U.S. Is Outgrowing Its Parks," *U.S. News & World Report*, June 10, 1955, p. 79.

8. Conrad L. Wirth, *Parks, Politics, and the People* (Norman: University of Oklahoma Press, 1980); Everhart, *National Park Service*, p. 26.

9. Child Jr. to W. M. Nichols, March 17, 1953, file "W. M. Nichols 1946–57," box YPC-2, YNP; W. M. Nichols to Child Jr., November 2, 1953, ibid.; Child Jr. to J. Q. Nichols and W. M. Nichols, December 16, 1953, ibid.; "Special List No. 7," August 9, 1953, file "VIPs 1953," box YPC-63, YNP; "Supplement to Special List No. 7," August 13, 1953, ibid.

10. Rogers to W. M. Nichols, November 3, 1953, file untitled, box YPC-149, YNP; Wirth to W. M. Nichols, December 3, 1953, March 10, 1955, ibid.; W. M. Nichols to Wirth, December 17, 1953, January 14, 1955, ibid.; W. M. Nichols to Galusha, March 19, 1955, ibid.

11. W. M. Nichols to Karl Kenyon, August 16, 1951, file "K," box YPC-150, YNP; Frank H. Collins to W. M. Nichols, August 9, 1930, file "Railroads 40 (3)," box YPC-13, YNP; "Annual Financial Report of the Yellowstone Park Company to the Department of the Interior, October 1, 1954 to September 30, 1955," file "NPS Correspondence 1956," box YPC-91, YNP; "Recapitulation of 1953 Budget," file "1953 budget," box YPC-59, YNP; B. O. Hallin to W. M. Nichols, September 2, 1952, file "historical 1," box YPC-3, YNP; W. M. Nichols to Rogers, April 1, 1954, file untitled, box YPC-149, YNP; W. M. Nichols to J. E. Haynes, March 1, 1955, file "Business Correspondence 1955," box YPC-35, YNP.

12. "Prospectus," file "W. M. Nichols 1946–57," box YPC-2, YNP.

13. Child Jr. to W. M. Nichols, February 21, 1955, March 24, 1955, file "W. M. Nichols 1946–57," box YPC-2, YNP; W. M. Nichols to J. E. Haynes, March 1, 1955, file "Business Correspondence 1955," box YPC-35, YNP; Haynes to W. M. Nichols, March 4, 1955, ibid.; "Is Yellowstone Really a Mess?" pp. 62–64.

14. "Is Yellowstone Really a Mess?" pp. 64–65; "Statement of Congressman Keith Thomson Wyoming," *Jackson Hole Courier*, September 22, 1955, p. 3; "Park Service Appropriation Key to Problem — Thomson," *Jackson Hole Courier*, September 22, 1955; "Wyoming Chief Raps Critics of Park Plan," *Salt Lake Tribune*, September 7, 1955;

Haynes to W. M. Nichols, March 4, 1955, YNP; Child Jr. to W. M. Nichols, February 21, 1955, ibid.; W. M. Nichols to Trevor Povah, August 29, 1955, file "Yellowstone Park Service Stations 1955–59," box YPC-19, YNP.

15. NPS memoranda, Wirth to all offices, February 18, June 27, 1955, file "2," box D-20, YNP; U.S. Department of the Interior, National Park Service, "Mission 66 for Yellowstone National Park," file "Yellowstone Concessions, Etc. 1966–81," box 5, Butcher collection, AHC; NPS press release, June 24, 1956, ibid.; Wirth, *Parks, Politics, and the People*, pp. 238–256.

16. Ise, *Our National Park Policy*, p. 547; "Dwight D. Eisenhower to Vice President and Speaker of the House of Representatives, February 2, 1956," file "M66 1955-59," box D-21, YNP; E. T. Scoyen to All Field Offices, March 7, 1956, ibid.; Wirth to All Field Offices, May 16, July 6, 1956, ibid.; W. G. Carnes to Wirth, May 18, 1956, file "4," ibid.; "Mission 66 Special Presentation," February 27, 1956, file "6-M66," box 27, Conrad L. Wirth collection, AHC; program, American Pioneer Dinner, February 8, 1956, Washington, D.C., file "Mission 66 1956–61," box 6, Butcher collection, AHC; "A Program for Parks," *American Forests* 61 (July 1955): 7, 32–33; Conrad L. Wirth, "Mission 66," *American Forests* 61 (August 1955): 16–17; Joe D. Morgan, "Mission 66," *American Forests* 61 (November 1955): 23, 58–60; "Mission 66 Gets Underway," *American Forests* 62 (March 1956): 58–60; Ernest G. Vetter, "Project in the Parks," *American Forests* 63 (September 1957): 16–18; James Winchester, "Park Man: Meet Conrad L. Wirth, Director of Uncle Sam's National Park Service," *Scholastic* 68 (April 1956): p. 6; "O'Mahoney Asks Nearly Half a Billion for National Park Use," *Jackson Hole Courier*, February 2, 1956; "Park Service Adopts Program Toward Observance of Golden Anniversary," *Jackson Hole Courier*, February 23, 1956.

17. "Statement of Current and Future Park Visitor Needs for Accommodations and Facilities in Yellowstone National Park: Report of Working Committee April 11–15, 1955," pp. 1–4, file no, 1, box D-20, YNP.

18. Ibid., pp. 3–4; W. M. Nichols to Weir, March 31, 1955, file untitled, box YPC-149, YNP; Wirth to W. M. Nichols, June 16, 1955, ibid.; "Mission 66 for Yellowstone National Park," pp. 5–6, AHC.

19. Wirth to W. M. Nichols, March 22, June 16, 1955, file untitled, box YPC-149, YNP; W. M. Nichols to Galusha, March 19, 1955, ibid.; W. M. Nichols to Weir, March 31, 1955, ibid.; Hugh D. Galusha Jr. to W. M. Nichols, July 18, 1955, file "General Correspondence 1958," box YPC-92, YNP.

20. W. M. Nichols to Galusha, March 17, 1955, YNP.

21. Galusha to W. M. Nichols, March 26, 1955, ibid.

22. Galusha Jr. to W. M. Nichols, July 18, 1955, YNP.

23. Chester A. Rude to Galusha Jr., August 18, 1955, file untitled, box YPC-149, YNP; W. M. Nichols to Wirth, August 31, 1955, file untitled, box YPC-150, YNP; Scoyen to All Field Offices, June 4, 1956, file "5," box D-20, YNP.

24. Galusha Jr. to Rude, September 7, 1955, file untitled, box YPC-149, YNP; "Review of Contract Renewal and Building Program — Canyon Village," August 31, 1956, file "NPS 1956," box YPC-91, ibid.

25. J. Q. Nichols to Wirth, February 3, 1956, file "Plans for Discontinuance, YPC 4/65," box C-7, YNP; transcription of telephone conversation, Tom Allen to Weir, January 26, 1956, file "NPS correspondence 1956," box YPC-91, YNP; Contract No. 14-10-0100-

603, February 3, 1956, ibid.; transcript of hearing, "Yellowstone National Park Contracts," U.S. House of Representatives, Committee on Interior and Insular Affairs, Washington, D.C., January 12, 1956, ibid.; "Review of Contract Renewal and Building Program — Canyon Village," ibid.; "Interior Department Submits Yellowstone Pact for Approval," *Cody Enterprise*, December 8, 1956, p. 5.

26. Loan Agreement, March 30, 1956, file "YPC background information," box YPC-97, YNP.

6. MISSION 66

1. Wirth, *Parks, Politics, and the People*, pp. 266–271.

2. Roy E. Appleman, "History of NPS Mission 66 Program," MS, pp. 37–44, box 34, Wirth collection, AHC; "Statement of Current and Future Park Visitor Needs," p. 4, YNP; NPS memorandum, "Summary of Mission 66 Objectives and Program for Yellowstone National Park," April 20, 1956, file "M66-5," box D-20, YNP.

3. Appleman, "History of Mission 66," pp. 31–32, AHC.

4. Ibid., pp. 24–44; Barnes, "Our Crumbling National Parks," pp. 11, 31; "National Park Service Plans for Future," *Salt Lake Tribune*, August 21, 1955, p. 16A; "Summary of Mission 66 Goals and Objectives," YNP; "Draft Statement of Goals and Plans for Mission 66 in Yellowstone National Park," file no. 3, box D-20, YNP, contains a complete account of all NPS plans for Yellowstone during the ten years of Mission 66.

5. Rogers to W. M. Nichols, April 5, 1956, file "NPS Correspondence 1956," box YPC-91, YNP; W. M. Nichols to Rogers, June 15, 1956, ibid.

6. Child Jr. to W. M. Nichols, February 23, March 10, 1956, file "HC Jr.," box YPC-2, YNP; W. M. Nichols to Child Jr., March 16, 27, 1956, ibid.; Child Jr. to Galusha Jr., October 2, 1956, ibid.; "Service Plans Park Projects," *Billings Gazette*, April 30, 1956, p. 3; "There Is Good News Today," *Jackson Hole Courier*, May 3, 1956, p. 5.

7. "Service Plans Park Projects," p. 3; "Mission 66 for Yellowstone National Park," p. 6, AHC; "The Master Plan for Yellowstone," *Casper Tribune Herald*, February 14, 1958, p. 1; NPS press release, June 24, September 26, 1956, file "M66 1955–59," box D-21, YNP; NPS press release, October 6, 1956, file "M66 1956–57," ibid.; map of Grand Canyon Area, Yellowstone National Park, file "General Correspondence 1958," box YPC-92, YNP.

8. Wirth, *Parks, Politics, and the People*, pp. 258–260, 271; NPS press release, June 24, 1956, file "Yellowstone Concessions Etc. 1966–81," box 5, Butcher collection, AHC; "Mission 66 for Yellowstone National Park," p. 4, ibid.

9. W. M. Nichols to Rogers, June 15, 1956, YNP; W. M. Nichols to Galusha Jr., May 29, 1956, file "NPS Correspondence 1956," box YPC-91, YNP.

10. NPS press release, September 26, 1956, YNP; Child Jr. to W. M. Nichols, April 27, 1956, file "HC Jr.," box YPC-2, YNP; "Service Plans Park Projects," p. 3.

11. NPS press release, June 24, 1956, AHC; draft, "Outline of Ground Breaking," May 24, 1956, file "M66 1955–59," box D-21, YNP; "Yellowstone Rite Launches Work," *Salt Lake Tribune*, June 24, 1956, p. 2; "Rites Launch New Era at Yellowstone," *Salt Lake Tribune*, June 26, 1956, p. 1.

12. NPS press release, June 23, 1956, AHC; Child Jr. to W. M. Nichols, February 23, 1956, YNP; Child Jr. to W. M. Nichols and J. Q. Nichols, November 8, 1956, file "HC Jr.," box YPC-2, YNP; "Special Provisions of Work Projects Located Within Yellowstone

National Park," addendum no. 1, file "General Correspondence 1959," box YPC-92, YNP; Rogers to Child Jr., May 25, 1956, file "Concessions Buildings and Other Facilities 1954–56," box C-14, YNP.

13. G. R. Brosius to YP Company, August 28, 1956, file "Travel Statistics 1956," box YPC-30, YNP; E. K. Campbell to Department of the Interior, October 8, 1956, ibid.; Mrs. Dennison B. Cowles to NPS, Yellowstone, October 3, 1956, ibid.; Leonard A. Falevitch to Superintendent, Yellowstone National Park, August 12, 1956, ibid.; Louis Margoles to YP Company, August 11, 1956, ibid.; Frank H. Partridge to Department of the Interior, August 31, 1956, ibid.

14. NPS press release, October 6, 1956, YNP; Child Jr. to W. M. Nichols and J. Q. Nichols, November 8, 1956, ibid.; NPS press release, December 20, 1956, file "M66 1955–59," box D-21, YNP; Child Jr. to J. Q. Nichols, November 28, 1956, file "HC Jr.," box YPC-2, YNP; "Many Improvement Projects Under Way in Yellowstone Park Under Mission 66 Plan," *Park County News* (Livingston, Montana), December 27, 1956, p. 1.

15. Canyon Ranger Station Daily Log, 1957, box W-19, YNP. The log contains numerous accounts of workers being expelled from the park for various infractions. The Yellowstone photo archive also contains pictures of construction vehicles after some of the frequent accidents along park roads.

16. Lemuel A. Garrison to Wirth, May 13, 1958, file "1958 Personal," box 24, Wirth collection, AHC; W. M. Nichols to Fred T. Burke, February 3, 1956, file "Business Correspondence 1956," box YPC-35, YNP; Child Jr. to W. M. Nichols, February 11, 1953, file "W. M. Nichols 1946–57," box YPC-2, YNP; W. M. Nichols to Child Jr., November 2, 1953, ibid.; Wesley A. D'Ewart to W. M. Nichols, March 2, 1953, ibid.; Child Jr. to W. M. Nichols, February 23, 1956, file "HC Jr.," ibid.; Child Jr. to W. M. Nichols and J. Q. Nichols, November 8, 1956, ibid.; Child Jr. to Trevor Povah, March 9, 1960, ibid. Joffe had worked in the park for over thirty years and regularly passed information to the concessioners throughout his tenure. Upon his retirement in 1960— Garrison tried to ease him out sooner, but to no avail — the YP Company, Hamilton, and Haynes hosted a dinner in his honor. They declined to contribute toward a gift, however; Joffe, in the words of Huntley Child Jr., was "certainly a good friend of the concessioners over the years and, I believe, has received ample repayment for this in gifts and other gratuities."

17. Garrison to J. Q. Nichols, August 6, 1957, file "Correspondence NPS 1957," box YPC-91, YNP; J. Q. Nichols to Garrison, August 10, 1957, ibid.; interview with John Good by Mark Barringer, July 27, 1994, Yellowstone National Park, Wyoming.

18. J. Q. Nichols to Warren Hamilton, February 27, 1957, file "NPS Correspondence 1957," box YPC-91, YNP; NPS press release, January, 1957, file "Park Travel Statistics 1956," box YPC-30, YNP; Child Jr. to J. Q. Nichols, November 28, 1956, file "HC Jr.," box YPC-2, YNP; YP Company announcement of officer elections, December 1, 1956, file "Business Correspondence 1946," box YPC-34, YNP; Galusha Jr. to W. M. Nichols, July 19, 1956, file "Business Correspondence 1956," box YPC-35, YNP; W. M. Nichols to Galusha Jr., July 23, September 6, 1956, ibid.; J. Q. Nichols to Galusha Jr., September 17, 1956, ibid.; Burke to W. M. Nichols, October 9, 1956, ibid.; W. M. Nichols to Burke, October 31, 1956, ibid.

19. Galusha Jr. to J. E. Haynes, April 22, 1958, folder 2, box 9, collection 1504, MSU- Bozeman; Good interview, July 27, 1994; Annual financial Report of Yellowstone Park

Company to the United States Department of the Interior, September 30, 1956, file "NPS Correspondence 1956," box YPC-91, YNP; Annual financial Report of Yellowstone Park Company to the United States Department of the Interior, September 30, 1957, file "NPS Correspondence 1957," ibid.; W. M. Nichols to Burke, April 23, May 6, 1957, file "Business Correspondence 1957," box YPC-35, YNP; Burke to W. M. Nichols, April 26, May 2, 1957, ibid.; Miotti to Burke, April 30, 1957, ibid.; W. M. Nichols to Galusha, May 2, 13, 1957, ibid.; Galusha to W. M. Nichols, May 6, 1957, ibid. The financial reports for 1952–1954 are in file "YPC 1949–59," box C-3, YNP.

20. NPS press release, January 1958, file "Park Travel Statistics 1957," box YPC-30, YNP; Robert J. Sevitz to Child Jr., August 1, 1957, file "W. M. Nichols 1946–57," box YPC-2, YNP; Child Jr. to Sevitz, August 10, 1957, ibid.; "Testimony of Hugh D. Galusha, Jr., Before the House Interior and Insular Affairs Committee, April 17, 1958, in Support of HR 10788," file "C," box YPC-150, YNP; "Canyon Village Dedication Aug. 31 with Wirth, Speaker," *Park County News* (Livingston, Montana), August 15, 1957, p. 8; "Yellowstone Travel 15% Ahead in August," *Park County News*, August 15, 1957, p. 7; "Director of National Parks to Speak at Dedication," *Salt Lake Tribune*, August 15, 1957, p. 4.

21. "Testimony of Hugh D. Galusha, Jr., April 17, 1958," YNP; "Review of Contract Renewal and Rebuilding Program — Canyon Village," August 31, 1956, ibid.; Thomas J. Hallin to J. Q. Nichols, December 4, 1958, file "General Correspondence 1958," box YPC-92, YNP; Garrison to J. Q. Nichols, October 8, 1958, ibid.; Good interview, July 27, 1994.

22. Garrison to J. Q. Nichols, November 25, 1957, file "NPS Correspondence 1957," box YPC-91, YNP; Garrison to Child Jr., February 21, 1958, file "Business Correspondence 1958," box YPC-35, YNP; "Yellowstone Park Inspection, 1959," file "Businesses Correspondence 1959," box YPC-36, YNP; William E. Cotton, "Development and Evaluation of the Company's Reorganization and Management Program," Report to the Board of Directors of the Yellowstone Park Company, October 1, 1959, file "HC Jr.," box YPC-2, YNP.

23. Child Jr. to J. Q. Nichols and Galusha Jr., April 2, 1958, file "HC Jr.," box YPC-2, YNP; J. Q. Nichols to Wirth, June 21, 1958, file "General Correspondence 1958," box YPC-92, YNP; Garrison to J. Q. Nichols, October 8, 1958, ibid.; "Percentage of Occupancy — Canyon Village — June, 1959," file "General Correspondence 1959," ibid.; J. Q. Nichols to Garrison, September 22, November 16, 1959, ibid.; Garrison to J. Q. Nichols, September 17, October 15, 1959, ibid.; Thomas J. Hallin to Howard Rundle, November 16, 1959, ibid.; NPS press release, August 9, 1960, file "Press Releases 1958–63," box K-22, YNP.

24. "A Prospectus for Grant Village," file "M66 1955–59," box D-21, YNP.

25. Ibid.; "Statement of Current and Future Park Visitor Needs," p. 4, YNP.

26. Swain, *Federal Conservation Policy,* pp. 130–134; Foresta, *America's National Parks and Their Keepers,* pp. 25–30. Ray Lyman Wilbur, in *Two Years of the Department of the Interior 1929–1931* (Washington, D.C.: U.S. Government Printing Office, 1931), illustrates the political advantages in keeping the public happy. One of the best accounts of tourist expectations in national parks is Pomeroy, *In Search of the Golden West.* Mark W. T. Harvey, in *A Symbol of Wilderness: Echo Park and the American Conservation Movement* (Albuquerque: University of New Mexico Press, 1994), provides the

best discussion of the Dinosaur controversy. See also Susan Rhodes Neel, "Irreconcilable Differences: Reclamation, Preservation, and the Origins of the Echo Park Dam Controversy" (Ph.D. diss., University of California at Los Angeles, 1990). For the role of the Sierra Club in various national parks issues, see Michael P. Cohen, *The History of the Sierra Club, 1892–1970* (San Francisco: Sierra Club Books, 1988). The idea of an "establishment" in conservation is noted by Fox in *John Muir and His Legacy*, but Fox neglects to include government agencies like the NPS, perhaps the most important component of all.

27. Miles, *Guardians of the Parks*, pp. 132, 187–193; Harvey, *A Symbol of Wilderness*, pp. 138, 150; Devereux Butcher, *Exploring Our National Parks and Monuments*, 2d ed. (Boston: Houghton Mifflin, 1947); Devereux Butcher, "In Defense of Dinosaur," *Audubon Magazine*, 53 (May 1951): 142–149; Samuel P. Hays, *Beauty, Health, and Permanence: Environmental Politics in the United States, 1955–1985* (New York: Cambridge University Press, 1987), pp. 13–39.

28. Miles, *Guardians of the Parks*, pp. 150–164, 189; Cohen, *History of the Sierra Club*, pp. 134–142; Devereux Butcher to Olaus Murie, August 1, 1960, box 5, file "YNP concessions," Butcher collection, AHC.

29. Harvey, *A Symbol of Wilderness*, pp. 287–301; Murie to Wirth, December 10, 1957, file "Mission 66 1956–61," box 6, Butcher collection, AHC; Murie to Wirth, January 7, 1958, file "Conservation Organizations," box 24, Wirth collection, AHC; Wirth to Harold E. Crowe, January 7, 1958, ibid.; Harry C. James to Wirth, January 31, 1958, ibid.; Scoyen to James, February 19, 1958, ibid.; Wirth to Sigurd Olson, March 24, 1958, file "1958 Personal," ibid.; Olson to Wirth, March 27, 1958, ibid.; Wirth to Olson, April 1, 1958, ibid.; Wirth to Harold C. Bradley, July 2, 1957, file "Sierra Club," ibid.; David Brower, "'Mission 65' is Proposed by Reviewer of Park Service's New Brochure on Wilderness; Calls Attention to Changes in Publication from Earlier Version and Urges Wilderness Bill Support," *National Parks Magazine*, March 1958, ibid.; Murie to Wirth, December 10, 1957, AHC.

30. Miles, *Guardians of the Parks*, pp. 132–189; Butcher to Duane Jacobs, October 5, 1959, file "Mission 66 1956–71," box 6, Butcher collection, AHC; Butcher to Homer Davis, August 25, 1960, file "Yellowstone Concessions, Etc., 1966–81," box 8, AHC; Davis to Butcher, November 1, 1960, file "YNP Concessions," box 5, AHC; Butcher to Murie, August 1, 1960, ibid.; Davis to Butcher, July 24, 1960, ibid.; Butcher to Wendell Anderson, July 20, 1960, ibid.; Butcher to Fred A. Seaton, July 30, 1960, file "Fred A. Seaton 1956–61," box 8, Butcher collection, AHC; Frank E. Masland Jr. to Wirth, May 31, 1960, file "1960 Personal," box 24, Wirth collection, AHC; Wirth to Masland Jr. June 3, 1960, ibid.

31. "Annual Report of the Superintendent of Yellowstone National Park to the Director of the National Park Service, June 16, 1959," YNP; Child Jr. to J. Q. Nichols, May 20, 1959, file "HC Jr.," box YPC-2, YNP; Luis A Gastellum to J. Q. Nichols, November 10, 1958, file "General Correspondence 1958," box YPC-92, YNP; Garrison to J. Q. Nichols, September 2, 1958, ibid.; Davis to A. Clark Stratton, June 6, 1959, file "YNP concessions," box 5, Butcher collection, AHC; E. T. Scoyen to Davis, June 19, 1959, ibid.; Butcher to M. C. Wilson, January 4, 1960, ibid.; Yellowstone Park Gateways Association to Butcher, May 16, 1960, ibid.; Galusha Jr. to J. Q. Nichols, November 19, 1958, folder 1,

box 9, collection 1504, MSU-Bozeman; Galusha Jr. to J. E. Haynes, April 22, 1959, folder 3, ibid.; "Group Organizes to Promote Tourist Attraction in Areas Adjacent to Parks," *Jackson Hole Courier*, September 18, 1958; "The Services in Yellowstone Park," *Billings Gazette*, July 17, 1960, p. 7; "Yellowstone Park Company Says Cities Hurt Business," *Billings Gazette*, July 12, 1960, p. 2; "Park Ads Lead to Protest," *Billings Gazette*, September 29, 1958, p. 1.

32. Masland Jr. to David Brower, June 10, 1960, file "Sierra Club," box 24, Wirth collection, AHC; Good interview, July 27, 1994.

33. "Mission 66 for Yellowstone National Park," AHC; Howard W. Baker to Superintendents, Region Two Field Areas, March 17, 1958, file no. 8, box D-21, YNP; Garrison to Staff Members, May 18, 1959, ibid.; Wirth to Washington Office and All Field Offices, February 27, 1959, file no. 9, box D-20, ibid.

34. J. Q. Nichols to D. R. Marquis, August 8, 1958, file "Business Correspondence 1958," box YPC-35, YNP; Galusha Jr. to Trevor Povah and J. Q. Nichols, August 27, 1958, ibid.; "Yellowstone Park Company Board of Directors, 1959," box YPC-150, YNP; J. Q. Nichols to Burke, May 4, 1959, file "Business Correspondence 1959," box YPC-36, YNP; "Annual Report, Yellowstone Park Company, 1960," ibid.; "Survey of Facilities and Operations for Yellowstone Park Company by Orr Pickering and Associates, Architects and Engineers, Billings, Montana," June, 1958, box C-7, YNP; Galusha Jr. report on financing, April 22, 1958, folder 2, box 9, collection 1504, MSU-Bozeman.

7. COLLAPSE

1. Clark C. Van Fleet, "Nature Out of Balance," *Atlantic Monthly*, February 1961, pp. 52–53; Paul Brooks, "The Pressure of Numbers," *Atlantic Monthly*, February 1961, pp. 54–55; Devereux Butcher, "Resorts or Wilderness?" *Atlantic Monthly*, February 1961, pp. 45–51; *Congressional Record*, Appendix, pp. A2142–A2143, file "1966–1976 NP Standards," box 6, Butcher collection, AHC.

2. Butcher to "Weldon," February 4, 1961, file "Conrad Wirth, 1936–63," box 8, Butcher collection, AHC; Homer Davis to Butcher, April 6, 1961, file "YNP concessions," box 5, AHC; Butcher to Davis, April 14, 1961, ibid.; Ferry B. Allen to Wirth, February 5, 1961, file "Correspondence 1961–62," box 8, Wirth collection, AHC; Wirth to Allen, February 10, 1961, ibid.; William H. Stringer, "'Interior' Veering," *Christian Science Monitor*, February 18, 1961, p. 6.

3. Wirth to Stewart Udall, March 10, 1961, file "Mission 66 1956–71," box 6, Butcher collection, AHC; Joseph Wood Krutch, "Which Men? What Needs?" *American Forests* 63 (April 4, 1957): 20–23.

4. Udall to Wirth, March 20, 1961, Butcher collection, AHC; NPS press release, April 24, 1961, ibid.; Don Hummel to Wirth, January 27, 30, February 14, 1961, file "1961 personal," box 24, Wirth collection, AHC; Henry Romney to Wirth, March 21, 1961, ibid.; Wirth to Albright, April 26, 1962, ibid.

5. La Marr Bittinger to All Department Heads, January 19, 1961, file "Transportation 1948–61," box YPC-19, YNP; Charles W. Marshall to Peter Johnson, January 9, 1961, ibid.; Marshall to J. Q. Nichols, June 22, 1961, ibid.; William Briscoe to Bittinger, October 26, 1961, ibid.; Bittinger to Garrison, July 15, October 27, 1961, ibid.; Eugene Laitala to Marshall, April 3, 1961, ibid.; Newell Gough, Jr. to A. O. Sheldon, April 11, 1961, ibid.;

Luis A. Gastellum to Bittinger, December 11, 1961, ibid.; Bittinger to A. T. Hibbard, December 11, 1961, ibid.; Hibbard to Bittinger, December 8, 1961, ibid.; Garrison to J. Q. Nichols, February 15, 1961, file "General Correspondence 1961," box YPC-92, YNP; Garrison to Bittinger, September 1, 1961, ibid.; Galusha, Higgins, and Galusha to Board of Directors, Yellowstone Park Company, November 3, 1961, file "YPC background information," box YPC-97, YNP; Ron Latimore to J. Q. Nichols, December 8, 1960, file "Railroads General," box YPC-31, YNP; contract between Western Fleetline and YP Company, April 24, 1957, file "Western Fleetline 1956–60 (Bruce Stoddard)," box YPC-21, YNP; Otto Brown to All Rangers, June 1, 1956, ibid.; J. Q. Nichols to William Wallace, May 2, 1956, ibid.; contract between YP Company and City School Bus System, April 29, 1960, file "LA City School Bus System," box YPC-23, YNP.

6. "Yellowstone Park Company Officers and Board of Directors," November 1, 1962, file "General Correspondence 1962," box YPC-93, YNP; Garrison to Beall, September 12, 1962, ibid.; Beall to Louis M. Lueders, October 11, 1962, ibid.

7. Edwin C. Kenner to Mrs. W. M. Nichols and Trevor Povah, December 21, 1961, file "General Correspondence 1961," box YPC-92, YNP; Galusha Jr. to Members of the Board, Yellowstone Park Company, March 13, 1962, box YPC-149, YNP; Galusha Jr. to Edwin W. Keleher, November 27, 1961, ibid.

8. George Beall to Garrison, November 23, 1962, file "General Correspondence 1962," box YPC-93, YNP; Beall to Garrison, January 31, 1963, file "General Correspondence 1963," ibid.; Isabel M. Haynes to Beall, March 19, 1963, ibid.; Beall to Isabel Haynes, March 22, 1963, ibid.; R. W. Carlson to Beall, November 26, 29, 1962, file "Approval of Capital Expenditures," box YPC-78, YNP; J. E. Haynes to Robert Henkel, March 30, 1962, file "Yellowstone National Park Council," box YPC-105, YNP.

9. "Yellowstone Park Company: A Blueprint for the Future," November 15, 1962, box YPC-149, YNP.

10. Garrison to Bittinger, September 1, 1961, file "General Correspondence 1961," box YPC-92, YNP; Bittinger to Garrison, September 5, 1961, ibid.; Bittinger to Lawrence C. Hadley, June 8, 1962, file "General Correspondence 1962," box YPC-93, YNP; E. D. C. Nichols to Wirth, August 24, 1962, ibid.; Eileen McGuire to E. D. C. Nichols, August 24, 1962, ibid.; Beall to Lueders, October 11, 1962, ibid.; Gastellum to Beall, March 1, 1963, file "General Correspondence 1963," ibid.

11. Beall to Gastellum, February 19, 1963, file "General Correspondence 1963," box YPC-93, YNP; Garrison to Beall, June 19, 1963, ibid.; Beall to Garrison, July 28, August 25, 1963, ibid.; Garrison to Hibbard, August 1, 1963, ibid.; E. Herrick Low to Garrison, August 29, 1963, ibid.; Art Bazata to Beall, November 19, 1963, file "Interior Department and NPS, January–June, 1964," box YPC-94, YNP.

12. "Details of Additions and Reductions in Plant and Equipment," September 30, 1961, box YPC-150, YNP; "Details of Additions and Reductions in Plant and Equipment," September 30, 1962, ibid.; Gastellum to Bittinger, November 2, 1961, file "General Correspondence 1961," box YPC-92, YNP; Wirth to Galusha Jr., March 22, 1962, box YPC-149, YNP; NPS press release, January 1961, November 2, 1962, file "Press Releases," box K-22, YNP; "Accommodations and Facilities Made Available During 1962," file "General Correspondence 1963," box YPC-93, YNP.

13. Beall to Garrison, August 7, 1963, file "Interior Department and NPS, July–December, 1964," box YPC-94, YNP; Gastellum to Garrison, September 9, 23, 1963, in binder, box

D-34, YNP; "Details of Additions and Reductions in Plant and Equipment," September 30, 1963, box YPC-150, YNP; NPS press release, January 2, 1963, file "Press Releases," box K-22, YNP.

14. Myron Gray to E. T. Scoyen, May 16, 1961, file "Plans for Discontinuance, YPC 4/65," box C-7, YNP; Paul E. Harris to Udall, June 21, 1961, ibid.; Mrs. William O. Cullen to Udall, June 25, 1961, ibid.; Carl R. Anderson to Udall, September 4, 1962, ibid.; Cecil and Nan Hunt to United States Department of the Interior, September 12, 1962, ibid.; E. P. Donahue to Frank E. Moss, July 3, 1961, ibid.; Harry F. Breen to Edward Derwinski, August 27, 1962, ibid.; Garrison to Bittinger, July 7, 1961, ibid.; William A. Myers to Jackson Price, September 7, 1961, file "General Correspondence 1961," box YPC-92, YNP; Price to Howard Baker, October 11, 1961, ibid.; Garrison to Bittinger, November 20, 1961, ibid.

15. "Inspection Report, Old Faithful Cafeteria, July 31, 1962," file "General Correspondence 1962," box YPC-93, YNP; Garrison to Bittinger, August 1, 1962, ibid.; Thomas S. Willett to Garrison, July 25, 1962, ibid.; inspection report, Canyon Village Lodge Eating Facilities, July 24, 1962, ibid.; inspection report, Fishing Bridge Cafeteria, August 15, 1962, ibid.; inspection report, Canyon Village Lodge, August 16, 1962, ibid.

16. Garrison to Mrs. William M. Nichols, August 30, 1962, file "Plans for Discontinuance, YPC, 4/65," box C-7, YNP; Garrison to Beall, October 15, 1962, file "General Correspondence 1962," box YPC-93, YNP; Beall to Garrison, November 26, 1962, ibid.

17. Garrison to Beall, July 25, 1963, file "Plans for Discontinuance, YPC, 4/65," box C-7, YNP. Photographs and announcements of the banquet and the Miss Yellowstone Pageant are in box YPC-129, YNP.

18. Beall to Wirth, October 11, 1963, box YPC-149, YNP.

19. Advisory Board on Wildlife Management, *Wildlife Management in the National Parks* (Washington, D.C.: U.S. Department of the Interior, 1963). Devereux Butcher had an ally on the Leopold commission, longtime friend and frequent correspondent Clarence Cottam, who provided him with advance copies of the report and discussed with him possible implications. See Butcher to Cottam, March 31, 1962, box 6, file "1944–76 National Parks Standards," Butcher collection, AHC; Department of the Interior press release, October 18, 1963, file "National Parks — General Problems, 1948–84," box 3, Butcher collection, AHC.

20. "Park Service Due for Big Changes," *New York Times,* October 17, 1963, p. 3; "New Director Is Named to Park Service," *Helena Independent,* October 20, 1963, p. 8; "Why Did Wirth Go?" *Deseret News,* October 21, 1963, p. 14A; Butcher to Udall, May 30, 1963, file "Stewart L. Udall," box 8, Butcher collection, AHC; Butcher to Udall, October 27, 1963, ibid.; Butcher to William M. Blair, November 18, 1963, file "Conrad Wirth Ousted from NPS Directorship," ibid.; "Remarks by Assistant Secretary of Interior John A. Carver," October 14, 1963, pp. 4–5, file "NPS Conference 1963," box 22, Wirth collection, AHC.

21. George B. Hartzog Jr., *Battling for the National Parks* (Mt. Kisco, N.Y.: Moyer Bell, 1988), pp. 74–79; "The Road to the Future: Long-Range Objectives, Goals, and Guidelines," box 6, Butcher collection, AHC.

22. Wirth to Udall, October 21, 1963, in notebook, box D-34, YNP; A. Clark Stratton to Members, Yellowstone Study Committee, November 19, 1963, ibid.; memo to Stratton, November 13, 1963, ibid.; Beall to Stratton, October 28, November 29, 1963, ibid.;

Stratton to Beall, November 18, 1963, ibid.; J. D. Ammerman to Beall, January 6, 1964, file "Interior Department and NPS, January–June, 1964," box YPC-94, YNP; Thomas Flynn to Beall, January 30, 1964, ibid.

23. "Agenda, Yellowstone Park Master Plan Study Meeting, January 25 and 26, 1964," in notebook, box D-34, YNP; Daniel J. Tobin Jr. to K. S. Chamberlain, February 25, 1964, ibid.; Beall to Price, March 18, 1964, file "Concessions Contracts and Permits, YPC 1964–65," box C-4, YNP.

24. "Memorandum of Discussion Between Supt. McLaughlin, A. T. Hibbard, and George Beall," June 5, 1964, file "Interior Department and NPS, January–June, 1964," box YPC-94, YNP; Hartzog to Beall, July 10, 1964, file "Concessions Contracts and Permits, YPC 1964–65," box C-4, YNP; Beall to Hartzog, July 15, 29, 1964, ibid.; Beall to Stratton, September 15, 1964, ibid.; McLaughlin to Stratton, July 15, 1964, in notebook, box D-34, YNP; Beall to Hartzog, October 30, 1964, file "Plans for Discontinuance, YPC 4/65," box C-7, YNP; Hartzog to Beall, November 3, 1964, ibid.

25. John A. Carver Jr. to William H. Orick, Jr., April 12, 1965, file "Concession contracts and permits, YPC 1964–65," box C-4, YNP; Gerald H. Trautman to Hartzog, May 11, 1965, ibid.; Hartzog to Trautman, May 21, 1965, ibid.; Low to Hartzog, April 21, 1965, file "Plans for Discontinuance, YPC 4/65," box C-7, YNP.

26. Low to Hartzog, April 21, 1965, YNP; Gough Jr. to Hartzog, June 4, 1965, file "Plans for Discontinuance, YPC 4/65," box C-7, ibid.

27. Beall to Hartzog, February 25, 1964, file "Interior Department and NPS, January–June, 1964," box YPC-94, YNP; Hartzog to Gough Jr., July 2, 1965, file "Plans for Discontinuance, YPC 4/65," box C-7, YNP; McLaughlin to Hartzog, July 1, 1965, ibid.

28. "Meeting with Directors of Yellowstone Park Company on July 22, 1965, in Yellowstone National Park," file "Plans for Discontinuance, YPC 4/65," box C-7, YNP; McLaughlin to Hartzog, August 19, 1965, ibid.; Hartzog to Gough Jr., September 22, 1965, ibid.; Hartzog to Gough Jr., October 8, 1965, file "NPS log," box YPC-94, YNP.

29. Minutes of concessioners meeting, January 11, 1961, file "1961 Staff Meeting," box YPC 101, YNP.

30. "Financial Audit, June 22, 1966," file "YPC Financial Audit, October 1, 1961 to September 30, 1965," box C-4, YNP; Hartzog to Udall, April 6, 1966, file "Concession Contracts and Permits, YPC 1966-67," YNP; memorandum, "Yellowstone Park Company," January 17, 1966, box YPC-149, YNP; Hartzog to Gough Jr., February 7, 1966, file "NPS log," box YPC-94, YNP.

31. Ronald R. Beaumont to McLaughlin, April 5, 1956, file "Concession Contracts and Permits, YPC 1966–67," box C-4, YNP; Bazata to Hamilton Stores, Inc., April 27, 1966, ibid.; Povah to Richard C. Pistell, May 16, 1966, ibid.; Pistell to Hartzog, May 16, 1966, ibid.; Hartzog to Povah, May 19, 1966, ibid.; Povah to Hartzog, April 25, 1966, ibid.; Hartzog to Pistell, May 18, 1966, ibid.; Povah to Bazata, June 7, 1966, ibid.; Bazata to Povah, June 8, 1966, ibid.

32. NPS press release, August 8, 1966, file "Concession Contracts and Permits, YPC 1966–67," box C-4, YNP.

CONCLUSION

1. See Dan R. Sholly, *Guardians of Yellowstone: An Intimate Look at the Challenges of Protecting America's Foremost Wilderness Park* (New York: William Morrow, 1991); Jim

Robbins, *Last Refuge: The Environmental Showdown in Yellowstone and the American West* (New York: William Morrow, 1993). Both discuss cogently the issues facing park managers at Yellowstone and elsewhere. Numerous articles and editorials have been published in newspapers and periodicals analyzing the continuing problems with winter use of the park. Todd Wilkinson, "Winter Paradox," *National Parks,* November–December, 1990, pp. 31–35, is representative. The literature on the 1988 fires is voluminous.

BIBLIOGRAPHY

ARCHIVAL COLLECTIONS

Maynard Barrows Collection, American Heritage Center, Laramie, Wyoming
Devereux Butcher Collection, American Heritage Center, Laramie, Wyoming
Arthur E. Demaray Collection, American Heritage Center, Laramie, Wyoming
Newton B. Drury Collection, American Heritage Center, Laramie, Wyoming
F. Jay Haynes Collection, Montana Historical Society, Helena, Montana
F. Jay Haynes Papers, Collection 1500, Burlingame Special Collections, Montana State
    University–Bozeman Libraries
Jack Ellis Haynes Papers, Collection 1504, Burlingame Special Collections, Montana State
    University–Bozeman Libraries
Howard H. Hays Collection, American Heritage Center, Laramie, Wyoming
Duane D. Jacobs Collection, American Heritage Center, Laramie, Wyoming
Merrill J. Mattes Collection, American Heritage Center, Laramie, Wyoming
Adolph Murie Collection, American Heritage Center, Laramie, Wyoming
National Park Service, Rocky Mountain Regional Office, Denver, Colorado
Conrad L. Wirth Collection, American Heritage Center, Laramie, Wyoming
Yellowstone National Park Research Library, Mammoth Hot Springs, Wyoming
Yellowstone Park Company Records, Burlingame Special Collections, Montana State
    University–Bozeman Libraries

INTERVIEWS

Darrell Bittner, July 26, 1994, Gardiner, Montana
John Good, July 27, 1994, Yellowstone National Park, Wyoming
Terry Pentilla, June 28, 1994, Denver, Colorado
Robert M. Utley, October 23, 1994, Albuquerque, New Mexico

ARTICLES AND CHAPTERS

Albright, Horace Marden. "The Great and Near-Great in Yellowstone." *Montana The
    Magazine of Western History* 22 (July 1972): 80–89.
Anderson, Terry L., and Peter J. Hill. "Appropriable Rents from Yellowstone Park: A Case
    of Incomplete Contracting." *Economic Inquiry* 34 (July 1996): 506–518.
Barnes, Len. "Our Crumbling National Parks." *Motor News,* August 1954, pp. 10–11.
Bartlett, Richard A. "Those Infernal Machines in Yellowstone." *Montana The Magazine
    of Western History* 20 (July 1970): 16–29.
———. "The Concessionaires of Yellowstone National Park: Genesis of a Policy,
    1882–1892." *Pacific Northwest Quarterly* 74 (January 1983): 2–10.
Bell, Tom. "The Lander-Yellowstone Transportation Company." *Wind River Mountaineer*
    (Fremont County, Wyoming), April 1, 1993, pp. 4–28.
Blodgett, Peter J. "Striking a Balance: Managing Concessions in the National Parks,
    1916–33." *Forest and Conservation History* 34 (April 1990): 60–68.
Brooks, Paul. "The Pressure of Numbers." *Atlantic Monthly,* February 1961, pp. 54–55.

Brower, David. "'Mission 65' is Proposed by Reviewer of Park Service's New Brochure on Wilderness: Calls Attention to Changes in Publication from Earlier Version and Urges Wilderness Bill Support." *National Parks Magazine,* March 1958, pp. 32–35.

Burke, Fred T. "Springtime in Yellowstone." *Yellowstone Gateway Post,* December 1993, pp. 13–16.

Burt, Struthers. "The Battle of Jackson's Hole." *The Nation,* March 3, 1926, pp. 225–227.

Butcher, Devereux. "In Defense of Dinosaur." *Audubon Magazine* 53 (May 1951): 142–149.

———. "Resorts or Wilderness?" *Atlantic Monthly,* February 1961, pp. 45–51.

Carty, Dave. "Spotlight on Yellowstone." *Western Outdoors,* February 1, 1994, pp. 42–56.

Cronon, William. "A Place for Stories: Nature, History, and Narrative." *Journal of American History* 78 (March 1992): 1347–1376.

———. "The Uses of Environmental History." *Environmental History Review* 17 (fall 1993): 11–22.

Czupryna, Louise, and Caryn Perry. "Nursing Practice in Yellowstone Park." *Journal of Emergency Nursing* 15 (July 1, 1989): 325–328.

De Voto, Bernard. "Let's Close the National Parks." *Harper's Magazine,* October 1953, pp. 49–53.

Dittl, Barbara H., and Joanne Mallmann. "Plain to Fancy: The Lake Hotel, 1889–1929." *Montana The Magazine of Western History* 34 (spring 1984): 32–45.

Dunn, Jerry Camarillo, Jr. "Wilderness Refined." *Westways,* December 1992, pp. 34–39, 73.

Du Puy, William Atherton. "The Growth of Our National Park System." *Current History* 30 (August 1929): 889–894.

Elder, Jim. "Yellowstone: Alive and Well." *Trailer Life,* March 1989, pp. 46–51.

"Expanding the National Park System." *Literary Digest,* June 1, 1935.

"Glimpses of Summer Playgrounds." *Literary Digest,* June 1930, pp. 16–20.

Grant, William E. "The Inalienable Land: American Wilderness as Sacred Symbol." *Journal of American Culture* 17 (spring 1994): 79–86.

Holly, Hazel. "National Parks Need $$ and Sense." *Woman's Home Companion,* May 1955, pp. 13, 15, 30, 60.

Hughes, Susan S. "The Sheepeater Myth of Northwestern Wyoming." *Plains Anthropologist* 45 (February 2000): 63–83.

Hultkrantz, Ake. "The Indians in Yellowstone Park." *Annals of Wyoming* 29 (October 1957): 125–149.

Hunt, William J., Jr. "Using Tourism as a Context for Historical Archeology." *CRM Bulletin* 17 (1994): 25–28.

"Is Yellowstone Really a Mess?" *Business Week,* October 1, 1955, pp. 62–65.

Julber, Eric. "The Wilderness: Just How Much Is Wild." *Forests and People* 21 (fourth quarter, 1971): 8–9.

Krutch, Joseph Wood. "Which Men? What Needs?" *American Forests* 63 (April 1957): 20–23.

Kunz, George F. "The Economic Value of Public Parks and Scenic Preservation." *Scientific Monthly* 16 (April 1923): 374–380.

Lambert, Kirby. "The Lure of the Parks." *Montana The Magazine of Western History* 46 (spring 1996): 42–55.

Langford, Nathaniel Pitt. "The Wonders of the Yellowstone." *Scribner's Monthly,* May–June 1871, pp. 1–17, 113–128.

Leavengood, David. "A Sense of Shelter: Robert C. Reamer in Yellowstone National Park." *Pacific Historical Review* 54 (1985): 495–513.

Malone, Michael P. "The Gallatin Canyon and the Tides of History." *Montana The Magazine of Western History* 23 (summer 1973): 2–17.

Mather, Stephen T. "A Glance Backward at National Park Development." *Nature* 10 (August 1927): 112–115.

McConnell, Grant. "The Conservation Movement — Past and Present." *Western Political Science Quarterly* 21 (1958): 463–478.

McIntosh, A. C. "Who Owns Yellowstone Park?" *American Mercury,* April 1936, pp. 493–496.

"Mission 66 Gets Underway." *American Forests* 62 (March 1956): 23, 58–60.

Morgan, Joe D. "Mission 66." *American Forests* 61 (November 1955): 58.

Nash, Roderick. "The American Invention of National Parks." *American Quarterly* 22 (fall 1970): 726–735.

Nelson, E. W. "The Economic Importance of Wild Life." *Scientific Monthly* 16 (April 1923): 367–373.

Netboy, Anthony. "Crisis in Our Parks." *American Forests* 61 (May 1955): 24–27, 46–47.

Oehlmann, H. "A Concessionaire Talks Back." *American Forests* 61 (July 1955): 13, 50–52.

O'Gara, Geoffrey, and Alexander Colhoun. "A Natural History of the Yellowstone Tourist." *Sierra* 81 (March–April 1996): 54–61.

Pack, Arthur Newton. "Bandits of the Border: Some More Thrills of the Glacier Park Expedition." *Nature* 12 (July 1928): 21–25.

"A Program for Parks." *American Forests* 61 (July 1955): 7, 32–33.

"The Public and the Parks." *Nature* 13 (April 1929): 255, 264.

Rast, Raymond W. "Vistas, Visions, and Visitors: Creating the Myth of Yellowstone National Park, 1872–1915." *Journal of the West* 37 (April 1998): 80–89.

Richardson, Elmo R. "The Struggle for the Valley: California's Hetch-Hetchy Controversy, 1905–1913." *California Historical Quarterly* 38 (1959): 249–258.

"Save the Yosemite." *Nature* 12 (July 1928): 30–31.

Schullery, Paul. "A Partnership in Conservation: Roosevelt & Yellowstone." *Montana The Magazine of Western History* 28 (summer 1978): 2–15.

Sellars, Richard West. "Science or Scenery? A Conflict of Values in the National Parks." *Wilderness* 52 (summer 1989): 29–38.

———. "The Roots of National Park Management: Evolving Perceptions of the Park Service's Mandate." *Journal of Forestry* 90 (January 1992): 16–19.

———. "Manipulating Nature's Paradise: National Park Management Under Stephen T. Mather, 1916–1929." *Montana The Magazine of Western History* 43 (spring 1993): 2–13.

"Should Our National Parks Be Closed?" *Every Week,* May 17, 1954, pp. 251–252.

Smith, Addison T. "Wanted — A Reservoir." *The Outlook,* January 19, 1927, pp. 77–79.

Steele, Rufus. "Summer Savages." *The Outlook,* May 12, 1926, pp. 56–58.

Stegner, Wallace. "We Are Destroying Our National Parks." *Sports Illustrated,* June 13, 1955, pp. 28–29, 44–46.

Swain, Donald C. "Harold Ickes, Horace Albright, and the Hundred Days." *Pacific Historical Review* 34 (August 1965): 455–465.

————. "The National Park Service and the New Deal, 1933–1940." *Pacific Historical Review* 41 (August 1972): 312–322.

Van Dyke, Henry. "A Meadow That Belongs to the People." *The Outlook*, January 19, 1927, pp. 79–80.

Van Fleet, Clark C. "Nature Out of Balance." *Atlantic Monthly*, February 1961, pp. 52–53.

Vetter, Ernest G. "Project in the Parks." *American Forests* 63 (September 1957): 16–18, 40–43.

Villard, Oswald Garrison. "A Park, a Man, and the Rest of Us." *Survey*, February 1, 1926, pp. 542–544.

Wack, Henry Wellington. "Travel Through Our National Parks and Scenic West." *Arts and Decoration*, June, 1930, pp. 68–106.

Watson, John. "The Friendly Bandit of Yellowstone Park." *American West* 24 (December 1987): 42–48.

"Western National Parks Invite America Out of Doors." *National Geographic Magazine*, July 1934, pp. 65–80.

White, Carl J. "Financial Frustration in Territorial Montana." *Montana The Magazine of Western History* 17 (spring 1967): 34–45.

Wilkinson, Todd. "Winter Paradox." *National Parks*, November–December 1990, pp. 31–35.

————. "Steven Fuller's Yellowstone: A Portfolio of a National Park Winterkeeper." *Backpacker*, February 1991, pp. 50–56.

Winchester, James. "Park Man: Meet Conrad L. Wirth, Director of Uncle Sam's National Park Service." *Scholastic* 68 (April 1956): 6.

Wirth, Conrad L. "Mission 66." *American Forests* 61 (August 1955): 16, 17.

Worster, Donald. "Two Faces West: The Development Myth in Canada and the United States." In *Terra Pacifica: People and Place in the Northwest States and Western Canada*, edited by Paul W. Hirt. Pullman: Washington State University Press, 1998.

Yard, Robert Sterling. "Economic Aspects of Our National Parks Policy." *Scientific Monthly* 16 (April 1923): 380–388.

————. "Congress and Conservation." *Survey*, April 15, 1929, pp. 133–134.

"Yellowstone: America's Crown Jewel." *Rocky Mountain Motorist*, May 1991, pp. 16–17.

"The Yellowstone Land Grab: A Lesson in Geography." *The Outlook*, October 20, 1926, pp. 393–394.

"The Yellowstone Grab: Beauty and the Beet." *The Outlook*, October 20, 1926, pp. 300–301.

GOVERNMENT DOCUMENTS

Advisory Board on Wildlife Management. *Wildlife Management in the National Parks.* Washington, D.C.: U.S. Department of the Interior, 1963.

Baldwin, Kenneth H. *Enchanted Enclosure: The Army Engineers and Yellowstone National Park: A Documentary History.* Washington, D.C.: Historical Division, Office of the Chief of Engineers, U.S. Army, 1976.

Clary, David A. *"The Place Where Hell Bubbled Up": A History of the First National Park.* Washington: U.S. Department of the Interior, National Park Service, Office of Publications, 1972.

Concessions in National Parks: Hearings Before a Subcommittee on Public Lands of the Committee on Public Lands, House of Representatives, Eighty First Congress, First Session, Making Study of Problems in Connection with the Public Lands of the United

States Pursuant to H. Res. 66, Held at Santa Fe, N. Mex., November 12, 1949. Washington, D.C.: U.S. Government Printing Office, 1950.

Cramton, Louis C. *Early History of Yellowstone National Park and Its Relation to National Park Policies.* Washington, D.C.: U.S. Government Printing Office, 1932.

Gannett, Henry. *Report on the Geographical Field Work in the Yellowstone National Park Extracted from the Twelfth Annual Report of the Survey for the Year 1878.* Washington, D.C.: U.S. Department of the Interior, U.S. Geological and Geographic Survey, 1883.

Jones, William A. *U.S. Army Corps of Engineers Report Upon the Reconnaissance of Northwestern Wyoming, Including Yellowstone National Park, Made in the Summer of 1873.* Washington, D.C.: U.S. Government Printing Office, 1875.

Mackintosh, Barry. *The National Parks: Shaping the System.* Washington, D.C.: U.S. Department of the Interior, 1985.

———. *Interpretation in the National Park Service: A Historical Perspective.* Washington, D.C.: U.S. Department of the Interior, National Park Service, History Division, 1986.

———. *National Park Service Administrative History: A Guide.* Washington, D.C.: U.S. Department of the Interior, National Park Service, History Division, 1991.

Olsen, Russ. *Administrative History: Organizational Structures of the National Park Service 1917 to 1985.* Washington, D.C.: U.S. Department of the Interior, National Park Service, History Division, 1985.

Paige, John C. *The Civilian Conservation Corps and the National Park Service, 1933–1942: An Administrative History.* Washington, D.C.: U.S. Department of the Interior, 1985.

Park Structures and Facilities. Washington, D.C.: U.S. Department of the Interior, National Park Service, Branch of Planning, 1935.

Tolson, Hillary A. *Laws Relating to the National Park Service and National Parks and Monuments.* Washington, D.C.: U.S. Government Printing Office, 1933.

———. *Historic Listing of National Park Service Officials.* Washington, D.C.: U.S. Department of the Interior, National Park Service, 1964.

U.S. Congress, Senate. Special Committee on Conservation of Wild Life Resources. *Consolidation in Federal Conservation Activities.* Report prepared by F. C. Walcott, Harry B. Hawes, Charles L. McNary, Key Pittman, and Peter Norbeck. 72d Cong., 2d sess., Report No. 1268, February 22, 1933. Serial set volume no. 9324.

U.S. Department of the Interior. *Annual Report of the Director of the National Park Service to the Secretary of the Interior for the Fiscal Year Ended June 30, 1929, and the Travel Season, 1929.* Washington, D.C.: U.S. Government Printing Office, 1929.

———. *Annual Report of the Director of the National Park Service to the Secretary of the Interior for the Fiscal Year Ended June 30, 1930, and the Travel Season, 1930.* Washington, D.C.: U.S. Government Printing Office, 1930.

———. *Annual Report of the Director of the National Park Service to the Secretary of the Interior for the Fiscal Year Ended June 30, 1931, and the Travel Season, 1931.* Washington, D.C.: U.S. Government Printing Office, 1931.

———. *Annual Report of the Director of the National Park Service to the Secretary of the Interior for the Fiscal Year Ended June 30, 1932, and the Travel Season, 1932.* Washington, D.C.: U.S. Government Printing Office, 1932.

———. *A Study of the Park and Recreation Problem of the United States.* Washington, D.C.: U.S. Government Printing Office, 1941.

———. *Draft Environmental Assessment for Community Plans for Canyon Village/East*

Entrance/Grant Village/Madison Junction/Norris Junction. Washington, D.C.: U.S. Department of the Interior, 1973.

————. *NPS Management Policies.* Washington, D.C.: U.S. Department of the Interior, 1988.

U.S. Department of the Interior, Yellowstone National Park, Office of the Superintendent. *Annual Report of the Superintendent, Yellowstone National Park, for the Year 1917.* Washington, D.C.: U.S. Department of the Interior, National Park Service, 1917.

Unrau, Harlan D. *Administrative History and Expansion of the National Park Service in the 1930s.* Denver: Denver Service Center, National Park Service, 1983.

Wilbur, Ray Lyman. *Two Years of the Department of the Interior 1929–1931.* Washington, D.C.: U.S. Government Printing Office, 1931.

Wilbur, Ray Lyman, and William Atherton Du Puy. *Conservation in the Department of the Interior.* Washington, D.C.: U.S. Government Printing Office, 1931.

Yellowstone Roads and Bridges: A Glimpse of the Past. Washington, D.C.: U. S. Department of the Interior, National Park Service, Historic American Engineering Record, 1989.

BOOKS AND DISSERTATIONS

Albanese, Catherine. *Nature Religion in America: From the Algonkian Indians to the New Age.* Chicago: University of Chicago Press, 1990.

Albright, Horace M., and Robert Cahn. *The Birth of the National Park Service: The Founding Years, 1913–33.* Salt Lake City, Utah: Howe Brothers, 1985.

Albright, Horace M., and Marian Albright Schenck. *Creating the National Park Service: The Missing Years.* Norman: University of Oklahoma Press, 1999.

Albright, Horace M., and Frank J. Taylor. *Oh, Ranger! A Book About the National Parks.* New York: Dodd, Mead, 1935.

Allin, Craig W. *The Politics of Wilderness Preservation.* Westport, Conn.: Greenwood Press, 1982.

Alter, J. Cecil. *James Bridger: Trapper, Frontiersman, Scout and Guide.* Columbus, Ohio: Long's College Book Co., 1951.

The Anceneys of the Flying D Ranch. Bozeman, Mont.: Gallatin County Historical Society, 1986.

Anderson, Benedict. *Imagined Communities: Reflections on the Origin and Spread of Nationalism.* New York: Verso, 1983.

Barnes, Christine. *Great Lodges of the West.* Bend, Ore.: W. W. West, 1997.

Bartlett, Richard A. *Nature's Yellowstone.* Tucson: University of Arizona Press, 1993.

————. *Yellowstone: A Wilderness Besieged.* Tucson: University of Arizona Press, 1985.

Brown, Mark H. *The Flight of the Nez Perce.* New York: Putnam's, 1967.

Buchholtz, C. W. *Rocky Mountain National Park: A History.* Boulder: Colorado Associated University Press, 1983.

Buel, J. W., ed. *Louisiana and the Fair: An Exposition of the World, Its People, and Their Achievements.* 10 vols. Saint Louis: World's Progress Publishing Company, 1905.

Burnham, Philip. *Indian Country, God's Country: Native Americans and the National Parks.* Washington, D.C.: Island Press, 2000.

Butcher, Devereux. *Exploring Our National Parks and Monuments.* 2d ed. Boston: Houghton Mifflin, 1949.

Carr, Ethan. *Wilderness by Design: Landscape Architecture and the National Park Service.* Lincoln: University of Nebraska Press, 1998.

Cassidy, James G. *Ferdinand V. Hayden: Entrepreneur of Science.* Lincoln: University of Nebraska Press, 2000.

Chase, Alston. *Playing God in Yellowstone: The Destruction of America's First National Park.* Boston: Atlantic Monthly Press, 1986.

Chidester, David, and Edward Tabor Linenthal, eds. *American Sacred Space.* Bloomington: Indiana University Press, 1995.

Chittenden, Hiram Martin. *The Yellowstone National Park.* Edited by Richard A. Bartlett. Norman: University of Oklahoma Press, 1964.

Cohen, Michael P. *The History of the Sierra Club, 1892–1970.* San Francisco: Sierra Club Books, 1988.

Conservators of Hope: The Horace M. Albright Conservation Lectures. Moscow: University of Idaho Press, 1988.

Cook, Charles W., David E. Folsom, and William Peterson. *The Valley of the Upper Yellowstone: An Exploration of the Headwaters of the Yellowstone River in the Year 1869.* Edited by Aubrey L. Haines. Norman: University of Oklahoma Press, 1965.

Cronon, William, ed. *Uncommon Ground: Rethinking the Human Place in Nature.* New York: Norton, 1995.

Cross, Coy F., II. *Go West, Young Man! Horace Greeley's Vision for America.* Albuquerque: University of New Mexico Press, 1995.

Demars, Stanford E. *The Tourist in Yosemite, 1855–1985.* Salt Lake City: University of Utah Press, 1991.

DeVoto, Bernard. *Across the Wide Missouri.* New York: Houghton Mifflin, 1947.

Dick, Everett. *The Lure of the Land: A Social History of the Public Lands from the Articles of Confederation to the New Deal.* Lincoln: University of Nebraska Press, 1970.

Dilsaver, Lary M., ed. *America's National Park System: The Critical Documents.* Lanham, Md.: Rowman and Littlefield, 1994.

Downs, Anthony. *Inside Bureaucracy.* Boston: Little, Brown, 1967.

Dunraven, Windham Thomas Wyndham-Quin, 4th Earl of. *The Great Divide.* London: Chatto and Windus, 1876.

Early, Katherine. *"For the Benefit and Enjoyment of the People": Cultural Attitudes and the Establishment of Yellowstone National Park.* Washington, D.C.: Georgetown University Press, 1984.

Ernst, Joseph W., ed. *Worthwhile Places: The Correspondence of John D. Rockefeller, Jr., and Horace M. Albright.* New York: Fordham University Press, 1991.

Everhart, William C. *The National Park Service.* Boulder, Colo.: Westview Press, 1983.

Forbes, B. C. *Men Who Are Making the West.* New York: B. C. Forbes, 1923.

Foresta, Ronald A. *America's National Parks and Their Keepers.* Washington, D.C.: Resources for the Future, 1984.

Fox, Stephen. *John Muir and His Legacy: The American Conservation Movement.* Boston: Little, Brown, 1981.

Freemuth, John C. *Islands Under Siege: National Parks and the Politics of External Threats.* Lawrence: University Press of Kansas, 1991.

Frome, Michael. *Battle for the Wilderness.* New York: Praeger, 1974.

———. *Conscience of a Conservationist: Selected Essays.* Knoxville: University of Tennessee Press, 1989.

———. *Regreening the National Parks.* Tucson: University of Arizona Press, 1992.

Hafen, LeRoy R., ed. *The Mountain Men and the Fur Trade of the Far West.* 10 vols. Glendale, Calif.: Arthur H. Clark, 1972.

Haines, Aubrey L. *The Yellowstone Story: A History of Our First National Park.* 2 vols. Yellowstone National Park, Wyo.: Yellowstone Library and Museum Association in cooperation with Colorado Associated University Press, 1977.

Hampton, Duane H. *How the U.S. Cavalry Saved Our National Parks.* Bloomington: Indiana University Press, 1971.

Harris, Burton. *John Colter: His Years in the Rockies.* New York: Scribner's, 1952.

Harris, Neil, ed. *The Land of Contrasts, 1880–1901.* New York: George Braziller, 1970.

Hartzog, George B., Jr. *Battling for the National Parks.* Mt. Kisco, N.Y.: Moyer Bell, 1988.

Harvey, Mark W. T. *A Symbol of Wilderness: Echo Park and the American Conservation Movement.* Albuquerque: University of New Mexico Press, 1994.

Haynes, F. Jay. *Catalogue of Views Mammoth, Imperial, Stereoscopic; Guidebooks, Souvenir Albums, Lantern and Window Transparencies, Photo-Gravures, Etc., of the Yellowstone National Park.* Fargo, Dakota Territory: F. Jay Haynes, 1887.

Haynes, Jack Ellis. *Haynes' New Guide to Yellowstone National Park.* Yellowstone National Park, Wyo.: Haynes, Inc., 1936.

Hays, Samuel P. *Conservation and the Gospel of Efficiency: The Progressive Conservation Movement, 1890–1920.* Cambridge, Mass.: Harvard University Press, 1959.

———. *Beauty, Health, and Permanence: Environmental Politics in the United States, 1955–1985.* New York: Cambridge University Press, 1987.

Hess, Karl Jr. *Rocky Times in Rocky Mountain National Park: An Unnatural History.* Niwot: University Press of Colorado, 1993.

Holloway, Harry, and John George. *Public Opinion: Coalitions, Elites, and Masses.* New York: St. Martin's Press, 1979.

Hummel, Don. *Stealing the National Parks.* Bellevue, Wash.: Free Enterprise Press, 1987.

Huth, Hans. *Nature and the American: Three Centuries of Changing Attitudes.* Berkeley: University of California Press, 1957.

Ickes, Harold L. *The Secret Diary of Harold L. Ickes: The First Thousand Days 1933–1936.* New York: Simon and Schuster, 1953.

Ise, John. *Our National Park Policy: A Critical History.* Baltimore: Johns Hopkins Press, 1961.

John, Arthur. *The Best Years of the Century: Richard Watson Gilder, Scribner's Monthly, and Century Magazine, 1870–1909.* Chicago: University of Illinois Press, 1981.

Johnson, Robert Underwood. *Remembered Yesterdays.* Boston: Little, Brown, 1923.

Kaiser, Harvey H. *Landmarks in the Landscape: Historic Architecture in the National Parks of the West.* San Francisco: Chronicle Books, 1997.

Kammen, Michael. *Selvages and Biases: The Fabric of History in American Culture.* Ithaca, N.Y.: Cornell University Press, 1975.

———. *Mystic Chords of Memory: The Transformation of Tradition in American Culture.* New York: Knopf, 1991.

Kaufman, Polly Welts. *National Parks and the Woman's Voice: A History.* Albuquerque: University of New Mexico Press, 1996.

Kaufman, Wallace. *No Turning Back: Dismantling the Fantasies of Environmental Thinking*. New York: Basic Books, 1994.

Keller, Robert H., and Michael F. Turek. *American Indians and National Parks*. Tucson: University of Arizona Press, 1998.

Kenney, Robert D. *From Geyserdom to Show-Me Land*. Clyde Park, Mont.: Robert D. Kenney, 1926.

Kirk, Ruth. *Sunrise to Paradise: The Story of Mount Rainier National Park*. Seattle: University of Washington Press, 1999.

Kittredge, William. *Owning It All*. St. Paul, Minn.: Graywolf Press, 1987.

Klein, Maury. *Union Pacific: The Rebirth, 1894–1969*. New York: Doubleday, 1990.

Krutch, Joseph Wood, ed. *Walden and Other Writings by Henry David Thoreau*. New York: Bantam Books, 1989.

The Land of Geysers: Yellowstone National Park. St. Paul, Minn.: Northern Pacific Railway, 1910.

Langford, Nathaniel Pitt. *The Discovery of Yellowstone Park*. Saint Paul, Minn.: Foundation, 1905. Reprint, Lincoln: University of Nebraska Press, 1972.

Leopold, Aldo. *A Sand County Almanac and Sketches Here and There*. New York: Oxford University Press, 1949.

LeUnes, Barbara Laverne Blythe. "The Conservation Philosophy of Stewart L. Udall, 1961–1968." Ph.D. diss., Texas A&M University, 1977.

Limerick, Patricia Nelson. *The Legacy of Conquest: The Unbroken Past of the American West*. New York: Norton, 1987.

Linenthal, Edward Tabor. *Sacred Ground: Americans and Their Battlefields*. Chicago: University of Illinois Press, 1991.

Lippmann, Walter. *Public Opinion*. New York: Macmillan, 1965.

Lowenthal, David. *Possessed by the Past: The Heritage Crusade and the Spoils of History*. New York: Free Press, 1996.

Lowenthal, David, and Martyn J. Bowden, eds. *Geographies of the Mind: Essays in Historical Geosophy*. New York: Oxford University Press, 1976.

Lowitt, Richard. *The New Deal and the West*. Norman: University of Oklahoma Press, 1993.

Lowry, William R. *The Capacity for Wonder: Preserving National Parks*. Washington, D.C.: Brookings Institution, 1994.

Lyons, Barrow. *Tomorrow's Birthright: A Political and Economic Interpretation of Our Natural Resources*. New York: Funk and Wagnalls, 1955.

Magoc, Chris J. *Yellowstone: The Creation and Selling of an American Landscape, 1870–1903*. Albuquerque: University of New Mexico Press, 1999.

Malone, Michael P. *James J. Hill: Empire Builder of the Northwest*. Norman: University of Oklahoma Press, 1996.

Malone, Michael P., and Richard B. Roeder. *Montana: A History of Two Centuries*. Seattle: University of Washington Press, 1976.

Marsh, George Perkins. *Man and Nature; or, Physical Geography as Modified by Human Action*. New York: Scribner, 1864.

Martinson, Arthur D. *Wilderness Above the Sound: The Story of Mount Rainier National Park*. Niwot, Colo.: Roberts Rinehart, 1986.

Marx, Leo. *The Machine in the Garden: Technology and the Pastoral Ideal in America*. New York: Oxford University Press, 1964.

McCutcheon, John T. *Drawn from Memory*. New York: Bobbs-Merrill, 1950.

McKibben, Bill. *The End of Nature*. New York: Doubleday, 1989.

McLaughlin, Andrew. *Regarding Nature: Industrialism and Deep Ecology*. Albany: State University of New York Press, 1993.

Miles, John C. *Guardians of the Parks: A History of the National Parks and Conservation Association*. Washington, D.C.: Taylor and Francis, in cooperation with the National Parks and Conservation Association, 1995.

Mills, Enos A. *The Rocky Mountain Wonderland*. Lincoln: University of Nebraska Press, 1991.

Muir, John. *Our National Parks*. Boston: Houghton Mifflin, 1916.

Murphy, Thomas D. *Three Wonderlands of the American West*. Boston: L. C. Page and Company, 1912.

———. *Seven Wonderlands of the American West*. Boston: L. C. Page and Company, Publishers, 1925.

Murray, W. H. *Geyserland: Yellowstone National Park*. Omaha, Nebr.: Union Pacific System, 1925.

Nash, Roderick. *Wilderness and the American Mind*. New Haven, Conn.: Yale University Press, 1967.

———. *The Rights of Nature: A History of Environmental Ethics*. Madison: University of Wisconsin Press, 1989.

———. ed. *American Environmentalism: Readings in Conservation History*. 3d ed. New York: McGraw-Hill, 1990.

Neel, Susan Rhodes. "Irreconcilable Differences: Reclamation, Preservation, and the Origins of the Echo Park Dam Controversy." Ph.D. diss., University of California at Los Angeles, 1990.

Nixon, Edgar B., ed. *Franklin D. Roosevelt and Conservation 1911–1945*. 2 vols. Hyde Park, N.Y.: General Services Administration, National Archives and Records Service, Franklin D. Roosevelt Library, 1957.

Norton, Harry J. *Wonder-Land Illustrated; or, Horseback Rides Through the Yellowstone National Park*. Virginia City, Mont.: Harry J. Norton, 1873.

Oelschlaeger, Max. *The Idea of Wilderness from Prehistory to the Age of Ecology*. New Haven, Conn.: Yale University Press, 1991.

Opie, John, ed. *Americans and Environment: The Controversy over Ecology*. Lexington, Mass.: D. C. Heath, 1971.

Penick, James, Jr. *Progressive Politics and Conservation: The Ballinger-Pinchot Affair*. Chicago: University of Chicago Press, 1968.

Pinchot, Gifford. *Breaking New Ground*. New York: Harcourt Brace, 1947.

Pomeroy, Earl. *In Search of the Golden West: The Tourist in Western America*. New York: Knopf, 1957.

Preserving Wilderness in Our National Parks. Washington, D.C.: National Parks and Conservation Association, 1971.

Price, Sir Rose Lambart. *A Summer on the Rockies*. London: S. Low, Marston and Company, 1898.

Prosser, Laurence Edwin Keith. "A Model for Planning and Managing National Parks." Ph.D. diss., University of Oregon, 1977.

Raban, Jonathan. *Bad Land: An American Romance.* New York: Random House, 1996.

Raftery, J. H. *A Miracle in Hotel Building: The Dramatic Story of the Building of the New Canyon Hotel in Yellowstone Park.* Yellowstone National Park, Wyo.: The Yellowstone Park Company, n.d.

Reiger, John F., ed. *The Passing of the Great West: Selected Papers of George Bird Grinnell.* New York: Scribner's, 1972.

Replogle, Wayne. *Yellowstone's Bannock Indian Trails.* Yellowstone National Park, Wyo.: Yellowstone Library and Museum Association, 1956.

Rescher, Nicholas. *Pluralism: Against the Demand for Consensus.* New York: Oxford University Press, 1993.

Richardson, Elmo R. *The Politics of Conservation: Crusades and Controversies, 1897–1913.* Berkeley: University of California Press, 1962.

———. *Dams, Parks and Politics: Resource Development and Preservation in the Truman-Eisenhower Era.* Lexington: University Press of Kentucky, 1973.

Righter, Robert W. *Crucible for Conservation: The Creation of Grand Teton National Park.* Boulder: Colorado Associated University Press, 1982.

Robbins, Jim. *Last Refuge: The Environmental Showdown in Yellowstone and the American West.* New York: William Morrow, 1993.

Robbins, Roy M. *Our Landed Heritage: The Public Domain, 1776–1936.* Princeton, N.J.: Princeton University Press, 1942.

Robinson, Edgar Eugene, and Paul Carroll Edwards, eds. *The Memoirs of Ray Lyman Wilbur 1875–1949.* Stanford, Calif.: Stanford University Press, 1960.

Rothman, Hal. *America's National Monuments: The Politics of Preservation.* Lawrence: University Press of Kansas, 1989.

———. *Devil's Bargains: Tourism in the Twentieth-Century American West.* Lawrence: University Press of Kansas, 1998.

Rubin, Charles T. *The Green Crusade: Rethinking the Roots of Environmentalism.* New York: Free Press, 1994.

Rudzitis, Gundars. *Wilderness and the Changing American West.* New York: Wiley, 1996.

Runte, Alfred. *National Parks: The American Experience.* Lincoln: University of Nebraska Press, 1979.

———. *Trains of Discovery: Western Railroads and the National Parks.* Rev. ed. Niwot, Colo.: Roberts Rinehart, 1990.

———. *Yosemite: The Embattled Wilderness.* Lincoln: University of Nebraska Press, 1990.

Russell, Osborne. *The Journal of a Trapper.* Edited by Aubrey L. Haines. Lincoln: University of Nebraska Press, 1964.

Salmond, John A. *The Civilian Conservation Corps, 1933–1942: A New Deal Case Study.* Durham, N.C.: Duke University Press, 1967.

Sax, Joseph L. *Mountains Without Handrails: Reflections on the National Parks.* Ann Arbor: University of Michigan Press, 1980.

Schama, Simon. *Landscape and Memory.* New York: Knopf, 1995.

Scheffel, Richard L., ed. *Discovering America's Past: Customs, Legends, History and Lore of Our Great Nation.* Pleasantville, N.Y.: The Reader's Digest Association, 1993.

Schullery, Paul. *Mountain Time.* New York: Nick Lyons Books, 1984.
———. *Searching for Yellowstone: Ecology and Wonder in the Last Wilderness.* Boston: Houghton Mifflin, 1997.
———. *Old Yellowstone Days.* Boulder: Colorado Associated University Press, 1979.
Schwantes, Carlos. *In Mountain Shadows: A History of Idaho.* Lincoln: University of Nebraska Press, 1991.
Sellars, Richard West. *Preserving Nature in the National Parks: A History.* New Haven, Conn.: Yale University Press, 1997.
Shankland, Robert. *Steve Mather of the National Parks.* 3d ed. New York: Knopf, 1970.
Shepard, Paul. *Nature and Madness.* San Francisco: Sierra Club Books, 1982.
Sholly, Dan R. *Guardians of Yellowstone: An Intimate Look at the Challenges of Protecting America's Foremost Wilderness Park.* New York: William Morrow, 1991.
Simons, Ian Gordon. *Interpreting Nature: Cultural Constructions of the Environment.* New York: Routledge, 1993.
Smith, F. Dupont. *Book of a Hundred Bears.* Chicago: Rand McNally, 1909.
Smith, Guy-Harold, ed. *Conservation of Natural Resources.* New York: Wiley, 1950.
Smith, Henry Nash. *Virgin Land: The American West as Symbol and Myth.* Cambridge, Mass.: Harvard University Press, 1950.
Smith, Neil. *Uneven Development: Nature, Capital, and the Production of Space.* New York: Basil Blackwell, 1984.
Spence, Mark David. *Dispossessing the Wilderness: Indian Removal and the Making of the National Parks.* New York: Oxford University Press, 1999.
Sprout, Harold Nance, and Margaret Sprout. *The Context of Environmental Politics: Unfinished Business for America's Third Century.* Lexington: University Press of Kentucky, 1978.
Stanley, Edwin J. *Rambles in Wonderland; or, Up the Yellowstone, and Among the Geysers and Other Curiosities of the National Park.* New York: D. Appleton and Company, 1878.
Stegner, Wallace. *The Uneasy Chair: A Biography of Bernard De Voto.* Garden City, N.Y.: Doubleday, 1974.
———. ed. *The Letters of Bernard De Voto.* Garden City, N.Y.: Doubleday, 1975.
Strahorn, Carrie Adell. *Fifteen-Thousand Miles by Stage.* New York: Putnam's, 1911.
Strahorn, Robert E. *The Resources of Montana Territory and Attractions of Yellowstone National Park.* Helena: Published by Direction of the Montana Legislature, 1879.
Strong, Douglas. *The Conservationists.* Menlo Park, Calif.: Addison-Wesley, 1971.
Strong, W. E. *A Trip to the Yellowstone National Park in July, August, and September, 1875.* Edited by Richard A. Bartlett. Norman: University of Oklahoma Press, 1968.
Swain, Donald C. *Federal Conservation Policy, 1921–1933.* Berkeley: University of California Press, 1963.
———. *Wilderness Defender: Horace M. Albright and Conservation.* Chicago: University of Chicago Press, 1970.
Taylor, Bob Pepperman. *Our Limits Transgressed: Environmental Political Thought in America.* Lawrence: University Press of Kansas, 1992.
Tilden, Freeman. *The National Parks: What They Mean to You and Me.* New York: Knopf, 1951.
———. *Interpreting Our Heritage.* Chapel Hill: University of North Carolina Press, 1977.

Thompson, Dennis L., ed. *Politics, Policy, and Natural Resources.* New York: Free Press, 1972.

Thoreau, Henry David. *The Writings of Henry David Thoreau.* 5 vols. Boston: Houghton Mifflin, 1906.

Turner, Frederick Jackson. *The Frontier in American History.* New York: Henry Holt, 1986.

Udall, Stewart L. *The Quiet Crisis.* New York: Holt, Rinehart, and Winston, 1963.

Utley, Robert M. *A Life Wild and Perilous: Mountain Men and the Paths to the Pacific.* New York: Henry Holt, 1997.

Vestal, Stanley. *Joe Meek: The Merry Mountain Man.* Lincoln: University of Nebraska Press, 1952.

Victor, Frances Fuller. *The River of the West: The Adventures of Joe Meek.* Missoula, Mont.: Mountain Press, 1983.

Watkins, T. H. *Righteous Pilgrim: The Life and Times of Harold L. Ickes 1874–1952.* New York: Henry Holt and Company, 1990.

———. *The Great Depression: America in the 1930s.* Boston: Little, Brown, 1993.

Weigle, Marta, and Barbara A. Babcock, eds. *The Great Southwest of the Fred Harvey Company and the Santa Fe Railway.* Phoenix, Ariz.: The Heard Museum, 1996.

White, Alma. *With God in the Yellowstone.* Zarephath, N.J.: Pillar of Fire, 1920.

White, Graham, and John Maze. *Harold Ickes of the New Deal.* Cambridge, Mass.: Harvard University Press, 1985.

White, Richard. *"It's Your Misfortune and None of My Own": A New History of the American West.* Norman: University of Oklahoma Press, 1991.

Williams, Peter W., and Randy Stutman, eds. *Perspectives on Concessions: Selected Papers.* Logan: Institute of Outdoor Recreation and Tourism, Utah State University, 1971.

Winser, Henry Jacob. *Yellowstone National Park: A Manual For Tourists.* New York: Putnam's, 1883.

Wirth, Conrad L. *Parks, Politics, and the People.* Norman: University of Oklahoma Press, 1980.

Worster, Donald. *The Wealth of Nature: Environmental History and the Ecological Imagination.* New York: Oxford University Press, 1993.

Wylie, William W. *The Yellowstone National Park, or The Great American Wonderland.* Kansas City, Mo.: Publishing House of Ramsey, Millett and Hudson, 1882.

Yard, Robert Sterling. *The Book of the National Parks.* New York: Scribner's, 1919.

Youngs, J. William T. *The Fair and the Falls: Spokane's Expo '74, Transforming an American Environment.* Cheney: Eastern Washington University Press, 1996.